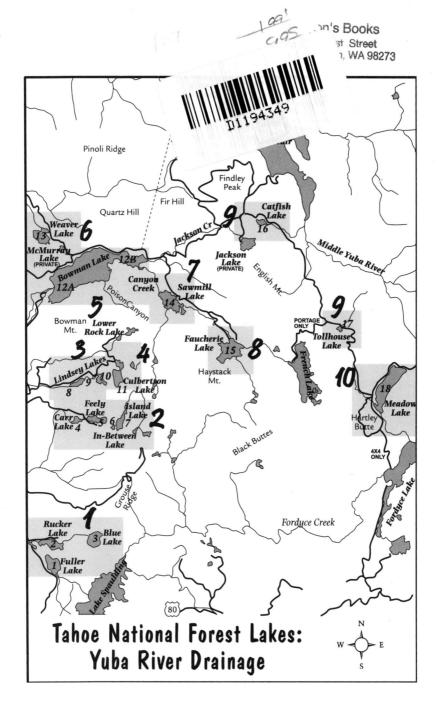

Pinoli Ridge

Findley Peak

Fir Hill

Quartz Hill

Catfish Lake

9

16

Weaver Lake **6**

13

Jackson Cr

Middle Yuba River

McMurray Lake (PRIVATE)

Bowman Lake **12B**

Jackson Lake (PRIVATE)

7

English Mt.

12A

Canyon Creek

PoisonCanyon

Sawmill Lake **14**

5

Bowman Mt.

Lower Rock Lake

9

PORTAGE ONLY

17

Faucherie Lake

Tollhouse Lake

3

Lindsey Lakes

9 **10**

Culbertson Lake **11**

4

15

8

Haystack Mt.

French Lake

10

8

Feely Lake

5 6

Island Lake

7

2

18

Meadow Lake

Carr Lake 4

In-Between Lake

Black Buttes

Hartley Butte

4X4 ONLY

Grouse Ridge

Fordyce Lake

Fordyce Creek

Rucker Lake

2

3 Blue Lake

1 Fuller Lake

Lake Spaulding

80

Tahoe National Forest Lakes: Yuba River Drainage

N
W — E
S

Dedication

Up the Lake, Vol. 3 is dedicated
to my lifelong friend and mentor: Mrs. Pat Jones.

———————————

Up the Lake with a Paddle

Canoe and Kayak Guide
Volume 3

**Tahoe National Forest—West
and the lakes within the
Yuba River Drainage**

By William Van der Ven

FineEdge.com

IMPORTANT LEGAL NOTICE AND DISCLAIMER

Outdoor activities are an assumed risk sport. This book cannot take the place of appropriate instruction for paddling, swimming, or life-saving techniques. Bodies of water, by nature, contain hazards and they change with time and conditions. Every effort has been made to make this guide as accurate as possible, but it is the ultimate responsibility of the paddler to judge his or her ability and act accordingly.

The author, editors, publisher, and distributors accept no liability for any errors or omissions in this book or for any injuries or losses incurred from using this book.

Credits

Cover photos: *William Van der Ven*
Photographs within text: *William Van der Ven*
Book Design: *Elayne Wallis*
Maps and Diagrams: *Sue Athmann*
Cover Design: *Melanie Haage*
Editors: *Elayne Wallis & Réanne Hemingway-Douglass*

Library of Congress Cataloging-in-Publication Data

Van der Ven, William, 1949–
    Up the lake with a paddle: canoe and kayak guide / by William Van der Ven. — 1st ed.
        p. cm.
        Contents: v.   1. Sierra Foothills and Sacramento Region
        ISBN-0-938665-54-5 (v.1)
        1. Canoes and canoeing—California, Northern—Guidebooks.
2.   Kayaking—California, Northern—Guidebooks.   3. California, Northern—Guidebooks.   I. Title.
GV776.C2V36 1998   98-16844
917.94—dc21   CIP

Address requests for permission to:
FineEdge.com, 13589 Clayton Lane, Anacortes, WA 98221
www.FineEdge.com
Printed in Canada
First Edition

TABLE OF CONTENTS

Acknowledgements	7
Introduction (Wilderness Ethics)	8
Using This Guide	10
The Meaning of Quiet Water Boating	12
Packing A Kayak, Loading A Canoe and Portaging	13
Lakes of the Yuba River Drainage	14

AREA 1: GROUSE RIDGE & S. YUBA RIVER DRAINAGE — **22**

Paddle Location 1: Fuller Lake	22
In the Eddy: Flumes, Canals & Pools of S. Yuba River Canyon	28
Paddle Location 2: Rucker Lake	33
Paddle Tip: Planning The Paddle with Photography In Mind	37
In the Eddy: Hikes from Rucker Lake	40
Paddle Location 3: Blue Lake	43

AREA 2: FALL CREEK MOUNTAIN & FALL CREEK DRAINAGE — **50**

Paddle Location 4: Carr Lake	50
In The Eddy: On The Portage Trail or The Joy of Kevlar	56
Paddle Location 5: Feeley Lake	60
Paddle Location 6: In-Between Lake	67
Paddle Location 7: Island Lake	70

AREA 3: FALL CREEK MTN & LINDSEY CREEK DRAINAGE — **76**

Paddle Location 8: Lower Lindsey Lake	76
Paddle Location 9: Middle Lindsey Lake	81
Paddle Tip: Lighting The Way for a Paddle at Night	88
Paddle Location 10: Upper Lindsey Lake	91

AREA 4: FALL CREEK MOUNTAIN & TEXAS CREEK DRAINAGE — **96**

Paddle Location 11: Culbertson Lake	96
In the Eddy: The Hike	107

AREA 5: BOWMAN MOUNTAIN & JACKSON/CANYON CREEK DRAINAGES — **110**

Paddle Location 12-A: Lower Bowman Lake	110
In the Eddy: A Paddle to Yellow Metal Mine	123
Paddle Location 12-B: Upper Bowman Lake	129
Paddle Tip: Transitioning from Flat Water to Moving Water	136

TABLE OF CONTENTS

AREA 6: PYRAMID PEAK & EAST FORK CREEK DRAINAGE   **138**
    Paddle Location 13: Weaver & McMurray Lakes   **138**

AREA 7: RED HILL & CANYON CREEK DRAINAGES   **148**
    Paddle Location 14: Sawmill Lake   **148**

AREA 8: HAYSTACK MTN & CANYON CREEK DRAINAGE   **156**
    Paddle Location 15: Faucherie Lake   **156**

AREA 9: ENGLISH MOUNTAIN & MEADOW LAKE ROAD   **167**
    Paddle Location 16: Catfish Lake   **167**
    Paddle Location 17: Tollhouse Lake   **171**

AREA 10: MEADOW LAKE HILL, HARTLEY BUTTE
          & FORDYCE CREEK   **176**
    Paddle Location 18: Meadow Lake   **176**

AREA 11: MIDDLE YUBA RIVER DRAINAGE & BALD RIDGE   **184**
    Paddle Location 19: Milton Reservoir   **184**

Appendices   **190**
Glossary   **208**
Bibliography & References   **215**
Other FineEdge.com Publications   **222**
About the Author   **224**

ACKNOWLEDGEMENTS

This volume was a joy to write, not only because of the material it covers, but for all the people I came in contact with who, in one form or another, contributed to its completion. I would first of all like to thank, as always, Louise, my wife and companion. Her steadfast belief in my endeavor continues to inspire me.

Mr. Arnold (Arn) Ghigliazza & Ms. Mary Duffield–you took a loopy high school student's aspirations seriously and opened a door to the joys of learning. The door continues to stay open; I thank you both.

Keith Miller, CEO & Big Dog of California Canoe & Kayak–you gave me the start so many years ago; many, many, thanks for your time, access to gear and continual support of "this writing project" . . . .

Kris Kringel, Manager, CCK, Sacramento–it is always a pleasure to walk into the store and see your upbeat self. I raise my paddle to you for all the help & humor during the ups and downs of writing this book.

Jenna Scimeca, your research endeavors were first rate. Kudos for the excellent digging into all those musty files. Best of luck with your studies at UCSC.

Hank Meals, fellow author and lover of the wilderness–you took on the task of checking the manuscript for historical accuracy. "Muchas Gracias Campadre."

Mike Scialfa, President of Crystal Range Associates–your advice is always appreciated, and carefully thought over. I feel humbled by your loyalty to my books.

Ann Denzer, bookkeeper & mom extraordinaire–the checks are *always* on time . . . . thank you.

Ms. Kim Parrino, my paddling partner & friend–I am in awe of your positive attitude and willingness to try out my schemes for the sake of the book: *"You want to cart that kayak where?"*

Bert Hall, I paddled, you hiked–what a team! The description of Yellow Metal Mine would not be as exciting or accurate without your knowledge. "Abrazos, amigo"!

Agnes Marenco–your positive attitude and willingness to paddle for the camera "just one more time" are greatly appreciated. Glenn Fleming, for all those wonderful memories paddling at Ahjumawi.

To all the staff at California Canoe & Kayak, Adventure Sports & Current Adventures–your help, good humor and overall support had not gone unnoticed. I thank you, one and all.

And, finally, despite the excellent staff work and editing, I bear full responsibility for the final outcome of the contents (or lack thereof) that appear in this book.

Wilderness Ethics

With the increased pressure on the use of our forests, lakes and backcountry, the need for a philosophy of use accompanied by common sense has become mandatory. It is not just the careless, casual camper who needs to be educated about wilderness preservation, but the experienced outdoors person who thinks he/she is following correct skills when indeed, he/she is not.

One such concept that has evolved to address the heavy impact on our landscape is based on the principle of *"going light."* The existence of a philosophy promoting "proper" etiquette in the wilderness has been around for many years. The first instructors were the Native Americans who passed down the "lore of the woods" to the early pioneers. Blending Native American teachings with European skills, the Mountain Man was able to survive many years in the wilderness before the demise of the beaver forced him to retire or take on the work of a trail guide for the many families migrating westward. On our continent's rivers, indomitable voyagers applied their knowledge of moving water and camp craft to guide their heavily laden canoes through miles of swollen rivers to the safe harbors belonging to either the Hudson's Bay Company or the Northwest Company.

Initially these teachings of camp craft and lore of the woods were geared for either survival or best use of the wilderness environment. As awareness of our heritage grew, so too did our sensitivity toward its future existence. The attention began to shift to a more evolved concept concerning shared stewardship of the land. As an example, the oncehallowed tradition of cutting pine branches for one's bed gave way to the use of lightweight sleeping mats.

Stewart Edward White, in his book, *The Forest,* written in 1903, devotes an entire chapter to *"The Science of Going Light."* Although emphasis was on gear, clothing and food, the premise behind the instruction was *"to go light, discard all but the really necessary articles."**

Originally this principle was geared toward the backpacker and camper, but has now taken over as the ethos for all participants in wilderness activities. With the modern realization that the wilderness is a finite resource and its very existence is determined by our present and future actions, "going light" wasn't enough. With guidelines worked out by the combined efforts of various organizations and State and Federal agencies, a new set of principles was adopted. These precepts are now found under the overall title "Leave No Trace" (LNT). Using education as the key to inform the public on correct behavior out-of-doors, the goal of LNT is to *"...spare the land and the sensibilities of other people. You choose your gear, your route, [or paddle] your schedule with the welfare of the wilderness in mind".* **

In addition to the above concept, the greatest impact on the wilderness by current users pertains to proper guidelines regarding hygiene and disposal of human waste. As we embrace the idea of "sparing the land," we must also keep in mind that our numbers create a health hazard, especially when it comes to our current practice of defecation in the wilderness.

As responsible users of wilderness areas, we must become current in modern methods of waste disposal. At the very least, families should invest in some sort of portable toilet system. This is not only a health issue, but also shows sensitivity to the pressures being placed by man on the environment. A good first source on the subject would be to read Roger Schumann's article in the December 1998 issue of *Sea Kayaker Magazine*. The piece is titled: "The Boombox by GTS: A Portable Toilet System." For an excellent introductory read on Leave No Trace camping, obtain the *2000 Beginner's Guide* to *Canoeing & Kayaking* published by *Canoe & Kayak Magazine*. On page 74 is a comprehensive article: "Keep it Clean With Leave No Trace," by Peter Stekel.

For an in-depth understanding of going light by using low-impact skills and the educational program of Leave No Trace Camping, read John Hart's *Walking Softly In the Wilderness* or contact the National Outdoor Leadership School (NOLS) at (307) 332-1292, or Leave No Trace Camping (LNT, Inc.) at (800) 332-4100. Their website is found at www.LNT.org

As you enjoy the paddles and journeys that your canoe and kayak may bring, remember to tread lightly on the land, and leave behind only the wake of your boat.

Sources

Sierra Club, *Going Light with Backpack or Burro.* Edited by David R. Brower. San Francisco, CA. 8th printing, 1964.

*The Forest, Stewart Edward White. McClure, Phillips & Company: New York. 1904 ed. Pg. 11.

**Excerpt taken from: *Walking Softly in the Wilderness,* by John Hart. Published by Sierra Club Books, San Francisco, CA. 3rd ed., 1998. Pg. 7.

USING THIS GUIDE

Up the Lake With a Paddle, Vol. 3 concentrates on many picturesque lakes within the Tahoe National Forest-West. Because these lakes are primarily all within the same region, I dispensed with the use of the chapters and substituted AREAS and PADDLE LOCATIONS.

AREA covers the broad setting using prominent geographical features and drainages as reference points. Each PADDLE LOCATION defines the specific lake/reservoir nestled with that AREA. For example: AREA ONE: GROUSE RIDGE & SOUTH YUBA RIVER DRAINAGE, PADDLE LOCATION 1: FULLER LAKE.

Prior to the start of the descriptions of the lakes, I include a brief overview of the Grouse Ridge Region within the Tahoe National Forest. An annotated listing of books and videos with content that explores the area in greater depth is also listed under For a Good Read.

Each paddle location begins with a highlighted fact section. This inset provides the reader with a quick overview on the difficulty, trip length, portage, distance/difficulty of portage, lake size, paddle distances, elevation, and the best season to paddle. This specific volume covers the lakes that may be attempted by paddlers of all skill levels. Weather conditions, however, will dictate the final decision to paddle a specific lake.

Trip Length includes driving time to assist you in deciding whether that paddle location is feasible as a day trip or if a longer stay would be more reasonable. Surprisingly, many of these lakes may be planned as a day paddle with an early arrival and a late afternoon departure. This day paddle venture is due in part to the overall small size of these lakes. Bowman Lake, the largest of the described paddle locations, is only 2.5 miles in length and ¾ of a mile wide. However, it is the quality rather than the quantity that should be the deciding factor. One may certainly circumnavigate Bowman Lake in one full day, but it would be at the expense of missing the subtle beauty and historical features surrounding the lake.

I include the Seasons in my fact section because weather dictates access and availability. The roads leading into many of these lakes are non-paved forest roads. They open late in spring and close early in the fall. Seasons also play a major role on the availability of water in these lakes. Using Bowman Lake again as an example, by planning your trip in late spring, your put-in/take-out will be at least 10 feet higher than the same location in late summer. Those 10 feet may be the difference between a gentle sloped gravel beach or a steep and muddy slick rock access point. In addition, an early spring in the Sacramento Valley may not correspond to the winter conditions still surrounding these alpine lakes. Therefore I have provided the Ranger District and the phone number under the National Forest heading.

A new feature included in this volume is the heading Portage. Although the majority of the lakes within the Yuba River Drainage Region are accessible by vehicle (either conventional, high clearance or 4x4) some are not. I came to the conclusion that to exclude the charm of Feeley Lake or the breathtaking beauty of Culbertson Lake only because their access requires a portage was not an option. However, I limited the choices to those lakes where the combination of driving access, difficulty and length of the portage is within the "do-able factor" of most readers.

All paddle locations requiring a portage are annotated. Each portage is listed in the text as well as on the map. Brief descriptions along with the length of the portages are provided.

Under Historical Background, I provide the reader with a short snippet pertaining to any known facts regarding the lake or immediate vicinity. I provide this information only on those lakes on which I was able to obtain some background. All primary sources that were used for a specific paddle location are listed under Area References at the end of each description. A more detailed account of technical references may be reviewed in the Annotated Bibliography located at the end of the book.

I moved the Map Section into two categories: Category 1 includes a list of USGS 7.5 Minute Topographical Section Sheets that pertain to each paddle location. The second category includes specific road maps and atlases covering that area. For a more detailed description on maps (topographical and road maps), where to order them, and pertinent web sites, turn to Appendix I located at the back of the book.

Under Access, I include the most direct route to each Area and Paddle Location. As mentioned previously, the majority of these lakes lie in areas where the roads are not paved and this may restrict the passage of standard vehicles. None of the lakes described in this volume require the use of an off-road 4x4 vehicle. I used a standard equipped Toyota pick-up (the choice of Afghani troops) to access these lakes. However, vehicles with a high clearance will provide a more comfortable and worry-free drive.

As for tracking the mileage, Bowman Lake Road, a.k.a. Forest Road 18, and the other Forest Service roads have mileage markers spaced every half-mile and mile.

Heads Up are helpful tidbits of quick-glance information that cover anything from the number and description of the campground sites to the location of the nearest phone, store and gas station.

The Description section contains the main information on each paddle location. This narrative includes the denotation of the shoreline and location of any hazards, visible plants and specific geological features, as well as any shoreline camping/picnic sites.

Sometimes additional information about a particular lake or area nearby will not fit into the Description section of the text. Such information includes detailed historical lore, or natural history features of the author's personal experiences. These writings are saved for the In the Eddy sections.

Each paddle location ends with a section titled Area References. These include all the primary sources I used when writing about that specific lake.

One additional new insert completes the Description Section of the book: Paddle Tips provides the reader with specific information on paddling a lake safely and enjoyably.

Additional information on botanical plant names, canoeing, kayaking and the regions covered in this volume can be found in the Glossary or the Appendices at the back of the book.

Meaning of Quiet Water Boating

Just what is "quiet water" boating and is quiet water really "quiet?"

Quiet water, flat water, and sometimes even non-moving water all have one thing in common: they are bodies of water that have little or no current. The main source of surface activity comes from wind gusts or is man-made. Lakes, ponds and reservoirs are the primary examples of this type of paddling location. When the speed of a current becomes too slow to measure, then even rivers may fall under the definition for quiet water paddling.

The primary hazards of open water boating–be it a quiet lake or flat

Is quiet water really quiet?

river–come from either the wind or sudden storms and the potential for a lightning strike.

The direction of the wind can make or break a paddler's day. Paddling into a continuous headwind blowing 10 to 15 miles per hour can become physically grueling and mentally draining, especially with the added worry of capsizing.

Wind is also the primary culprit in inducing rapid changes in the weather. This is especially evident when the wind ushers in the unstable air that forms those potentially dangerous summer storms, so common to the Sierra. Man, too, plays a part in defining the conditions of a particular lake, reservoir or section of river. A person's behavior, when in control of a high-speed boat or other motorized watercraft in close proximity to a non-motorized boat, will directly influence the safety of the paddlers.

In my description of paddling on the lakes and reservoirs for this volume, I include a description of wind, weather and any other obstacles that I encountered when paddling there.

Packing a Kayak, Loading a Canoe & Portaging

Before I began writing this chapter, I thought about several memorable paddles I had been on recently and about what helped to make them that way. One characteristic they had in common was how well my boat responded even with gear aboard, and the ease with which I could obtain items when needed. Both of these points are directly related to how I packed my boat and the containers that held my gear. Before I get into the "how" of packing a kayak or canoe, I will discuss some of the items available to hold gear securely and keep them dry.

Unless you have an unlimited budget, it is very expensive to buy all the top-quality dry bags you need to hold your gear. To get around this outlay of money, you learn to mix-n-match. Purchase dry bags for gear that absolutely needs to be protected and dry: your sleeping bag, camera and film, extra clothing. For the other items, an excellent alternative is the use of double-lined leaf bags. Avoid the thin plastic economy bags–they tend to stretch and tear easily.

For smaller items such as batteries, flashlights and even film, use the new zipper-lock bags that have a plastic slider; they work extremely well. For bulky items such as trip diaries, small books, gloves or socks, use the freezer storage bags that contain a built-in pouch.

Before you put that dent in your wallet purchasing top-quality dry bags, consider a visit to a good Army-Navy surplus store. If you take your time and examine the surplus gear carefully, you may walk out with some terrific storage items–some even protected by Gore-Tex (a waterproof breathable layer). The majority of items, however, are either nylon or heavy-duty plastic and in

Getting the boats and gear ready for a day on the water.

your choice of camouflage, black, or OD green.

When you are ready to make a purchase of the real thing, know that dry bags come in a variety of shapes, sizes and material. If you are a kayaker, look for brands that are designed with few or no buckles that fit easily into a kayak's hold. Unlike standard dry bags, these bags have bottoms that are tapered rather than round. For a canoeist, look for bags that may be attached easily to your boat's lash points. For larger bags, it is worth the extra cost of a multiple-use bag that allows you to wear it as a backpack when portaging.

For kayakers, bag size is very important. To create a waterproof seal, the tops of the bags must be rolled down a certain number of times. This affects the storage capacity of the bag. Also, sizes large through extra-large when filled become bulky and may not fit through a kayak's storage hatch.

In addition to size, the bag's material composition affects its price. Dry bags made from soft plastic are less expensive than those manufactured out of vinyl. Both plastic and vinyl are less expensive than treated nylon. In extreme cold however, plastic and vinyl bags tend to become brittle. Their main quality, besides the cost, has to do with their durability. Unlike the more expensive nylon, the plastic/vinyl bags are very puncture resistant. If ease of storage is an issue, consider nylon bags. Plastic/vinyl bags have a tendency to rub and stick together when pressed against each other. Canvas is yet another option. Bags made of this material, while durable and water resistant, are not waterproof.

Traditionally, top-quality dry bags have their seams sewn and then taped. This was very labor intensive and therefore, expensive. Today, the majority of bags are heat-welded (see the March, 1998, *Canoe & Kayak Magazine* article by Bryan Chitwood, listed below under Sources).

Last but not least, purchase bags of different colors. This allows you to keep track of which bag contains what gear.

Gear Storage

Whether it is a kayak or a canoe, where and how you place the gear will determine the boat's stability. Placing the heaviest items such as water jugs, food, and kitchen gear low and as close to the center as possible will ensure your ability to steer the boat with better control. *Note: Taking along a water purifier eliminates the need to carry large and heavy amounts of water.* If the craft is a kayak, pack the heavy gear close to the bulkheads and pack outward; this will allow the boat to ride over waves instead of punching through them. As a matter of fact, a boat containing a properly displaced load is *more stable* than an empty one.

As you center your heavy gear, be careful not to place too much weight on one side or the other. Reserve the ends and the sides of the boat for light gear or you will be paddling a boat that will have a tendency to porpoise or cant to one side. In kayaks, because the space reserved for gear is rather small and confining, the tendency for it to shift is less of a problem, especially if the gear was sealed in dry bags or other containers. In canoes, gear is

Loaded and ready to begin the portage. Note that heavy gear is placed toward the stern.

usually lashed or buckled to thwarts or pre-attached D-rings that are glued to the bottom or attached to the side of the craft. Leave the far ends of the boat for your lighter goods such as sleeping bags and foam pads.

In kayaks, reserve the space behind the seat and backrest for your first aid and emergency tool/repair kits. In a canoe, I put my first aid kit in a dry bag attached to the rear thwart and keep my tool kit under the seat.

The deck space on a kayak contains a bungee cord that may be used for the attachment of light items such as a jacket or sponge. *(Be wary of this practice if paddling during a strong wind or in heavy chop. The wind, breaking waves, or an accident may cause you to lose those items.)* For additional commodities, it is better to attach a deck bag. Some of these deck bags function similarly to a dry bag but have straps or other means of attaching to the deck rigging of the kayak (see photo). Deck bags are made for canoes also. They usually attach under the seat or to the thwarts.

Packing a Canoe or Kayak for a Cart Portage

Many of the portage trails described in this book can be negotiated through the use of a canoe/kayak cart* (see photo) made by several different manufacturers. For a list of these companies, check the advertisement or gear section of a paddling magazine, read the Periodicals Section in the Appendices of this book, or visit a retail paddle-sport store.

The first step to correctly portage a paddle-craft on a cart is to place the boat on the cart in such a manner that you may pull it with relative ease. Strapping more than half the boat's length onto the cart usually accomplishes this. The cart acts as a fulcrum and the boat becomes a lever equalizing the effort of lifting the weight of the load (see photo).

How you pack the gear in the boat will determine the ease of transporting the entire load to your destination. If the boat is a canoe, begin loading from the rear toward the mid-section. Start with the heaviest gear first, ending with the lightest gear packed at the mid-point or a little forward of the boat's center (see photo). If you packed properly, as you pick up the bow it should lift with little or no effort.

To make the pulling of the boat a bit easier especially over rough ground, fix a sling under the grab handle or bow thwart. Make the sling long enough to go around your shoulder leaving enough slack to pull the boat and cart comfortably and with a consistent motion (see photo).

With a kayak, load the heavy gear in the rear compartment stuffing the heaviest bags as far back toward the stern as you can. If you are able, strap some of the medium-weighted bags onto the afterdeck (see photo). Save the cockpit area for the light gear and the forward compartment for the lightest stuff. The use of a sling, as on the canoe, allows you to control the motion of the strapped boat over the portage trail.

Finally, work out the kinks of boat attachment to the cart, placement of gear, and negotiating the loaded cart at home or a lake close to home before attempting your first portage in a wilderness setting.

Good Luck & Happy Trails!

*I used the cart manufactured by PRIMEX of California under the Deluge logo. They may be reached at: www.deluge.com / 1(800)422-2482.

With a sling over the shoulder, the boat's motions are easier to control. Sometimes you have to pack gear on the afterdeck for easier boat handling. Note deckbag in front of cockpit.

Sources

For an in-depth description of carts available for portaging, please read:

Rice, Larry, "Roll On Buddy," *Canoe & Kayak Magazine,* July 1999. pg. 90.

Chitwood, Bryan, "Increasingly Sophisticated: Dry Bags Come Of Age," *Canoe & Kayak Magazine*, March 1998. pgs. 72-76.

Hanson, Jonathan, "Packing For Performance," *Sea Kayaker Magazine,* February 1996. pgs. 33-35.

Knapp, Andy, "Long Haul Packing," *Canoe & Kayak Magazine,* August 1996. pg. 10.

Lakes Of The Yuba River Watershed Region

A portion of the Grouse Ridge Basin from Grouse Ridge. The view is to the north, looking down on Island and Feeley lakes. Fall Creek Mountain (7,490') dominates the horizon.

Of the more than 4,000 lakes* located in the high Sierra, the majority of lakes within the Yuba River Watershed share the distinction of being man-made. In addition, these reservoirs were initially constructed to provide water for hydraulic mining activities occurring in the lower foothills. When this destructive form of mining was banned by a court order (United States Circuit Court Order dated: January 9, 1884), the use of the reservoirs changed too. The impoundment of water for electrical power and fresh drinking water became big business for the municipal utility companies serving the rapidly growing communities of Grass Valley, Nevada City & smaller outlying areas.

I have included a description of a hike, (In The Eddy, Paddle Location 1), to one of the flume systems that used to cover the region. It is worth the effort to visit because it gives you an appreciation for the engineering skills and construction hardships that were endured by the early workers. A little-known fact about the construction of many canal and flume systems is that they were built literally into the sides of steep granite gorges using very primitive techniques. The workers, who were primarily Chinese, had honed their construction skills building the Western Pacific Railroad through the Sierras. (Read Huggins & Olmsted's, *Adventures on & off Interstate 80*, pgs. 172-173).

For those of you that enjoy the history of early mining, I also include a description of a paddle to a historical mining site that still retains a standing stamp mill and rail line for the ore carts. (See: In The Eddy, Paddle Location 12-A.)

It wasn't long before visitors from these expanding towns and other communities began discovering the sublime majesty of this section of the high country. Old wagon roads and trails into former mining camps were expanded and utilized by the growing numbers of tourists seeking the beauty of the Sierra High Country. Bowman Lake Road, a cobble-strewn washboard of a road, sometimes has more traffic on it during a summer weekend than the adjacent California State Highway 20! Indeed, before Interstate 80 was constructed, there was talk of widening Henness Pass Road–that Bowman Lake Road is a part of–to four lanes! (See For A Good Read, *Sierra Crossing First Roads to California,* by Thomas F. Howards)

Today, the rugged beauty of the Grouse Ridge Area (located within the Yuba River Watershed and the Tahoe National Forest), may be enjoyed either by paddling the waters of the reservoirs, biking or four-wheeling the former logging roads, or hiking the old trails built by early miners. Remnants of historical mining towns, camps, and sites may still be found on one of your explorations thanks mainly to the remote location and lack of paved roads into many of these lakes.

*This number is derived from: *High Mountain Lakes and Streams of the Sierra Nevada: A guide to the aquatic ecosystems,* compiled by the USDA-Forest Service, Pacific Southwest Region. pg. 1.

For A Good Read

Caras, Roger, *The Forest.* Holt, Rinehart & Winston, 1979. 179 pp.
Through stories about the many life forms, the author introduces the reader to the natural history of a conifer forest in the West. A great book to read to children, especially over a campfire.

Hinkle, George & Bliss, *Sierra Nevada Lakes the American Lakes Series.* Indianapolis, MA: Bobbs-Merrill Company, Inc., 1949. 383 pp.
The authors use the lakes as a reference point to write historical sketches of the surrounding area. Their concise history on the rise and fall of Meadow Lake/Summit City mining town will broaden your appreciation of Meadow Lake.

Howard, Thomas Frederick, *Sierra Crossing: First Roads to California.* Berkeley, CA: University of California Press, 1998. 218 pp.
A scholarly and fascinating read of the overland routes through the mountains into California.

McPhee, John, *Assembling California.* New York, NY: Farrar, Straus and Giroux, 1993, 3rd paperback ed., 1998. 303 pp.
The fourth book of a tetralogy on the new geology based on the theories of Plate Tectonics and Sea-Floor Spreading. The author uses Interstate 80 as the focal point

as he travels in the company of Eldridge Moores, a geology professor at the University of California, Davis. McPhee explains the geologic history of the Sierras and surrounding area of the Grouse Ridge lakes.

Meals, Hank, *Yuba Trails 2: A Selection of Historic Hiking Trails in the Yuba River Watershed.* Self published, 2001.To order: (530) 470-0632.
A professionally published upgraded version of the 1993 book of the same name. The author includes a description of the history and archaeology as well as the flora, fauna of the Yuba River Watershed. As an added bonus, the author includes trails with descriptions pertaining to the North Fork of the American River.

Muir, John, *The Mountains of California.* Sierra Club Publications, The John Muir Library ed., 1988. 292 pp.
A library of the Sierras is incomplete without at least one copy of a work by John Muir. The Mountains of California *was his first book & his exuberance for the wilderness makes the text sing.*

Snyder, Gary, *Mountains and Rivers Without End.* COUNTERPOINT Publishers, distributed by Publishers Group West, 1996. 164 pp.
Written by one of the Sacramento Valley and foothill's most distinguished poets. His epic speaks of landscapes, birth and death, and the majesty of just being.

Video
Stories of the Yuba, prod. & Dir. Greg Schiffner, 1hr., 15min., GANDL Productions, videocassette. To order: (530) 265-3638.
A history of the South Yuba River in three acts: Act I – Geography/History, Act II – Recreation/Inspiration, Act III – Preservation/Development.

Cassette
TripTape The Native's Guide Donner Pass I-80 from the Foothills over the Sierra. 65min. Echo Peak Productions, Fair Oaks, CA. 1992.
Narration of the history and natural history of the area bordered by Interstate 80 from the foothills beginning at Newcastle near Auburn and ending at Donner Lake.

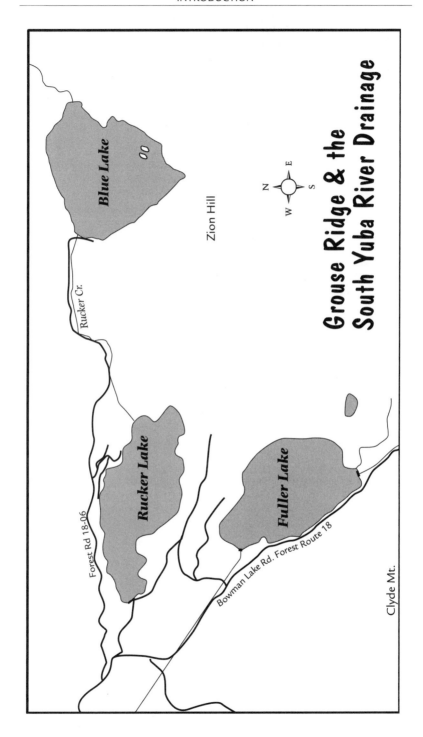

Grouse Ridge
& South Yuba River Drainage

PADDLE LOCATION 1
Fuller Lake

Difficulty: All skill levels, however, paddlers should be aware of current created by the discharge of water from Bowman-Spaulding Tunnel.
Trip Length: An excellent day paddle.
Lake Size: 5 x .25 miles
Paddle Distance:
From the dam to the extreme NW end, the lake is 0.5 mile long
Lake Elevation: 5,600'
Season: Spring through fall, or until heavy snowfall closes the road.
Historical Background: Constructed before 1871 by the Meager Mining Company for hydraulic mining purposes. Named after one of the mining company officials.
County: Nevada
National Forest: Tahoe National Forest, Nevada City Ranger District (530) 265-4531
Maps: USGS 7.5 Minute Topographical Sheet: Blue Canyon
National Forest Service Maps: Tahoe National Forest, South Yuba River Recreation Guide
Road Maps: Compass Maps Inc.: Nevada and Sierra counties; Nevada–Sierra counties Street and Road Atlas
American Auto Assn. (AAA) Maps: Northern California/Bay & Mountain sections

Access: Take Interstate 80 East. Drive past the Yuba Gap Exit and turn off onto Hwy. 20 West. Continue on Hwy. 20 for 4.0 miles and turn right onto Bowman Lake Road (Forest Service Road 18N18). Follow the road for 4.0 miles. Road conditions and the type of vehicle will determine where you park. If there is snow and ice on the road, and your vehicle does not have 4-wheel drive or the proper tires, park near the gate located approximately 100 yards before the entrance to the lake. Past the gate the road starts to climb and you run the risk of losing traction and sliding off the road. The portage to the lake is not far and the piece of mind is well worth it! If no snow and ice are on the road, drive into the day-use parking area located near the dam and to your right (see map). The put-in/take-out is to your left as you face the dam.

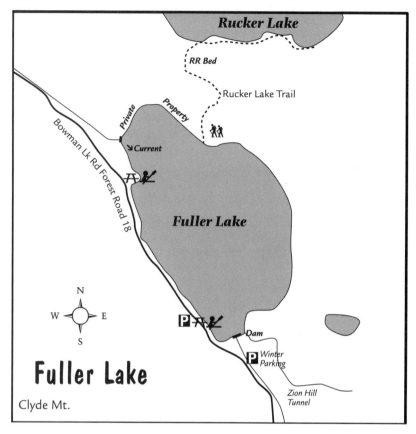

Heads Up

- A perfect lake for family outings.
- Paved road with access almost year round.
- The surrounding forest provides a windbreak.
- Day use only, no overnight camping.
- Small boats only: 10 MPH speed limit.
- Access to nearby lakes. (Rucker and Blue Lakes are within hiking and driving distances)
- In the fall and spring, you can see variety of migratory birds including Bald Eagles.
- Respect surrounding private property and stay clear of nearby flumes and tunnels.

Description: By late fall, there are few Sierra lakes or reservoirs that contain enough water for an enjoyable paddle. Others are difficult to reach due to snow or sudden changes in the weather. Come Thanksgiving, it sure would be nice to take the family or visiting friends for a paddle on a high-country lake that doesn't have the look of a bathtub ring. Fuller Lake offers such an opportunity, and more! In an autumn without numerous heavy snowfalls, Fuller Lake is accessible by any family vehicle. Although this lake can be paddled throughout the spring and summer months, you will have to share its beauty with numerous other visitors.

The lake is fed by the constant inflow of water from the Bowman - Spaulding Canal therefore, its drop-off is minimal. In addition, the shoreline's scrape zone is shallow, allowing the forest vegetation to create a natural zone around the lake which gives Fuller Lake the appearance of a natural (rather than man-made) reservoir, which in fact is the case.

As you take in the view of the lake, note that its size makes it perfect for a leisurely paddle. With the short amount of daylight available, you can still paddle the full length of the lake, take in a hike, enjoy a pleasant lunch, and depart before the day grows colder.

Set your boat on its course and paddle to the small, shaded cove located on the south end of the dam. Often perched on one of the dead snags standing at the lake's edge is a resident Bald Eagle *(Haliaeetus leucocephalus)* whose size and markings of snow-white head, throat and tail along with its yellow bill are sure indicators of its adult status. If the bird is present, don't make any sudden moves or use loud voices. As you train your binoculars or telephoto lens on the eagle, you may experience a disconcerting feeling from the sight of the eagle staring directly back at you! I have drifted silently in my canoe, observing the bird for over fifteen minutes, before the eagle became tired or bored with my presence and finally spread its wings and flew off in a majestic glide across the lake.

From this small cove, shaded from the morning sun, let your boat drift toward the middle of the lake. Note the sharp contrast of light against dark produced by objects covered in snow lying in the shadows cast by the tall conifers. Look down into the lake's depths and you will see the amazing clarity of the water. Huge stumps of former trees lie submerged—a reminder that this is a reservoir created as a water source for the inhabitants of Nevada City, Grass Valley and neighboring communities.

Bordering the lake, patchy spots of color mark the transition from summer as the leaves of various deciduous trees take on their fall hues. Stretching endlessly onto the flanks of the surrounding ridges, tall conifers of various height, shape, and shades of green, give this lake a feeling of being in a wilderness.

By the time you have drifted to the lake's center, you have noticed the tall ridges and peaks that dominate the skyline. To orient you, the long ridgeline-stretching north to south is Clyde Mountain (6,052') the highest peak surrounding the lake. As you look toward the dam, the small knoll on the left (5,678') has no official name, but is a part of the larger and more prominent peak visible to the southeast, Zion Hill (6,204').

From here you may choose any direction to paddle or continue enjoying the scenery as your boat glides across the lake. If you paddle across to the southeastern shore, the snow lies heavy in the dense forest. Locate the section of shore that contains the frost-burned sedges *(Family Cyperaceae)*; they are growing along the bank in the foreground of the forest. Once you are out of your boat, hike carefully into the shaded under-story. These woods receive little to no human presence in the fall after deer season; subsequently, after the first light snowfall, many stories become evident by the tracks left in the snow. You may find not only where the deer come to drink, but also how the coyote *(Canis latrans)* tracked its victim, and the pile of feathers to prove its success. Snow scuffed around a trail of tracks and droplets of frozen blood may indicate where a small rodent became an owl's dinner.

When you begin to feel the cold through your layers of clothes, hike back out into the sun-warmed shore of the lake. As you take in the beauty of the tranquil surface of the lake, you will note the small bobbing motions of the small black and white objects visible on the far side of the lake. These ever-moving, changing objects are actually ducks. During the fall and winter, flocks of migrating ducks and other waterfowl land for periods of rest. The birds are enroute to their winter-feeding grounds. You may spot anything from a common mallard *(Anas platyrhynchos)* to Canvasbacks *(Aythya valisineria)*, or, as in my case, a mixed flock of common mergansers (Mergus merganser) and buffleheads (Bucephala albeola).

It was interesting to sit and watch the flock of ducks as they reacted to the overhead flights of the Bald Eagle. Whenever the eagle lifted off his perch to cruise the lake, a chorus of duck calls would precede the whistling sounds of the ducks' wings. Eventually, the small clusters of ducks would join into one flock before swooping down to the opposite end of the lake. This game of "tag" continued on several occasions, each time however, neither did the ducks leave the lake, nor did the eagle display any overt threat to the ducks. Eventually, the eagle tired of the noise and attention veered to the Northeast and disappeared past the horizon. The flock of ducks, quickly breaking up into small groups, began to scatter and catch up on their feeding and preening.

The winter sun's angle allows for the cove on the far northeast side to receive the maximum benefit from the afternoon sun. This end of the lake is also the shallow end. Growing off the bottom, dense mats of Elodea *(Anacharis canadensis)*, or waterweed, provide a food source for dabbling ducks such as the mallards. This thick mass of aquatic plant life also acts as a haven for many small fish, amphibians, crustaceans and insects; diving ducks, such as the mergansers and buffleheads, in turn, hunt them.

If you are interested in observing these different ducks from a close vantage point, paddle to the small point located past the clearing containing the sedges, but before the wooden boat dock. The point's shoreline con-

A December outing on Fuller Lake. Snow still dusts the top of Zion Hill (6,204').

tains a nice sandy beach and level area to take-out. The conifers provide a windbreak and act as a natural blind, screening your presence from the birds. The clearing at the point is the last public access on this northeast side of the lake. The clearing also marks the location of your put-in for the trail leading to Rucker Lake. (See Paddle Location 2, In the Eddy: The Hikes From Rucker Lake).

As you continue your paddle, follow the contour of the cove that makes up this end of the lake and you will pass several cabins with their respective boat docks jutting out into the cove. Posted "No Trespassing" signs, unfortunately, mark the border separating the U. S. Forest Service land from the Restricted Use Area. At the public Day Use Area, located on the northwest upper end of the lake, a Public Notice explains in detail the division of the lake.

When you round the southwest end of the cove, you will spot the mouth of the channel where water from the Bowman-Spaulding Tunnel enters the lake. Be cautious as you paddle past this inlet. If you look down into the clear depths of the lake, you will note that the bottom has been scoured of sediments and is free of vegetation. You can trace the flow of the current by the underwater slope of piled sediments visible on both sides of the channel. The strength of the current here may vary based on the release levels emanating from Bowman Lake.

The cluster of green buildings set within the belt of conifers and along the edge of the channel belongs to the Grass Valley Rod & Gun Club. This organization of sportsmen goes back many years and is a historical fixture at the lake. A similar organization, The Grass Valley Sportsmens Club, Inc., has its lodge at Weaver Lake (see Paddle Location 13).

Once you have passed the channel and left the club's structures behind, look to your right for a glimpse of the picnic tables and barbecues that make up the Day Use Area. This site contains the aforementioned picnic tables and barbecues as well as a cinder block toilet with facilities for the handicapped. If it has not already been taken, the best site is located underneath the huge pine growing on the point facing southeast. From the picnic table you have a clear view of the lake, and the barren slopes that make up a portion of Zion Hill.

When you depart from the use area, be sure to obtain a last glimpse of the point with its giant ponderosa, yellow pine *(Pinus ponderosa)* and neighboring conifers as they cast a mirror image on the tranquil surface of the lake.

Ahead are the last section of shoreline and the approaching details of the dam. By now, the late afternoon sun has cast this side of the lake into deep shadow. The mantle of snow on the logs and rocks stands in sharp relief against the gloom of the tree line. You soon pass a small patch of winter-dead stands of cattails *(Genus Typha)* and tall sedges. Their golden patina contrasts against the deep shadows of the trees.

A short distance before your take-out, the subtle colors of the forest and shoreline retreat against the sudden splash of red coming off the sideboards of an old summer cabin. The cabin is all boarded up— either for the winter, or due to lack of use. Its once-level foundation is now askew but, there is still a look of tired dignity to the setting. Before taking out, the final scene before you will consist of the dam and maybe a few fisherpersons making their last casts onto the sun-dappled waters of the lake.

Area References

The Reader's Digest Association, Inc., *Book of North American Birds,* 5th printing. Pleasantville, NY: The Reader's Digest Association, Inc., 1993. 576 pp.

Palmer, Laurence E., *Fieldbook of Natural History,* 2nd ed. Revised by H. Seymour Fowler. New York: McGraw-Hill Book Company, 1975. 779 pp.

IN THE EDDY

The Flumes, Canals & Pools of South Yuba River Canyon

"To the men of the 'fifties, . . . the development of techniques of washing the Tertiary gravels was of more immediate interest.

This type of mining rested directly on the placer methods used in working the deposits along the contemporary watercourses.

. . . it was made possible by the diversion and harnessing of a fair fraction of the water in the Sierran streams. Ditching, damming, and fluming began as a means of supplying ordinary placer claims. Their more spectacular results were in the attack upon the Tertiary gravels."

—John Walton Caughey, *Gold Is The Cornerstone*, pg. 257.

The majority of lakes within the Grouse Ridge region were dammed to act as catch basins for a steady supply of water for hydraulic mining. A series of wooden flumes and canals carried this water for miles, crossing ridges and canyons, flowing through the forests to where the *diggings* were. Before you start your ascent to the first of these lakes (see map), you may view the remnants of these flumes by hiking a trail through a mixed coniferous forest consisting of: California or White Alder; Bigleaf Maples; California Laurel or Oregon Myrtle; California Black Oak; Canyon Live Oak; Incense Cedars; Ponderosa; and Jeffrey Pines. As an added bonus, on the return leg of the hike, you may enjoy the emerald-green waters of some deep-water pools created by the erosional handiwork of former glaciers and more recently by the combined waters of the South Yuba River, Jordan Creek and Rucker Creek.

Approximately one mile after you turned off from Highway 20 onto Bowman Lake Road, park under the conifer grove in front of the last house just before you cross the bridge and descend into the South Yuba River Canyon. The bridge crosses the South Yuba Canal/Flume. Located to the left of the house and paralleling the road is a metal flume. This updated version of the old flume system now carries drinking water to the many inhabitants of Grass Valley and Nevada City. You can also view the remains of the original rock cribbing by crossing the road and scrambling underneath the metal flume. The stacked rock foundation running parallel with the modern flume once supported a wooden flume that carried water to the mine operations.

To obtain a grand view of the South Yuba River Canyon and the remnants of the original flume that was constructed onto the side of a bare rock

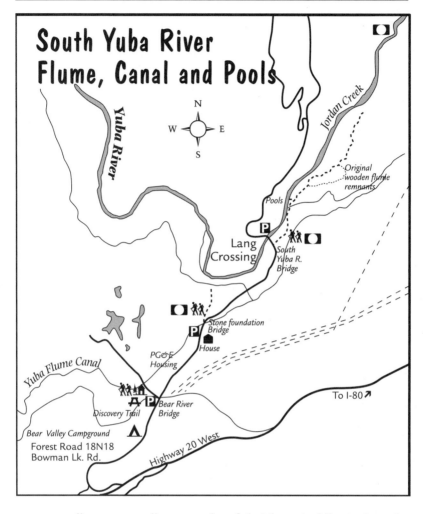

South Yuba River
Flume, Canal and Pools

gorge as well as some excellent examples of glacial terrain, hike up the rocky knob on your left after crossing the bridge. Before you cross the bridge, look for a line of whitish rock approximately 3 feet wide visible to the right, at the base of the knob and extending upward. Now let your eyes follow that white line of rock to the far slope of the canyon visible in the distance. That is the same deposit as the one in front of you. Geologists call this feature a dike. Dikes are formed when molten minerals are injected into weak zones or fissures located in the parent rock. If you follow this dike to where it drops off into the sides of the gorge, look to your left for the timber debris that marks the line of the old flume.

As you begin your hike up the rocky knob, notice the polished and scratched surface of the bedrock. When you reach the top of the knob, note that the surface—indeed all the bare rock visible throughout the canyon—has been scraped to a fine polish. Grooves of various depths are interspersed as lines of fractures running roughly north-south. These grooves and striations were also the work of glaciers as they ground their way down the river canyons.

If you examine the bedrock at your feet, the primary rock type is a mixture of various metamorphic or changed rocks. The predominate type is a metaquartzite, however, those rounded boulders of various heights lying scattered on the surface are primarily granite and they don't belong here! These *erratics*, as geologists call them, were transported to their present location by glacial movement. When the glaciers retreated, they dumped their loads of rock.

The Flumes, Canal & Pools

The trailhead for this hike begins at the historic site listed on the topographical sheet as Lang Crossing. The site was named for John Lang who, in 1882, purchased the surrounding property then known as Culbertson Station. To reach the trailhead leading to the remains of the original flume system as well as to some deep and inviting pools, you may drive or hike down Bowman Lake Road and park adjacent to the blue gate visible on your right. Additional parking is located across the South Yuba River Bridge and on the right. The trailhead is located on the other (north) side of the gate.

Before you cross the gate to begin your hike, walk to the edge of the canyon and note the former concrete abutments. Unfortunately, these concrete blocks are all that remain of the former bridges that were used to cross this historical section of the river. Even the roadbed has been rebuilt and widened in recent years.

To reach the area of the original flume, stay on the trail that used to be a road. You will be hiking through a section of forest containing a variety of different species of trees. A short distance along the trail, you will cross a small stream. Look to your right for a lone stump set back away from the edge of the path. If you examine the stump, which appears to be an Incense Cedar, you can see the notches cut into the sides of the stump. These were used to hold springboards that, in turn, supported the loggers as they cut down the tree.

When you reach the second stream crossing, take note that this meager flow is all that's left of the once powerful South Fork of the Yuba River. The majority of the river's water makes its way quietly within the confines of the concrete canal, visible along Highway 20. Just before you cross the stream, look to your left for a short path that leads to a clearing located slightly above the trail. This is one of two access paths that leads to the deep-water pools of the former river channel. The second access, and the one with the stunning first view of the pools, is located across the streambed and a short distance up the road. Just before you reach the top of the hill, look left for a narrow trail that leads through the belt of trees toward the edge of the stream channel. When you hike out of the tree line, you will spot the emerald pool shimmering below and to your left.

To reach the area of the former flume, cross the stream, hike up the inclined road past the path to the pool overlook. Hike under the transmission

Close-up of an inviting pool on the South Fork of the Yuba River.

line and look to your right for a partially overgrown jeep trail. This indistinct but cobble strewn path intersects the main road just before it bends to the left. Take this jeep trail and follow it for approximately 1/4 mile as it winds its way through the dense oak and conifer forest. You will intersect a cleared path running north-south and the base of a granite cliff. Look left through the cleared area of the path, and you should spot the stacked rock that marks the location of a retaining wall. This same rock retaining wall braced the level stone foundation (visible above the stacked rock), which supported the wooden framing of the Omega Mining Canal. The canal was built to carry water to the Alpha and Omega hydraulic gold diggings (California Historical Landmarks 628 and 629).

If you pass this first access point, continue following the main road until it reaches the cleared overlook of the dry riverbed. Turn right and follow the cleared area through the trees in a southeasterly direction for approximately 200 hundred yards. Eventually you will reach the base of a granite ridgeline. This is the same granite ridge that contains the dry stacked stone foundation of the old canal. Indeed, chances are that the piles of rotting wood you have been stepping over to reach the base of the ridge are all that is left of the canal and its framework. If you examine some of the wood closely, you will find square-headed nails and other metal still imbedded in the timbers. Some of these timber pieces even have rectangular holes carved through them.*

If you follow the stone foundation and timber remnant to its source, it will lead you to the dam site of Lake Spaulding. The downstream end follows the South Yuba River Canyon. If you look south up to the rim of the ridge, you will spot the modern, enclosed flume that resembles a giant pipeline. This

31

Standing on what used to be the bed of a former wooden flume, high on the wall of the South Yuba River Canyon.

is the successor to the old flume that made up a part of the vast system of flumes and canals belonging to the South Yuba Canal Water Company and is now part of Nevada Irrigation District (NID) and the Pacific Gas And Electric Company's** vast hydroelectric system.

Notes

Because of the important historical significance of this site, please do not attempt to remove any of the artifacts. Not only are you destroying history, but it is illegal. Lastly, the condition of these timbers is fragile at best. Do not walk or place any weight on them.

**Due to the recent (2001) energy debacle, Pacific Gas & Electric (PG&E) filed for bankruptcy. As part of their effort to regain solvency, they are in the process of selling off their watershed lands. Some of these land holdings may include parcels along the Yuba River Watershed.*

Sources

California State Parks. *California Historical Landmarks,* California State Parks, Office of Historic Preservation, 1996. 346 pp. (pg. 148)

Caughey, John Walton. *Gold Is The Cornerstone,* Berkeley, CA: University Of California Press, 1948. 321 pp.

Peattie, Donald Culross. *A Natural History of Western Trees,* Boston, Mass: Houghton Mifflin Company, 1981 Edition. 751 pp.

PADDLE LOCATION 2

Rucker Lake

Difficulty: All skill levels
Trip length: Great day paddle
Lake Size: 3350' x 2750'
Paddle Distances:
From put-in at the FS campground to the meadow and Rucker Creek Trailhead: 0.15 mile
Take-out for hike to the knob: 0.45 mile
Rucker Lake Dam site: 0.56 mile
Elevation: 5,462'
Season: From the time the snow melts through fall; optimum time is late spring and late fall when crowds are gone.
Historical Background: The Meager Mining Company developed the reservoir site and constructed the dam before 1871 as a reliable water source for hydraulic mining.
County: Nevada
National Forest: Tahoe National Forest, Nevada City Ranger District: (530) 265-4531
Maps: USGS 7.5' Topographical Section: Blue Canyon Quadrangle, 1979 (photo revision)
National Forest Maps: Tahoe National Forest Service Map, South Yuba River Recreation Guide
Road Maps: Compass Maps Inc.: Nevada and Sierra Counties, Nevada-Sierra Counties Street and Road Atlas

Access: Take Interstate 80 East, drive past Yuba Gap and Crystal Road turnoff. Exit right onto Highway 20 West. Continue on Highway 20 for 4.0 miles and turn right on Bowman lake Road, (Forest Service Route: 18N18). Follow the road for approximately 5 miles. Turn right onto Forest Service Road 18-06 (a.k.a.: Blue Lake Road). *(Note: the 18-06 rd. turnoff is 3/10's of a mile from the posted 4.5 Mile Marker).* Drive an additional 4/10th's of a mile, passing two water tanks, to a Y-fork. Take the right fork and drive 2/10ths of a mile to a second Y-fork. The left fork leads to a day use parking area. The right fork takes you to the entrance of the U.S. Forest Service campground. Look for a Forest Service green gate on your left, located approximately 1/10th of a mile from the fork. Don't be mislead by the Forest Service sign regarding group camping visible on your right before you turn into the campground. This sign marks the entrance to Liahona, a private camping area.

Heads Up

- Only small motorized and paddle craft are allowed.
- A great family lake with easy access.
- Located near other lakes.
- Campground has fire rings and new cinder block vault toilets.
- Campfire permit is required for any overnight camping.
- Bear country: pack and camp smart.
- Mountain biking and hiking on nearby roads and trails.

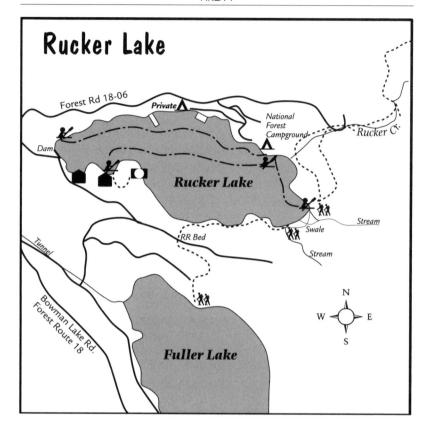

Rucker Lake

Forest Rd 18-06
Private
National Forest Campground
Rucker Cr.
Dam
Rucker Lake
Tunnel
RR Bed
Swale
Stream
Stream
Bowman Lake Rd. Forest Route 18
Fuller Lake

N
W E
S

■ Excellent short hike from Rucker Lake to Fuller Lake. This hike
follows an old flume and narrow gauge railroad grade.

Description: Both Rucker and Fuller lakes are situated so close to one another (a mere 800 feet) that you may paddle two lakes for the price of one.
(See Area One, Paddle Location 1, for a description of Fuller Lake.) If it
weren't for the conifer forest and a small ridge providing a screen between
the two lakes, you would be able to view paddlers on either lake. Set in a
basin completely surrounded by conifers with a shore view of rock-walled
Grouse Ridge, Fuller Lake is a grand getaway for the paddler. The secondary dirt road access is maintained due to nearby residences, and the lake is
located only a short driving distance from the paved Bowman Lake Road.

The lake is well screened by the tall conifers growing along the edge of
the lake. The predominate trees surrounding the lake are stately Ponderosas,
tall Lodgepoles, and lighter hued Incense Cedars. Interspersed between
the main tree belts and usually set back from the edge of the lake, are
smaller stands of California Black Oaks, individual types of fir and the
occasional Quaking Aspen *(Populus tremuloides)*. The presence of all these

different tree types growing intermixed with each other is a indicator that you are in a particular plant community known as a mixed-conifer forest.*

Once past this screen, the kidney-shaped contours of the lake are readily visible. This same belt of trees that hugs the shore also provides a wind-break against the afternoon breeze that sweeps the surface of the lake. This breeze appears to be prevailing from the north, the same location as the spillway and housing cluster. Speaking of houses, the western shoreline of the lake contains several cabins and houses that are discreetly set back from the lake. Only one major house and grounds are distinctly viewable from the water. With the exception of the visible spillway and the two small docks, it is hard to believe that the lake is inhabited. This changes however as the snow melts off the roadways and the days become warmer. By early summer, this and the nearby Fuller Lake are primary destination points for local families, especially during the weekend. The better time to enjoy these two lakes is either during the week or in the spring and fall.

Lake view

From the campground entrance, the first feature that beckons your eye is the prominent red-hued rounded rock knoll clearly visible on the west end of the lake. The larger tree-covered hill some distance to the west and partially screened by the forest is Clyde Mountain (6,052'). Tucked into the trees to the left (south) of the rock knoll are several cabins whose presence may be deferred by the break in the trees that border the entire shoreline of the lake. As you continue to follow the contour of the lake southward, you will notice that the shoreline makes a bend to the southeast where a meadow

View uplake from the knob. The small clearing is the grass and sedge-covered mouth of Rucker Creek. Zion Hill (6,204') is in the background.

35

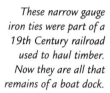

These narrow gauge iron ties were part of a 19th Century railroad used to haul timber. Now they are all that remains of a boat dock.

is clearly visible. The clearing that breaks the monotony of trees also marks the southeastern border of the lake. As you follow the shoreline upward to your present location, you will notice several small coves. During the early morning when these coves are still shaded from the rising sun you may observe White Egrets *(Casmerodius albus)* and Great Blue Herons *(Ardea herodias)* poised for a quick thrust with their bill as they patiently await their prey. Dabbling in the water, feeding on the sedges that grow along the lake's edge, or just resting on the surface, are family groups of Mallards, Common Mergansers and Canada Geese *(Branta canadensis)*.

Returning to the rocky knoll, the right edge of the knoll hides a part of the shoreline. This section of lake contains a small well-shaded cove and is the take-out for the hike to the top of the knoll. A small A-frame cabin sits on the northern edge of this cove. The view of the northeastern shoreline reveals the visible horizontal slash that identifies the location of the dam and spillway. Several old stumps and a couple of docks mark the location of the beach that is part of the Liahona Campground.

Now that you have scanned and become aware of the prominent features that surround the lake, it is time to ready your craft and become familiar with the rest of the lake.

Down Lake Views

PADDLE TIP

Paddling with Photography in Mind

If you want to do some photography, plan your paddle around the availability of light and shade. By observing the sunlight as it penetrates and retreats around the lake, you can plan your paddle around the changes in the sun's position during the course of the day. In the morning the rising sun highlights the lower lake around the dam. As the day progresses, the upper lake and eastern shoreline lose their cover of shade and become sunlit. By the late afternoon, the upper lake and meadow become sunlit providing many photographic opportunities.

As you begin your paddle toward the lower lake and dam, you will pass the small docks of the campground. Immediately past them you will notice what appears to be the stumps of trees standing in the waters of the lake. By paddling closer, you will note that these "stumps" are actually the remains of trees that were logged during the creation of the reservoir. This slash pile now provides an anchor for plants and a hiding place for the lake's watery inhabitants.

Upon reaching the edge of the dam, if you wish to explore the area on foot, you may take out at the upper east end of the dam. From there, you will be able to walk along the footpath leading to the bridge spanning the release site. The belt of conifers surrounding the dam site is primarily Incense Cedars and Lodgepole Pines.

If you paddle the length of the dam be wary of partially submerged rocks that may scrape your canoe or kayak. Occasionally, you may spot a shimmer coming from the shallow bottom. If you take the time to examine the cause, you will be rewarded with a lure that some unlucky fisherperson lost to these same submerged rocks. When you reach the dam's lower end and turn your boat toward the direction of the small cove that becomes the west shoreline, you will pass the landscaped grounds of a private residence. Because this cove is so well protected from the wind, its surface stays calm and flat. If you are paddling here in the springtime, your boat's bow will cleave through the thick cover of yellow pollen that was released by the surrounding conifers.

When you round the small point that separates this cove from the adjacent one, you will pass another smaller A-frame cabin tucked in the copse of pines. Continue to follow the shoreline of this small cove. If you are interested in hiking to the top of the rocky knoll whose sheer rock wall dominates this end of the lake, beach your craft along the shoreline opposite the cabin site. A faint but discernable trail leads from the shore following the high ground to the top of the knoll. As you hike a few yards into the tree line, look for a large trunk of a mature Black Oak *(Q. kelloggii).* The trail to the ridge top follows beside it.

Before reaching the top, you will pass a vegetative belt consisting of two types of manzanita (Spanish for *"little apple,"* referring to the plant's apple-like fruit*)* growing nearby. The taller shrub-like variety is Greenleaf Manzanita *(Arctostaphylos patula),* and the ground-hugging type known as Pinemat Manzanita *(Arctostaphylos nevadensis).* These plants are easily identifiable by the deep red hue of the bark, the leather-like texture and waxy feel of their broad leaves. Upon passing the manzanita you emerge onto the cleared knob of the knoll. From here you have a spectacular view of the lake, the outspread forest and the craggy flank of Zion Hill (6,204'). *Note: If you sit to enjoy the view, be wary of the many aggressive large black ants (Family Formicidae) whose presence may be painfully felt, if you linger too long. Be sure to keep the zippers and drawstrings of any packs shut to these ants from catching a ride in your boat.*

Walkaround the sparsely covered knob and you will notice the large rounded clusters of erratics spread around the area. Many of these glacial erratics were transported many miles from their origin before they came to rest here.

Back in your boat, as you paddle around the base of the knob, take note of the composition of the rock that makes up this geologic feature. The entire outcrop appears to be a single mass of quartzite whose presence may be attributed, in part, to the scouring effects of former glaciers. Be wary of partially submerged rocks as you round the knob. Suddenly, you leave the sculpted rocky wall of the knob behind, pass through several standing trunks of former conifers, and enter into another tree-lined cove.

A short paddle following the shoreline will place you in an area of the cove where a submerged tree leans out toward the center of the lake. Here, too, the waters are deeper and therefore cooler than the surrounding warm shallow area along the shoreline. Let your boat drift, keep your movements to a minimum, and watch the water around the area of the submerged tree. You should be able to spot several large trout *(Family Salmo)* that will pass under you as your craft silently moves past the submerged trunk. Several of these fish appear to be trophy sized.

As you paddle past the area of the trout, you will pass the cove and work your way around a shallow point before entering the next cove. Looking at the shoreline you should be able to spot two tall and imposing Ponderosa Pines that grow near the shoreline. Set back a short distance will be a standing snag that now serves as a hotel for many birds in the area.

Directly ahead of you lies the grass and sedge-covered mouth of Rucker Creek. A partially covered entryway is located along the right shoreline. Look for a group of willows lining the far right bank. Passing through the brush-covered entrance, Red-winged Blackbirds *(Agelaius phoeniceus)* vocally protest your entry and occasionally, strafe your boat. Follow the stream until it becomes too narrow for paddling. Here under the sparse, but scented, canopy of a young pine you may enjoy the unobstructed view of he lake. As the breeze picks up, pack your gear, turn your boat around, and paddle back onto the

The meadow offers a nice lunch spot with a clear view of Rucker Lake.

main body of the lake. Crossing the wet meadow you catch a nice glimpse of Zion Hill as it begins to redden from the late afternoon sun. Close to the water, leaf blades from sedges shimmer in the sunlight with the same passing breeze. Bobbing up and down as they feed on the sedges, a small flock of Canada Geese, the same flock you observed earlier, ignores your passing.

You enter a small cove that is protected from the wind and possibly startle a Great Blue Heron standing immobile in the shallows near the shore. From here, it is but a short paddle to your original put-in. Before you finish, however, you may spot the strangely constructed boat dock located a short distance away. Paddling to the site, you notice that the entire dock was built from railroad ties. There you have it! The mystery of what happened to those missing ties, (In The Eddy: The Hikes From Rucker Lake), is now at least, partially solved.

Area References

Gudde, ErwinG. *California Place Names.* Revised and enlarged by William Bright. Berkeley, CA.: University of California Press, 1998. 467 pp.

Grater, Russel K. *Discovering Sierra Mammals,* Yosemite Association, Sequoia Natural History Association, 1978. 174 pp.

Thomas, John Hunter & Dennis R. Parnell, *Native Shrubs of the Sierra Nevada,* Berkeley, CA: University of California Press. 1974. 127 pp. (pg. 89)

Whitney Stephen, *Western Forests,* A National Audubon Society Nature Guide. Alfred A. Knopf, Inc.: New York, 1997. 670 pp.

IN THE EDDY

The Hikes From Rucker Lake

If you want to explore the forest surrounding the lake, the wet meadow at the mouth of Rucker Creek presents an ideal location for two hikes. From here, the trail to Fuller Lake may be intersected as well as the trail to the former railroad bed and flume line. If hiking through the forest does not appeal to you, then a hike following the bed of Rucker Creek will be of interest (see map).

Trail to Fuller Lake With Side Treks
to Old Logging Railroad Bed & Flume Line

The trail to Fuller Lake may be reached by first hiking the shoreline trail along Rucker Lake. You may reach this trail by following the inlet you paddled in on where it ends at the forest margin. Look for a faint but discernable path on the right (southwest) end of the inlet. You will hike past several boulders and intersect the shoreline trail paralleling the lake. Follow this trail until you reach a small stream. Take the upper fork that begins to climb up the ridge. You are now on the trail that leads to Fuller Lake. Where the trail crests the ridge, look for an outcrop of boulders. The trail should make a bend around this outcrop before descending down toward Fuller Lake. Examine the ground closely as you round this bend. Look for the remnants of timber that were the crossties holding the iron rails of a former logging rail line.

A short distance past the bend the trail drops off to the right but the rail bed continues to follow the ridge crest. Continuing on the trail to the lake, you cross a berm running roughly north to south and at a right angle to the trail. You are now crossing one of many flume beds that were built to carry water for hydraulic mining, then later, as part of an integrated water source for drinking and hydroelectric use. If time and energy permits, you may follow the flume bed as it parallels the ridge separating the two lakes. From where you first intersect the flume bed, the trail drops down and intersects the Fuller Lake shoreline trail. A few short steps across this trail, passing the belt of conifers that border the shoreline, is a gorgeous view of Fuller Lake.

The Hike Along Rucker Creek

From the take-out at the inlet, follow the small stream as it flows through the grassy meadow past the stand of dead wood where it disappears in the forest. As you make your way along the soggy ground, you may spot small oval earthen furrows running in random directions all along the expanse of the meadow. This is the work of the California Mole *(Scapanus latimanus)*, an animal that spends its entire life underground. Just before you reach the shaded canopy of the forest, look for the budding stalks of Corn Lilies *(Veratrum californicum)* growing in scattered bunches at the edge of the meadow. Entering the tree line near the creek, you can't help but notice all the fallen timber lying scat-

Portions of an old flume bed along the trail between Rucker and Fuller Lakes.

tered all around the edge of the forest. My guess is that the rising levels of the lake have rotted the root systems of these trees. The stressed trees, already weakened, were further susceptible to attacks by insects and diseases. If you have a set of binoculars, wait a few minutes and you may observe the antics of the woodpeckers *(FamilyPicidae)* as they hunt for insects hiding in the dead wood. On some of the dead trunks huge blisters of Red-belted Polypore, *(Fomitopsis pinicola)* fungus provides further proof of tree decay.

Treading your way through the downed trees, look for trunks lying on the ground containing huge cavities or with evidence of being shredded. There is a good chance that you are viewing the work of a bear as it tore apart a tree trunk in search of ant nests and other insects.Once past the edge of the wetland, the creek takes on a new vibrancy as it tumbles and falls over the various-sized boulders. Small waterfalls are evident along with frothy whirlpools that form along eddy lines. The light now becomes muted and coolness is felt as you progress deeper into the woods. When you step out into a sunlit clearing, look down at your feet and see if you can spot the delicate yellow petaled form of a Pine Violet or Yellow Wood Violet, *(Viola lobata)*. Eventually you will reach the visible stonework that marks a small debris dam. This dam was built to prevent debris and silt from entering Rucker Lake during the construction of the dam at Blue Lake located further upstream. From here you may either continue on to Blue Lake, or cross over the stream and pick up the jeep trail that will lead back to the open meadow and mouth of Rucker Creek. On your return, just before you pass through a small stand of mature Jeffrey Pine, take the time to view their silhouette and admire their girth. Then, as you pass between them, place your nose into a furrowed trunk and breath in the aroma of vanilla, butterscotch or pineapple.

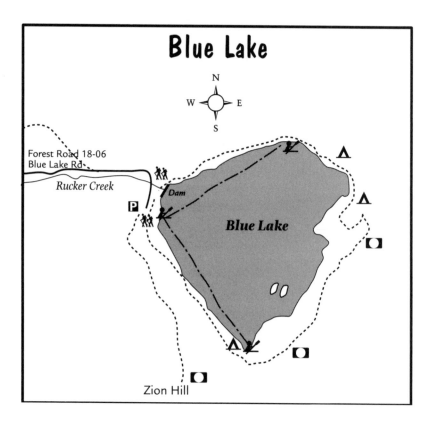

PADDLE LOCATION 3

Blue Lake

Difficulty: All skill levels
Trip Length: Day use or longer
Lake Size: Approximately 4/10ths of a mile in circumference.
Paddle Distances:
From the put-in to FS Campground, SE end of lake: 0.35 mile
Take-out for ridge hike & primitive camping area: 0.33 mile
Elevation: 5,920' at the spillway
Season: Spring, after the snow melts, into summer before water levels drop creating steep banks.
County: Nevada
National Forest: Tahoe National Forest, Nevada City Ranger District (530) 265-4531
Maps: USGS 7.5 Minute Topographical Sheet: Blue Canyon Quadrangle
National Forest Service Map: Shown on the Tahoe National Forest Service Map. Jurisdiction may reside with Pacific Gas & Electric (PG&E).
Road Maps: Compass maps Inc.: Nevada & Sierra Counties
American Auto Assn. (AAA) Maps: Northern California/Bay & Mountain sections

Access: Take Interstate 80 East, drive past Yuba Gap & Crystal Road turnoff. Exit right onto Highway 20 West. Continue on Highway 20 for 4.0 miles and turn right on Bowman Lake Road, (Forest Service Route: 18N18). Follow the road for approximately 5 miles. Turn right onto Forest Service Road: 18-06 (a.k.a.: Blue Lake Road). *(Note: the 18-06 road turnoff is 3/10th's of a mile from the posted 4.5 Mile Marker).* Drive an additional 4/10th's of a mile, passing two water tanks, to a Y-fork. Stay to the left until you reach a clearing that served as a stacking center for logs. At the end of the clearing the road comes to another Y-fork. The left fork is the old jeep trail that is marked on the 7.5 Minute Quadrangle. Take the right fork, *not marked on any of the maps*, cutting through the edge of the clearing. Here the road begins to climb as it parallels Rucker Creek. You will cross one or more small intermittent streams before reaching the final crossing of Rucker Creek. Look for several huge boulders visible across the creek and on your right. The rebuilt dam and spillway will be visible above the creek on your left. Unless erosion has altered the crossing point, you may drive across and park at the western edge of the dam.

Heads Up

- Small picturesque lake ideal for day or weekend use.
- Paddle only when full. Drawdown creates steep banks unsuitable for easy exit and beaching of boat.
- Short hikes along granite ridges with spectacular scenery of Lake

Spaulding, Fordyce Canyon, & prominent Sierran Peaks.
- Lakeside primitive camping.
- Bear country: pack & camp smart.
- Campfire permit advisable.
- Additional lakes located within a short driving distance.

Description: The decision to paddle on Blue Lake is not the end-all of your destination get-away. The lake is small and oval shaped, creating a foregone conclusion of where and what you will explore. The real reason for choosing Blue Lake is not just the paddling, but also the chance to surround you, your family and friends, with a full camping experience. This is one of the few picturesque lakes located within a short driving distance off Bowman Lake Road and may be reached with almost any family vehicle. The small size of the lake makes it an ideal choice to take small kids and teach them proper boat camping skills. Everything about the layout of the lake seems tailor-made for either the development or improvement of one's boating and camping skills.

Upon arrival and parking, there is a short portage down from the parking area near the dam to the put-in/take-out at the lake's edge. Although a hiking trail follows the entire shoreline of the lake, paddling your gear-filled boat is definitely the preferred method of transport to your choice of campsite. With the exception of the tree-screened sites along the northeast end of the lake, all the other camping spots are readily

View of Blue Lake looking east toward the ridge described in the text. The tip of Red Mountain looms in the distance.

From a nearby ridgetop you can enjoy this incredible view of Fordyce Creek Gorge. Grouse Ridge (7,000') flanks the left (north) side of the valley, and the half-dome of Old Man Mountain (7,789') is visible in the distance.

visible as you paddle along the shoreline. Because of this method of transport to your site, proper loading of the boat becomes imperative. (See Packing a kayake, loading a canoe, and portaging, pg. 13.)

Once the boat or boats are packed and on the water, as you paddle along the shoreline the entire family may provide an input to the best choice of campsite. If locating the camp is the primary order of business, I suggest that you follow the west shoreline first. Choice sites appear only a short paddling distance from your put-in. This end of the lake contains a level stretch of gravel beach screened by a background of tall conifers and the imposing mass of Zion Hill (6,204').

The area has suitable quantities of downed wood for a campfire and the rugged brush covered terrain keeps the kids on the beach and within your sight. Take along a set or two of binoculars and a couple of good guidebooks on birds and trees. The entire belt of pines and cedars contains scores of birds whose activities are easily viewed from your camp. The variety of the conifers growing in short proximity to each other produces an assortment of pinecones of various shapes and sizes. In addition to making excellent fire-starters, these cones could be used to identify the trees. The birds and trees and the variety of rocks should pique the interest of adult and child alike. Due to the unique geology of the area, Blue Lake is situated at a contact zone between the young Sierran granite and the altered remnants of older layers of former geologic events (see Area Reference Section). Because of this, one may find interesting rock types having such names as: metaquartzite, schist, gneiss, greenstone, hornblende, pegmatite, diorite; as well as the ubiquitous granite.

Depending on your needs, the best area for a campsite is located at the far southwest end of the lake. Here you have a level gravel beach, shelter and shade provided by the trees and the mountain; subsequently, you are in close proximity to a granite ridge containing accessible hiking trails. Unfortunately, none of these trails lead to the top of Zion Hill. If you have an interest in hiking to this summit, the trail begins at the far end of the turn-around where you portaged your boat to the lake (see map).

To break up the monotony of paddling "just on the lake," there are two very small islands readily visible from the put-in located on this southwest end of the lake. Be careful of your approach to these barren rocky knobs; there are many partially submerged boulders surrounding the islands. As you follow the southern shoreline, be sure to beach your boat and make time to hike up the readily accessible granite ridge that parallels this end of the lake. Not only will the hike be a welcome diversion to the paddle, but also there is an excellent reason for making this hike. As you work your way up the granite slope, note the presence of the Sierra Juniper/Western Juniper (Juniperus occidentalis), a tree not found on the opposite end of the lake. Also note the small size of the pines growing nearby. This stunted growth is due in part to the open location where the trees grow. Their diminished size is, in part, a survival trait against severe wind exposure and the result of repeated frost damage that occurs to the growing shoots of the trees.

As you thread your way through the rubble of weathered granite, pay close attention to where you place your feet. During my hikes through the area, I have been rudely reminded of my complacency by the sudden dry "rasping" sound of a Western Rattlesnake (Crotalus viridis).

Interspersed amongst the piles of granite and stunted conifers, are areas of level ground where the granite has eroded and left a base of poorly sorted granules called grus. Some of these areas are large enough to be used as a campsite. In fact, if you look further, you may spot the telltale remnants of former campfires by the piles of ash and their rings of stone. Eventually you reach the top of the ridge, and the reason for the hiking effort becomes clear: stretching outward as far as the eye can see are the glacial valleys and imposing peaks of the North-Central Sierra Nevada Mountain Range. To obtain the best view, wait for the late afternoon sun to highlight the area. From this vantage point you may look down onto the shimmering waters that make up Lake Spaulding (described in *Up the Lake, Vol.1*). Rising above the lake looking south are a series of ridges whose tops are bisected by the horizontal lines of the Transcontinental Railroad and Interstate 80.

To the northeast, you may follow the line of the broad U-shaped valley that marks the location of Fordyce Creek. The spectacular ridge that characterizes the northern flank of the valley is Grouse Ridge. It trends for two miles in a south to southwest direction, at an average height of 7,000'. The peak in the immediate foreground, directly across from Grouse Ridge and with the reddish hue on its top, is Brady Mountain (5,956'). Sitting alone in the distance with a profile similar to Yosemite's famous Half-Dome is Old Man Mountain (7,789').

Continuing on with your paddle, when you reach the steep banks that mark the channel of an intermittent stream flowing into the lake (southeast shoreline), look for a beach to take out. You may either follow up the channel of this stream or hike up the banks of the lake's shore. Either way, located a short distance into the tree line, is a primitive campground complete with picnic tables and iron fire-rings. When I explored the area in 2001, there were several camp chairs carved out of tree stumps located in various campsites. They all faced the lake and were quite comfortable.

This campground contains at least six sites scattered in various locations within the small belt of conifers. The stream drainage acts as a

Picturesque benches were carved from stumps near the campsites. From one of these thrones the camper may enjoy a grand view of the lake.

natural dividing line separating the sites. Screened by the pines and brush, the flank of Grouse Ridge Peak (7,181') rises behind the campground. From here to the dam, you will be paddling along side the sloping contours of the peak. The entire shoreline is hidden under a thick cover of manzanita (*Genus Arctostaphylos*), and various species of pines.

Area References

Alt, David & Donald W. Hyndman, *Roadside Geology of Northern and Central California*. Missoula, MT: Mountain Press Publishing Company, 2000, 369 pp. (See; Introduction, pgs 1-4 & Chapter 2, pgs 9-17)

Arno, Stephen F. & Ramona P. Hammerly, *Timberline Mountain and Arctic Forest Frontiers*, Seattle, WA: The Mountaineers, 1993, 4th printing. 304 pp.

Chesterman, Charles W., *The Audubon Society Field Guide to North American Rocks and Minerals*. New York, NY: Alfred A. Knopf, Inc., 1978, 2nd Printing. 507 pp.

Storer, Tracy I., & Robert L. Usinger, *Sierra Nevada Natural History*, Berkeley, CA: University of California Press, 1963. 374 pp.

Whitney, Stephen, *National Audubon Society Nature Guide: Western Forests*. New York, NY: Alfred A. Knopf, Inc., 1997, 670 pp.

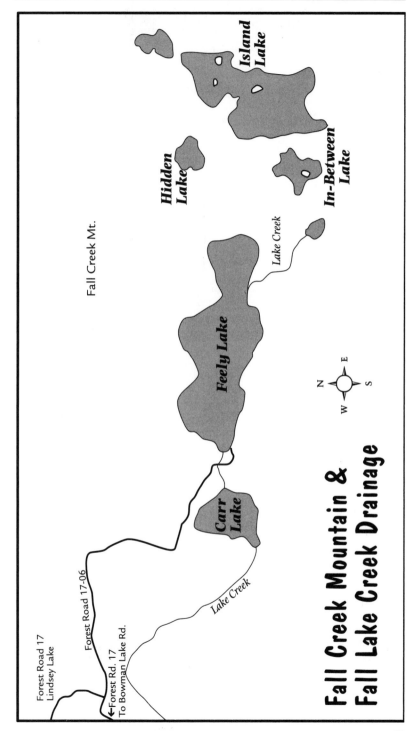

Island Lake

Hidden Lake

In-Between Lake

Lake Creek

Fall Creek Mt.

Feely Lake

N E S W

Carr Lake

Forest Road 17-06

Lake Creek

Forest Road 17
Lindsey Lake

←Forest Rd. 17
To Bowman Lake Rd.

**Fall Creek Mountain &
Fall Lake Creek Drainage**

Area 2

Fall Creek Mountain & Fall Creek Drainage

PADDLE LOCATION 4

Carr Lake

Difficulty: Except for an occasional strong afternoon wind, for boaters of all skill levels
Trip Length: The reservoir itself is too small for anything but a day paddle, however, the long drive time makes it an overnight destination spot.
Paddling Distances:
From the put-in north end of lake to dam and take-out for ridge hike: 0.17 mile.
Season: From snow melt through mid-summer before the water levels drop. Best time is in the spring when reservoir is fullest and the wildflowers are blooming.
Lake Size: 950' X 800'
Elevation: 6,664'
County: Nevada
National Forest: Tahoe National Forest, Nevada City Ranger District (530) 265-4531
Maps: USGS 7.5 Minute Topographical Section: Graniteville Quadrangle
Adjoining section: English Mtn. Quadrangle
National Forest Service Map: Tahoe National Forest
Road Maps: Compass Maps, Inc.: Nevada and Sierra Counties; Nevada–Sierra Counties Street and Road Atlas
American Auto. Assn. (AAA) Maps: Northern California/Bay & Mountain Section

Access: Interstate Highway 80 East to California State Highway 20 West. Exit at Yuba Gap toward Nevada City. Continue on Highway 20 West for four miles, exit onto Bowman Lake Road / Forest Road 18. The exit for Carr and Feeley Lakes, Forest Road 17, will be on your right just past the 8.5 Mile Marker. *Note: This last four mile section is a rough dirt and cobble road.* Continue on FR 17 for approximately 3 miles. You will come to a Y-fork. Take the right fork that becomes FR 17-06. About 4/10ths of a mile from this first intersection you will come upon another Y. Stay to the right. After one mile, FR 17-06 terminates in the parking area for Carr and Feeley Lakes. Overflow parking is located in a cleared area just below the Carr–Feeley Lakes Trailhead Sign. To access Carr Lake, hike past the gate containing the information board, and the lake will appear on your right. If you are planning to camp, your campsite will serve as your put-in. Put in at the nearest vacant access point if you are interested in paddling the lake for the day only.

Heads Up
- Fire permit required for any fire or stove use.
- The nearest phone and groceries are at the small country store on Crystal Lake Road. The exit is at Yuba Gap off I-80 West. Gas, sundries and fast food may be obtained at the Shell Station off I-80 below Yuba Gap in Nyack.
- Primitive camping sites, containing a fire ring only, are dispersed around the edge of the lake (see map).
- Vault toilet, no water facilities.
- Bear country: pack and camp smart.
- Wind may be a problem in the mid morning and afternoon.
- Good fishing, Brookies and Rainbows. Best spot appears to be near the mouth of Fall Lake Creek.
- Access to lakes nearby. See Paddling Locations 5–8.
- Some great mountain biking and hiking nearby.
- Impressive view from the dam site of the ridges, canyons and forest surrounding the South and Middle Forks of the Yuba River.

Description: Pick two days in spring, but wait no later than the first week in June. Time those days to a full moon, and drive out to Carr Lake. Time your arrival so that you are at the lake in the early evening.

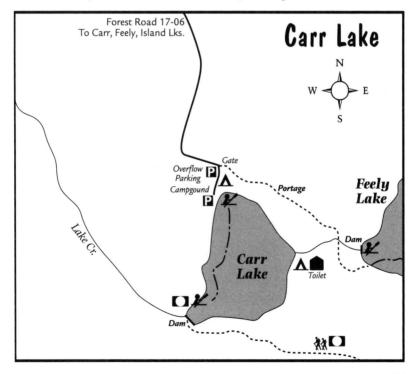

Carr Lake sits high, surrounded by a forest of pine, cedar, and fir.

Ignore the hordes of mosquitoes that serve as the welcoming committee. Pack your gear and hoist your boat for the short walk to the shoreline of Carr Lake.

If a toilet facility is part of your comfort margin, then portage down the road toward Feeley Lake Dam. There are at least four campsites that share a small vault toilet at the lower west end of the dam site. Unfortunately there is no access to Carr Lake from any of these sites.   Otherwise, pick a spot at the northeast edge of the lake nearest the road, or, pack the boat and paddle toward Carr Dam visible at the western end of the lake. Just before the dam, look for an opening in the trees surrounding that portion of the lake. In a clearing, containing a field of Bracken ferns *(Pteridium aquilinum)* is a small section of beach ideal for a take-out. Walk in a short distance and find a suitable campsite. Try to stay as close to the dam as possible.

As dusk approaches, quickly set up camp. When night falls and the globule moon begins to rise over the ridgeline, brew up your favorite hot beverage and walk across the top of the dam. Tromp over the lip of the berm, and enjoy your well-earned view! For an additional sensory overload, repeat the same performance in the morning before the sun reaches too high and washes out the vista. Be sure to bring a camera, binoculars, wildflower field guide, and a daypack containing water, hat, lip-balm, and a snack. Wear lightweight long pants for bush whacking and a light jacket as protection against the wind.

As you crest that same berm of rocky soil, take a deep breath and inhale the rich aroma emanating from acres of variously hued wild flowers whose faces bow against the force of the wind. Every feature stands out in sharp relief from the Transcontinental Railroad and Interstate 80 in the foreground, to the distant peaks of the Sierra Buttes (8,587').

When your eyes focus on the varieties of wildflowers carpeting the slope of this former glacial moraine, their individual names spring to mind. The larger yellow daisy-like flowers with the enormous softly hairy leaves are Mules Ears. There are seven species growing in the area, subsequently, *Wyethia mollis* is the only one to grow above low montane elevations, from 4000-10,500.' The plant was named after Nathaniel Wyeth, a 19th Century American explorer. The plant with the smaller, brighter, yellow flower heads is Balsam Root, *Balsamorhiza sagittata* (referring to its sticky cap and arrow shaped leaves.) Interspersed around these daisy-like plants, are stems of blue Torrey's lupine, *Lupinus lepidus var. sellulus.* This species was also named after a 19th Century figure, John Torrey, an American chemist and plant taxonomist.

Standing apart from the clusters of lupines and growing at the base of scattered rock piles, are small clusters of Applegate's Paintbrush/Wavy-leaved Paintbrush, *(Castilleja applegatei)*. Carpeting the ground, Pussy Paws, *(Calyptridium umbellatum)* show off their rounded clusters of pink flowers. Their shape resembles the upturned pads of cat paws. An interesting feature of this plant is the ability of the ground lying stems to heat up, then slowly rise to an almost vertical position lifting the flowers away from the radiant heat of the ground.

Two additional flowering plants are the clusters of white flowers belonging to the phlox family. This plant is known as Granite Gilia, *(Leptodactylon pungens)* or sometimes *"prickly phlox."* The plant with the tiny clusters of yellow dots for flowers is Lomatium, *(Lomatium utriculatum)*, a member of the carrot family.

The varieties of different rocks denote their movement by the past action of moving glaciers as they plucked rocks from one location and transported them to another. If time permits, follow the meandering trail to the top of the ridge. Deer initially created these random trails as they continue to browse their way alongside the ridge face. Hikers have widened them and now a distinct series of pathways winds to the top. If you have worn the lightweight long pants (recommended earlier), you will save your legs from being *sliced and diced* by the many branchlets and thorns sticking out along the route. The view from the top of the ridge allows you to have an unsurpassed observation of both Carr and Feeley lakes. To the northeast, the far distant jagged outline of the Sierra Buttes stands out in sharp relief.

Back on the water, paddling the circumference of the lake allows you to obtain a good perspective of the lake's personality. Swarms of midges *(Chironomus sp.)* and other hatches rise from the sun-touched shallows. Sometimes these swarms become so thick you literally breath-in and spit out multitudes of the emerging insects. Members of the dragonfly family such as Green Darners *(Anax junius)*, damselflies like the Northern Bluets *(Enallagma*

Early spring on Carr Lake. Fall Creek Mountain (7,490') is seen in the background.

cyathigerum), and Vivid Dancers *(Argia vivida)* flit and jet past you in search of food or mates.

How do you tell the dragonflies apart from the damselflies? The dragonflies have a more robust body; when resting, dragonflies hold their wings outstretched and damselflies fold theirs vertically to the rear. For readers wishing to learn more about this fascinating order of insects, check out an award-winning website devoted exclusively to dragonflies: http://www.sonic.net/dragonfly.

Unfortunately, except for one small clearing at the southern bend of the lake (see map), this steep section of shoreline does not allow for an easy take-out. Your exploration will have to be done using your boat, however, the paddling is easy and the scenery just glides by. Eventually you reach the area of a steep barren rock wall that dominates the southern end of the lake. If the light is right, you will spot sections of the wall that glisten as if polished. This is indeed the case! As glaciers carved their way down this valley, the combination of the weight of the ice and the grit imbedded in it scoured the rock to a fine polish. This glacial polish just adds to the evidence of former climatic patterns that existed thousands of years ago. Now Bracken Ferns or Brake *(Pteridium aquilinum),* Scarlet Penstemon *(Penstemon rostriflorus),* and clumps of manzanita *(Genus Arctostaphylos)* dot the crevices of the rocky ledges. Passing the rock wall but before you reach the mouth of Fall Lake Creek, you will pass a steep brushy bank. Located behind this screen of rock and brush are the clusters of campsites grouped around the only toilet facility in the area of the two lakes.

When you reach the mouth of Fall Lake Creek, be wary of partially submerged rocks that surround the creek's entrance. Let your boat drift, and see if you can spot a stubby gray bird resting on either the rocks or bare limbs at the stream's edge. The American Dipper *(Cinclus mexicanus)*, or by its British name of the *Water Ouzel*, possesses the unique ability to dive into the water and run along the bottom catching insects with its partially open wings.

Passing the creek, you paddle past a thick growth of Lemmon Willow *(Salix lemmonii)* and Aspen *(Populus tremuloides)*. Located behind the brush are several campsites and the partially obscured old road and portage trail leading to Feeley Lake. The two small clearings immediately past the aspen grove are your take-outs. The campsites behind the screen of brush at the take-outs are the only sites on this side of the lake with easy access to the water.

Area References

Biggs, Kathy, *Common Dragonflies of California*. Sebastopol, CA: Azalea Creek Publishing, 2nd printing, October 2000. 96 pp.

Blackwell, Laird R., *Wildflowers of the Sierra Nevada and the Central Valley*. Edmonton, AB, Canada: Lone Pine Publishing. 1999. 288 pp.

Durham, David L., *Place-Names of California's Gold Country Including Yosemite National Park*. Clovis, CA: Quill Driver Books/Word Dancer Press, Inc., 2000. 369 pp.

On the last leg of the drive to Carr Lake.

Freeman, Jim, *North Sierra Trout Fishing.* San Francisco, CA: Chronicle Books, 1972. 80 pp.

National Audubon Society, *Western Forests,* author: Stephen Whitney. New York, NY: Alfred A. Knopf, Inc. 9th printing, march 1997. 670 po.

_____, *Field Guide to North American Birds, Western Addition,* author, Miklos D. F. Udvardy. New York, NY: Alfred A. Knopf, 17th printing, January 1992. 852 pp.

Storer, Tracy I. & Robert L. Usinger, *Sierra Nevada Natural History.* Berkeley, CA: University Of California Press, 1963. 374 pp.

⟐ IN THE EDDY ⟐

On the Portage Trail or The Joy of Kevlar

As I studied the topographical sheet looking over the next group of lakes I would paddle, I saw that portages were involved. Based on my research, the distances varied from 1/10 of a mile on the former road to Feeley Lake, all the way to almost 1 mile of varied route conditions for Culbertson Lake. But the best news pertained to the trail conditions for each of the portages. All the portages were on established trails, as the maps seemed to indicate. None, to my relief, required blazing my own trail . . . canoe and all!

In addition to all the positive terrain variables, I also possessed two key pieces of equipment that would relieve some of the grunt work on any portage—my 32lb Kevlar* Advantage** canoe and the all-aluminum take-apart boat cart! So with a smug smile on my face, I stepped out of my pickup, set up the cart, and loaded my canoe. With the canoe sling strapped snugly over my shoulder, I ventured forth on the first leg of a two-part portage.

The former road leading to Feeley Lake from the newly established gate at the entrance to Carr Lake reinforced my belief that these two portages were a "piece of cake." Eventually, my first real test came when I started up the small incline leading to the basin rim of Feeley Lake. Large cobbles, firmly imbedded in the soil, were heaped all across the trail. "No problemo," I said aloud to myself.

I could see the last section of the trail before the put-in; consequently, like the plow horse heading for the barn, I increased my efforts. The first group of boulders was negotiated with little to no effort, so I tugged harder on the sling. With a resounding "whap," the cart came to a sudden halt! My back, being turned away and facing the trail, I heard the sound, did not stop in time; subsequently, with all the grace of a puppy at the end of a leash, I came to a screeching halt with my butt firmly on the ground! "Gad," how ignoble! Looking about to see if anybody observed this farce on the trail, I quickly dusted the tender portion of my anatomy and with a few choice epitaphs, limped over to check for damages.

Apparently, in my sudden haste to negotiate this last group of cobbles, I did not examine their layout and size. When the two wheels of the weighted cart rode up to the two side-by-side cobbles, one of the cobbles was too large for the wheel to negotiate. The proverbial law of the portage trail took over–namely, the law of moveable cart encountering immovable object, equals a bruised ego and a sore butt.

With the wheels firmly abutted against the cobbles, the folding frame of the cart, well . . . folded. This action threw the weighted canoe down on the cobbles and initiated a breaking reaction on my body. Luckily, no damage occurred to the cart, the canoe or any of the packed gear. To re-strap the canoe however, I first had to unload it so that I could fold down the axle and lift the boat back onto the cart. By the time all this was completed and I was ready to proceed, the sun had set below the tree line. I negotiated Fall Lake Creek (the stream below Lake Feeley Dam) without any further travail and arrived at the end of the first leg of the portage.

With the exception of the hasty attempt to reach the lake, my plan was working well. The cart proved to my satisfaction that it could carry the weight of a fully loaded canoe, negotiate a cobble-strewn trail, and ford a flowing stream. I now had to unload the gear before paddling to my campsite at the far end of the lake, near the second and final portion of the portage trail. This last section however, would either prove or disprove all the past hype I gave on the benefits of a light Kevlar canoe.

The following morning, I left the majority of my gear in camp. Packing only a daypack and paddle, I hefted my canoe to my shoulder and proceeded to follow the stream until I cut the main trail. Unlike the easy road leading to Feeley Lake, this portage to Island Lake involves being off-trail at different portions of the portage. It was at these sections of the portage that the worth of carrying a Kevlar canoe came to the fore. As I climbed the ridge leading to the upper lakes, I had to not only watch where I placed my feet, but also keep track of the angle of my canoe–all the while negotiating through dense trees.

The route became steeper and the section of trail began to narrow. On two occasions I climbed over fallen trunks. When one side of my shoulder became fatigued, I carefully turned the canoe onto the other side. After crossing the same stream I again followed off-trail and crunching over a section of snow pack I finally arrived at the shoreline of In-Between Lake.*** A short paddle across, I once again picked up my canoe, stepped out of the trees and straight into the face of a bug-eyed mule! I yelped, it bucked, the dog barked, and the rider swore as he held on for dear life! After the dust cleared, I learned that the rider was on his way to Carr Lake on the return loop of the Round Lake Trail.****

After we said our goodbyes, I stepped across the section of trail where the near mishap occurred, and beheld the splendid view of my destination: Island Lake. My description of this beautiful lake may be read in Paddle Location 7.

"With the wheels firmly abutted against the cobbles, the folding frame of the cart, well...folded."

Needless to say, after an enjoyable full day of paddling, it was time to retrace my steps and begin the portage back to my campsite at Feeley Lake. It is with great relief that I may write to my readers, of only one incident on the return leg of the portage. This incident occurred on the same section of the portage where I tested the durability of the cart. I was carrying the canoe to the set-up cart and overheard a group of hikers as they came up behind me. One hiker as soon as he spotted me on the trail said to the other: "Hey, how would you like to carry that on the trail?" "No thanks, these packs are bad enough," said the other hiker. I just smiled to myself and acknowledged   . . . the joy of Kevlar.

Sources

* DuPont patents Kevlar. It is a synthetic fiber with resistance to tension and shock but not especially resistant to compression and abrasion. It is used in the manufacture of bulletproof vests, in the aerospace industry, auto racing and paddling helmets (See: *Paddler Magazine*, January/February 2001 issue, pg. 96).

** Advantage is the name of a 16'- 6" solo canoe manufactured by We No Nah Canoe Company of Wenonah, Minnesota. For a copy of their free brochure call: (507) 454-5430, fax: (507)454-5448. E-mail: info@wenonah.com /internet: www.wenonah.com

*** No such lake with the name of In-Between-Lake exists on the 7.5 Granitville Topo sheet. I created the name for the sake of clarity and continuity when describing the portage and the lake.

**** The Round Lake Trail is part of a much larger trail network visible in the free handout: *Trails – Nevada City Ranger District, Tahoe National Forest*. This and other free materials may be picked up at the Nevada City Ranger District Office, 631 Coyote St. Nevada City, CA: 95959 or you may request a copy by telephoning: (530) 265-4531. The office may also be contacted at: www.r5.fs.fed.us/tahoe

Video

"We-No-Nah Canoe: Canoe Repair," videocassette 35:05 minutes. Wenonah Canoe Company, Winona MN. 35:05 min. To obtain, phone: (507) 454-5430 / fax: (507)454-5448. *Although made by the Wenonah Canoe Company using their boats, this excellent video shows you step-by-step how to do proper gel-coat repair, place skid plates, repair cracked ribs; canoe assembly is also included with the proper installation of yokes, foot braces, and seat replacement. As a final treat, you receive a mini tour of the Wenonah factory and observe the construction of a fiberglass canoe.*

PADDLE LOCATION 5

Feeley Lake

(Portage Required)

Note: *The spelling for this lake may also appear as "Feely Lake." This confusion is due to the way it is spelled on the 7.5 Minute Granitville Quadrangle. On the topographical map the spelling is Feely; almost everywhere else it appears as Feeley.*

Difficulty: With the exception of strong afternoon wind, for boaters of all skill levels

Trip Length: The entire lake may be paddled in half-a-day.

Portage: From gate at Carr Lake to Feeley Lake Dam Put-in: 0.26 mile

Paddling Distance:
From the dam put-in to the take-out at mouth of Fall Creek for the portage to In-Between Lake and Island lake: 0.41 mile. The portage is on a former Forest Service access road. There are a few cobbles and a stream crossing on the route (see In the Eddy, On the Portage Trail).

Season: From late spring, when the snow melts off the access roads, to mid-summer before the water levels drop. The optimum time however, is in the spring when the lake is fullest, the crowds not present, and the wildflowers are blooming.

Lake Size: 3000' X 1200'

Elevation: 6,724'

Historical Background: Although the lake has been deepened with the creation of a dam, it is one of the few glacier-carved natural lakes within driving distance.

County: Nevada

National Forest: Tahoe NationalForest, Nevada City Ranger District (530) 265-4531

Maps: USGS 7.5 Minute Topographical Section: Graniteville Quadrangle

Adjoining section: English Mtn. Quadrangle

National Forest Service Map: Tahoe National Forest

Road Maps: Compass Maps, Inc.: Nevada and Sierra Counties; Nevada–Sierra Counties Street and Road Atlas

American Auto. Assn. (AAA) Maps: N. California/Bay and Mountain sections

Access: Interstate Highway 80 East to California State Highway 20 West. Exit at Yuba Gap toward Nevada City. Continue on Highway 20 West for four miles, exit onto Bowman Lake Road / Forest Road 18. The exit, Forest Road 17, for Carr and Feeley Lakes will be on your right just past the 8.5 Mile Marker. *Note: This last four mile section is a rough dirt and cobble road.* Continue on FR 17 for approximately 3 miles. You will come to a Y-fork. Take the right fork, which becomes FR 17-06. After one mile, this forest road terminates in the parking area for Carr and Feeley lakes. Additional parking is also located in a cleared area just below the Carr–Feeley Lakes Trailhead sign.

To prevent increased congestion at both lakes, the Forest Service wisely closed vehicular access directly to Carr and Feeley lakes. A green gate now forces the public to park and hike to their prospective campsites. This is not a problem for Carr Lake, located just a short walk over the lip of the berm separating the lake from the parking area. With Feeley Lake, however, a brief but attention-getting portage is necessary.

To reach Feeley Lake, cart or carry your boat and gear following the road adjoining Carr Lake on the opposite side of the locked gate. The distance is approximately 1/10 of a mile. The put-in is located across Fall Lake Creek, on top of the berm to your left.

Heads Up

- A campfire permit is required for open fires and camp stoves.
- Groceries may be purchased at the small country store on Crystal Lake Road. There is also a phone there. The exit is at Yuba Gap off I-80 West. Gas, sundries and fast food may be obtained at the Shell Station off I-80 below Yuba Gap in Nyack.
- A short 1/10-mile portage is necessary to access the lake with a canoe or kayak.
- Dispersed camping only, (see map).
- Impressive views surrounding the lake.
- Less crowded than Carr Lake.
- Camp is near access trail to other backcountry lakes, i.e.: Island Lake.
- This is bear country: pack and camp smart.

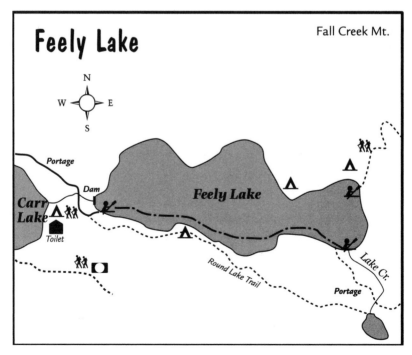

View of upper Feeley Lake through the pines.

Description: It is well worth the short portage to be able to paddle Feeley Lake. Once you have skirted the small stream and trudged up the rocky berm of the dam, your first glimpse of the lake should bring a smile to your face. Stretching out toward the distant ridge, the sun-speckled waters of the lake appear inviting. Rising high above the forest that surrounds the lake, red-hued Fall Creek Mountain (7,490') dominates the northern horizon. Along the southwestern shoreline, a forest of conifers, predominantly White Fir *(Abies concolor)*, borders the lake. The trunks of these trees are covered with neon-yellow Wolf Lichen; Staghorn Lichen *(Letharia vulpina)*, that seem to glow in the morning sun. All around you are the songs and calls of many birds whose presence may be heard rather then seen.

Thanks in part to the Forest Service, the recent closure of the road that leads to the lake ensures a less crowded paddling experience. Your decision to make the short portage will now provide you with a memorable time on the lake. If you are paddling the lake in the morning and plan on taking photographs, I recommend following the southwest shoreline. The morning sun will highlight the northeastern shore and provide shade against glare on your side of the lake. The tall trees filter most of the bright sunlight allowing you to take decent photographs and enjoy the view without the harsh reflection.

The main hiking trail (Round Lake Trail) to Island Lake and the lakes below Grouse Ridge follows along the southwest shoreline before ascending the lake's southern ridge. Look for hikers on the trail and you will have a good idea of its location should you attempt to hike on the trail. Midway down the lake, you will skirt a small finger of the shoreline jutting into the lake. A small campsite sits partially obscured by the trees and boulders visible from the water's edge. Eventually you will reach the southern edge of the lake where a small stream spills into the lake. The stream flows from a small pocket lake that sits adjacent to the portage trail leading to Island Lake (see map and Paddle Location 7).

If you are here in the springtime, beach your boat and spend a little time exploring the area. Walk past the bare branches of the willows and stoop down to view the many delicate wildflowers growing out from the pine duff of the forest floor. These flowers, some of the first to bloom after the snow melts, belong to the genus *Erythronium*, are known by their common name of Plain-leaf Fawn Lily. An interesting characteristic of this species of flower is their ability to change color after fertilization. When they first bloom their petals are a creamy white. One to two weeks later, after fertilization takes place, the petals turn pink, then purple.

The small headlands has excellent campsites.

Take-out at upper end of Feeley Lake for the portage to In-Between and Island lakes.

Make time to hike the short but steep trail to the top of the rocky knob that dominates the lower southwestern shoreline. Although trees and soil cover the southern slope of this knob, its shape is still discernable. When viewed in profile from the water the knob takes on a gentile streamlined slope on one end and a steep, rough side on the other. All these features are characteristics of a *Roche moutonee* (sheep rocks). These rocks, named after a wavy French wig popular in the 18th Century, and the fact that the smaller knobs resemble sheep in a field *". . .are common at the bottom and along the flanks of glaciated valleys."**

To reach the top, follow the faint trail leading upward from the right bank of the stream. Cut across the portage trail and guide yourself to the top of the knoll. Hike past the large erratics strewn about, and make your way to the lip of the knoll that faces the lake. From here, you have an unobstructed view of Feeley Lake. Walk to the cluster of large erratics facing Fall Creek Mountain (easterly) and examine these fine examples of glacially dumped boulders. Their composition appears to be granitic (formed beneath the earth's surface), but the bedrock that they are sitting on is primarily quartzite, a metamorphic *(changed)* rock that was altered by heat and pressure from its original composition as quartz. Note the darker oval shapes that randomly imbed the boulders. Geologists call these dark shapes inclusions. They are pieces of older rock, sometimes basalt that became imbedded and did not fully melt in the rising mass of molten granite.

The small stream that you pass on the way back to your boat is Fall Lake Creek. It originates from a small pocket lake located higher up on the ridgeline and just off the main trail to Island Lake. To my knowledge, this is the primary stream that provides the necessary water for Feeley Lake.

If you are planning on camping at the lake but haven't located a campsite, your next take-out may provide you with one. From the stream, paddle across the cove to the grassy beach visible on the opposite shore. The beach is located directly below the clearing that separates the two stands of conifers growing at the base of Fall Creek Mountain. When you beach your boat and walk up to the first grove of trees, you will find the first of several fire rings that are scattered about the area. Located here in the "flats" close to the water are two established campsites. The other two are located to your right facing southeast and up in the grove of mature Red Fir *(Abies magnifica)* standing above the beach. John Muir called this fir the Magnificent Silver Fir and its close cousin the White Fir was given the name Silver Fir.

If you take the time to hike into the forest growing at the north base of the mountain, you will notice that in addition to the conifers, there are numerous deciduous trees and flowering shrubs growing at the fringe of the forest. Burdened with numerous clusters of white flowers, whose heady scent is carried down by the breeze, Buck Brush, *(Ceanothus cuneatus)* creates a flowery wall that hides the talus slope.

The Hike to Hidden Lake

If a hike is in order, I recommend following the deer trail up the ridge directly behind you facing southeast. Follow the trail upward and to the left aiming toward the saddle coming off Fall Creek Mountain. Once you have completed the first pitch past the outcrop of scree the going is rather easy. Eventually you will come out on top of an erratic covered granite knoll. From here you have a fantastic view of Feeley Lake on one side and Island Lake on the other.

If you continue down the granite slope, Hidden Lake, a natural tarn, will come into view to your left. The lake is aptly named because it lies concealed by a screen of conifers and the talus slope of Fall Creek Mountain. Hiking past the lake you will intersect the trail to Penner Lake by way of Island Lake, whose shimmering waters are in front of you. At this time, you can either double back or take the intersected trail west to the Round Lake Trail and down to Fall Lake Creek, where it flows into Feeley Lake.

After a day or two of camping with many memorable views, you are ready to pack the boat and paddle the short distance to the dam and your take-out. If you follow the northeastern shoreline, not only will you be blocked from any head wind, but be able to obtain a view of the former fire lookout on Grouse Ridge (7,712').

Area References

*Hambrey, Michael & Jurg Alean, *Glaciers.* New York, NY: Cambridge University Press, 1994 reprint. pg. 129.

Blackwell, Laird R., *Wildflowers of the Sierra Nevada and the Central Valley.* Edmonton, AB., Canada: Lone Pine Publishing, 1999. 288 pp.

_____ *Wildflowers of the Tahoe Sierra,* Redmond, WA: Lonepine Publishing, 1997. 144 pp.

Durham, David L., *Place-Names of California's Gold Country Including Yosemite National Park.* Clovis, CA: Quill Driver Books/Word Dancer Press, Inc., 2000. 369 pp.

Lanner, Ronald, M., *Conifers of California.* Los Olivos, CA: Cachuma Press, 1999. 274 pp.

Maley, Terry, *Field Geology Illustrated.* Boise, ID: Mineral Land Publications, 1994. 316 pp.

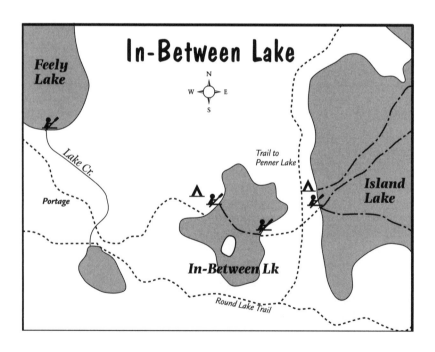

PADDLE LOCATION 6
In-Between Lake

*Note: There is no In-Between Lake listed on the 7.5 English Mtn. Topographical Section Sheet. I created the name for clarity and continuity when describing the portage and the lake.

Difficulty: The only thing difficult about this lake is getting to it. Once you have arrived, it provides a nice interim until you complete your last leg of the portage to Island Lake.
Trip Length: A day paddle if you are willing to endure portaging up as well as down the ridge from Feeley Lake.
Portage: From take-out at mouth of Fall Creek, Feeley Lake to put-in, In-Between Lake it is 0.28 mile. This portage requires a moderately strenuous hike following a narrow trail adjacent to Fall Creek. A creek crossing occurs where the trail intersects a small tarn. From here to In-Between Lake, approximately 0.01 miles is off trail.
Paddling Distance:
Distance from put-in to take-out, east end of lake: 0.07 Miles.
Season: After the snow melts through mid-summer before the water levels drop.
Lake Size: 650' X 800'
Elevation: 6,920'
Historical Background: One of the few natural lakes in the area. There are no dams that impound the water, or any other man-made structures controlling the level of the lake. This small gem is probably a tarn lake left over from the last glacial period.
County: Nevada
National Forest: Tahoe National Forest, Nevada City Ranger District (530) 265-4531
Maps: USGS 7.5 Minute Topographical Section: Graniteville Quadrangle
Adjoining section: English Mtn. Quadrangle
National Forest Service Map: Tahoe National Forest
Road Maps: Compass Maps, Inc.: Nevada and Sierra Counties; Nevada–Sierra counties Street and Road Atlas
American Auto Assn. (AAA) Maps: Northern California/Bay & Mountain sections

Access: Your portage begins at the mouth of Fall Lake Creek where it empties into Feeley Lake. The mouth of Fall Lake Creek is located on the south end of Feeley Lake, adjacent to a small rocky beach. *Note: This section of Fall Lake Creek is not shown on the 7.5 Minute sheets; use the map provided in the guidebook to locate the location of the creek.* From here you must route your way following the creek until you intersect the main hiking trail to Island Lake and the Five Lakes Basin.

Follow the trail to the top of the ridge located approximately 300 yards from your take-out. You have crested the ridge when you intersect a small grassy pocket lake. Continue on the trail until you spot the surface water of In-Between Lake. The lake is on your left (north) through the belt of Lodgepole pines that surround the lake. The best put-in is at the small clearing,

The small island of In-Between Lake. A small campsite is located in the clearing to the right of the large boulder.

which faces west and has a well-built stone fire ring.

Heads up:
- An excellent stopover between Feeley and Island lakes.
- Has one small campsite with a rock fire ring on the lake's west end.
- Use it as a paddling shortcut on the portage to Island Lake.

Description: After the portage up the ridge from Feeley Lake, the sight of this small oasis in the forest is a welcome one. The best put-in for In-Between Lake is located on the midsection of the southwest side of the lake (see map). Look for a built-up stone fire ring in a clearing near the shoreline. If you are portaging during the heat of the day, the water is refreshing but not icy cold. The last leg of the portage is visible directly across the lake from a small clearing facing east (see map). Once ashore, you will be able to glimpse the surface of Island Lake. Because this is such a short and last leg of the portage, take a break and become familiar with this miniature alpine lake.

By now you will have noticed the small island with the grove of Lodgepole Pines growing in the center and bordered by granite boulders. There is a small fire ring located on the eastern edge of the island. Growing as small shrubs surrounding the edge of the lakes shore line, Alpine Laurel (*Kalmia microphylla*) puts on a colorful display with its small, bright pink flowers. The waters clarity allows you to see small fingerlings swimming in the warmer shallows. When you paddle across, if you skirt the island on the right, be wary of several boulders that are difficult to spot until you are nearly on top of them. They are off the southeast tip of the island. When you begin to hear voices or spot movement in the clearing to the east of In-Between Lake, then you have also located the hiking trail leading to Island Lake.

Your take-out and return put-in is located in the small shallow cove facing east. When you step out of your boat, take your last view of this pristine alpine delight, then walk across the main trail for a view of Island Lake.

Area References

Blackwell, Laird R., *Wildflowers of the Sierra Nevada and the Central Valley*. Edmonton, AB, Canada: Lone Pine Publishing. 1999. 288 pp.

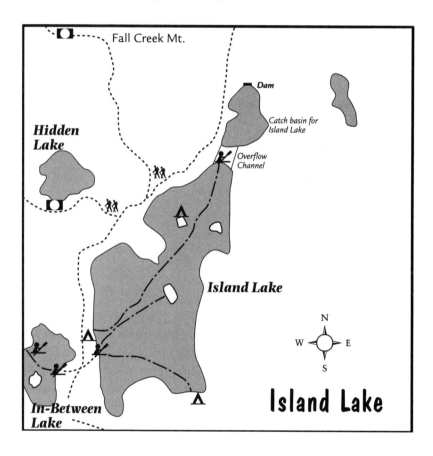

PADDLE LOCATION 7

Island Lake

(Portage Required)

Difficulty: Including the portage, the major difficulty to paddling Island Lake involves the wind. Strong afternoon gusts may create a problem for novice boaters. The combination of wind and frigid water are the two major hazards to this paddle.

Trip Length: A day paddle, if you are willing to endure portaging up as well as down the ridge from Feeley Lake.

Portage: From your take-out at east end of In-Between Lake to put-in at southwest end of Island Lake: 0.17 mile. This short portage crosses the multi-use trail to Penner Lake, before a short descent to the water's edge. The ground is free of obstacles, but be wary of horses, llamas and mules.

Paddling Distances: (see map)

From the put-in, SW end to Islands: 0.13 mile;

North end of lake: 0.35 mile; Campsite, SE end: 0.52 mile

Season: In spring after the snowmelts through early summer before water levels drop.

Lake Size: 2,250' in length

Elevation: 6,875'

Historical Background: Island Lake is another example of a tarn: a lake formed by a glacier carving a bowl into the terrain. To the best of my knowledge, this is one of the few natural lakes in the region–a lake that has not been drastically altered by construction of a dam.

County: Nevada

National Forest: Tahoe National Forest, Nevada City Ranger District (530) 265-4531

Maps: USGS 7.5 Minute Topographical Section: Graniteville Quadrangle

Adjoining section: English Mtn. Quadrangle

National Forest Service Map: Tahoe National Forest

Road Maps: Compass Maps, Inc.: Nevada and Sierra Counties

Nevada–Sierra Counties Street and Road Atlas

American Auto Assn. (AAA) Maps: Northern California/Bay and Mountain sections

Access:

Your portage begins at the mouth of Fall Lake Creek where it empties into Feeley Lake. The mouth of Lake Creek is located on the south end of Feeley Lake, adjacent to a small rocky beach. From here you must route your way following the creek until you intersect the main hiking trail to Island Lake and the Five Lakes Basin. Follow the trail to the top of the ridge located approximately 300 yards from your take-out. You have crested the ridge when you intersect a small grassy pocket lake. Continue on the trail until you spot the surface water of In-Between Lake. The lake will be visible on your left (north) through the belt of Lodgepole pines that surround the lake. The best put-in is at the small clearing, containing a well built stone fire ring, and facing west.

This diagonal slash of younger rock called a dike intrudes into the older granitic bedrock.

Paddle around the small island toward the miniature cove facing east. Behind the cove is a small clearing. Walk through the pines growing at the lake's edge where you will intersect the main hiking trail to Penner Lake and have your first view of Island Lake. Located on the other side of the hiking trail is a path leading toward the lake. Follow it downward and you will spot the put-in/take-out spot.

Heads Up:
- Requires a short but rugged portage (read *In the Eddy*, pg. 57).
- A fire permit is mandatory for stoves and campfires.
- Dispersed camping only.
- Bear habitat: pack and camp smart.
- Windy in the afternoon.
- Multiple trails for hiking on all sides of the lake.
- The all-day hike to the top of Fall Creek Mountain is worth every sore muscle.
- The shorter hike to Hidden Lake is a must, have your lunch on the knoll overlooking Island and Feeley lakes . . .Supremo views!

Description: Island Lake requires considerable effort to reach just to have a paddle, however, your exertion will pay off with memorable scenery and the pride of self-accomplishment. Once you have completed the portage and are standing on the granite knoll overlooking the lake, you will be glad of your undertaking. When you step across the track of the main hiking trail from your short paddle across In-Between Lake, walk down a few feet on the side trail leading down to Island Lake. Set your boat and gear down, then walk to the flat surface of the knoll to your right (south). From this vantage point, you will have an unobstructed view of the entire lake. You now may plan your paddle to those areas beyond the lake that bear further exploration. You may also decide on the general area for a campsite or picnic area.

Pack your boat and gear to the lake's edge. Unfortunately, there is no easy put-in. The bank leading down to the water is steep and once you have floated your boat, there is no easy access into the boat. The only alternative is a longer portage either up the trail in a southerly direction, or, further down the trail, toward the base of the rocky finger extending outward into the lake.

From whatever put-in you decide on, your best paddling strategy should include the direction of the wind. The wind starts as a freshening breeze about 8:00 AM and slowly increases in intensity to intermittent gusts by 10:00 AM. Peak strength lasts till around 4:30 PM. As the suns heat loses its grip, the gusts disappear and the lake becomes glassy. The prevailing wind is from the north, right through the gap below the western base of Fall Creek Mountain. If you are beginning your paddle during the windy portion of the day, I recommend a clock-wise direction of travel. On the other hand, if the lake is calm at the time of your put-in, then head for the island visible from the shore. When the wind picks up, the island becomes too windswept and loses its appeal. The best place to put-in at the island is a small pocket cove located on the southeast side. Here, too, is a small, somewhat protected granite bench extending at an angle into the water. This makes an ideal swimming and diving spot.

If you are interested in finding a campsite, paddle toward the cove located at the extreme south end of the lake. Upon beaching your boat, you should find several campsites to the right of the beach. From here you may explore the cove or hike up the eroding benches that mark the bare rock walls of the ridge. Head for the two stunted Jeffrey Pines that are visible on the horizon. From their location, you obtain a nice shady bench to enjoy the view of the lake and profile of Fall Creek Mountain.

While you are enjoying the view, you may detect the scent of vanilla, butterscotch or maybe even pineapple. Don't worry; your nose is not playing tricks on you! The scent is coming from the bark of the Jeffrey Pine tree. This aroma is one of the distinguishing features that help in identifying the tree. For an understanding of how these scents are produced, read the subtitled

This is your first view of Island Lake from In-Between Lake. The largest of three islands is partially visible to the left of the silhouetted pine tree.

section: South Shore (Bowman Dam Sites), located in Paddle Location 12-A: LOWER BOWMAN LAKE.

As you cast your gaze across the lake to the flank of Fall Creek Mountain, you will spot the piles of white boulders sitting on the reddish surface that makes up the south east ridge of the mountain. If you are interested in hiking the area, follow the ridge you are standing on upward until you intersect with the Long Lake Trail. Follow this trail down until you reach the area of your cove, then find your way back to the beach and your boat. Back in your boat, paddle adjacent the granite sidewall that makes up the southeast end of the cove. You will come across a wide slice of reddish rock thrusting diagonally into the exposed sidewall of stained granite. At first glance, this feature appears to be an excellent example of a dike. Dikes are created when molten material is squeezed or thrust into a fracture or weak zone within the overlying bedrock. Usually this molten material comes from an igneous (rocks that form from a molten mass) source. This particular intrusion appears to be composed of quartzite, a rock type altered or changed, (*metamorphosed* in geology speak) from its original state as sandstone.

To the author's knowledge, quartzite does not readily form dikes or fill fractures in parent rock. Since the "dike" disappears below the surface of the lake, geologists may only surmise the origins of this particular geologic feature.

Lying to the west of the cove and your campsite, the shoreline rounds a small finger of exposed rock jutting into the lake. Be careful paddling around this finger due to the many partially submerged granite pieces hidden beneath the lake surface. This same finger separates the cove containing your campsite from a narrower but longer cove. Located on the right shore of this narrow cove is a trail that leads to the top of the ridge, and then cuts across a barren knoll of granite before stopping at the water's edge of In-Between Lake.

Continuing past the cove, you soon pass the site of your original put-in and arrive at the sidewall of the large peninsula reaching outward towards the lake. Don't miss the highlighted erratic sitting alone on top of the ridge of the peninsula. Round the point and enter into a wind-sheltered cove with broad slopes covered by a dense mat of manzanita.

Turning your head toward the lake, you locate the remaining two islands that give the lake its name. Both islands are large enough to beach a boat on and explore. The larger of the two contains a fire ring from previous overnight visitors. Prior to departing Island Lake, consider examining the historic 19th Century rock crib dam built at the northeast end of Island Lake. The dam is actually on the end of the small pour-over flood lake that is located behind the small pine-covered berm at the tail end of Island Lake (See *Hike to Hidden Lake*, in Paddle Location 5.)

Area References

Durham, David L., *Place-Names of California's Gold Country Including Yosemite National Park*. Clovis, CA: Quill Driver Books/Word Dancer Press, Inc., 2000. 369 pp.

Lanner, Ronald, M., *Conifers of California*. Los Olivos, CA: Cachuma Press, 1999. 274 pp.

The Audubon Society, *Field Guide to North American Rocks and Minerals*. Charles W. Chesterman & Kurt E. Lowe, New York, NY: Alfred A. Knopf, Inc. 2nd printing. 850 pp.

Thomas, John Hunter, & Dennis R. Parnell, *Native Shrubs of the Sierra Nevada*. Berkeley, CA: University of California Press, 1974. 127 pp.

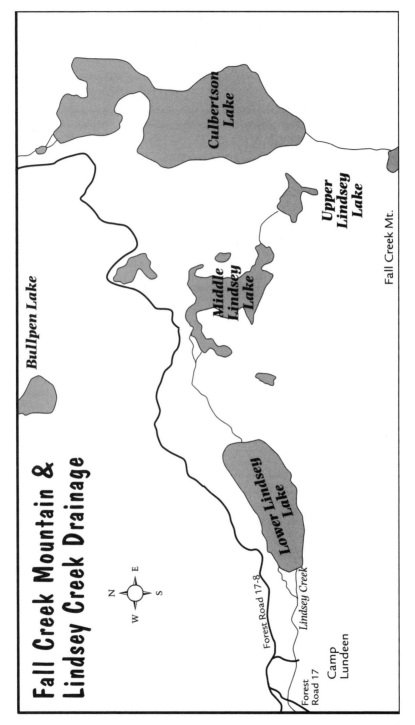

Fall Creek Mountain &
Lindsey Creek Drainage

Bullpen Lake

Culbertson Lake

Upper Lindsey Lake

Middle Lindsey Lake

Lower Lindsey Lake

Fall Creek Mt.

Lindsey Creek

Forest Road 17-8

Forest Road 17

Camp Lundeen

Area 3

Fall Creek Mountain & Lindsey Creek Drainage

PADDLE LOCATION 8
Lower Lindsey Lake

Difficulty: Except for the daily afternoon wind, for boaters of all skill levels
Trip Length: Lower Lindsey is too small for anything except a day paddle. Due to the long driving time, the Lindsey Lakes should be planned as overnight destinations.
Paddling Distances: (see map) From the put-in/boat launch to:
Campsite across lake (SE side, mid-lake): 0.13 mile;
Mouth of Lindsey Ck, NE end: 0.22 mile;
Circumnavigation of lake (counter-clockwise): 0.91 mile
Lake Size: 1900' x 500'
Season: From snow melt off the roadway through the fall. The optimum time would be in late spring, when the reservoir is at its fullest.
Elevation: 6,236'
Historical Background: The lakes were named for Robert Lindsey, a water agent for the Eureka Lake (now known as French Lake) Company in the late 1800's.
County: Nevada
National Forest: Tahoe National Forest, Nevada City Ranger District (530) 265-4531
Maps: USGS 7.5 Minute Topographical Section: Graniteville Quadrangle
Adjoining Section: English Mtn. Quadrangle
National Forest Service Map: Tahoe National Forest
Road Maps: Compass Maps Inc.: Nevada and Sierra Counties; Nevada-Sierra Counties Street and Road Atlas
American Auto Assn. (AAA) Maps: Northern California/Bay and Mountain sections

Access: Interstate 80 East to California State Highway 20 West. Exit is at Yuba Gap immediately after driving over the highway over-crossing. Your turnoff is west toward Nevada City. Continue on Highway 20 for 4 miles, exit onto Bowman lake Road (Forest Road 18). Continue on Bowman Lake Road for 10.5 miles (look for brown mile markers on the side of the roadway). Take the Loney Meadow turnoff on your right, approximately 40 feet past the 10.5 Mile Marker. You are now on Forest Road 17-8. *Note: once you have turned-off of Bowman Lake Road/Forest Rd 18, you will need a vehicle with sufficient ground clearance to complete the drive to Lindsey Lakes.* Drive past the vandalized remains of an old house until you reach the fork in the road. Turn right and

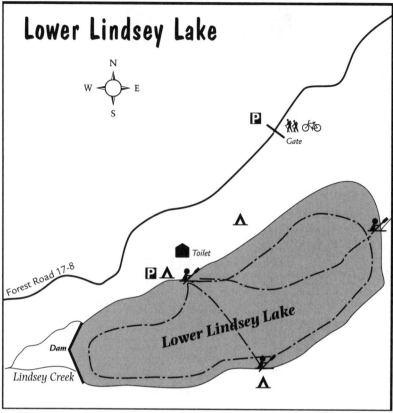

Lower Lindsey Lake

Forest Road 17-8

Toilet

Gate

Lower Lindsey Lake

Dam

Lindsey Creek

continue for approximately 1 mile until you reach the T-intersection and the final road section to Lower Lindsey Lake. From here to the campground is the worst section of road. Take your time and watch for cobbles and deep ruts. The road you intersect at the "T" is Forest Road 17 that leads to Carr and Feeley lakes and then connects with Bowman Lake road at Mile Marker 8.5. You may take it on your way out instead of Forest Road 17-8. *Note: If you are towing a trailer or in a large RV, park in the spaces just before making the final climb to the lake and campground. There is no room for a turnaround at the lake.*

Heads Up:
- Campfire Permit is mandatory even for camp stoves.
- Bear country: pack and camp smart.
- Bring mountain bikes; the trail to Middle Lindsey and beyond is great for biking.
- Each site contains a metal fire ring and picnic table.
- One cinder block vault toilet for entire campground.
- For those seeking a bit more privacy and quiet, consider paddling across the lake and choose your own campsite (see map).

The main body of Lower Lindsey Lake is shown with the southwest flank of Fall Creek Mountain (7,490') looming in the background.

■ Nearest phone and groceries located at the grocery store at Yuba Gap Exit on I-80 West.
■ Excellent fishing at Middle Lindsey and Culbertson Lakes.
■ Incredible display of wild flowers in spring and early summer. Best bet for flower variety is below the dam at Upper Lindsey Lake.

Description: If variety is your game, then pack up and make tracks to the Lindsey Lakes. For all the effort it takes to make the drive, your rewards are many. For starters, you have the option of paddling at least two lakes; subsequently, with a bit more effort on the portage trail, you may dip your paddle into two additional lakes. In one three-day weekend, you will have paddled a grand total of four lakes! For all you Type-A personalities, what a great way to drain off some of that adrenalin.

If moderation and the slow lane are your getaway priorities, then a campsite directly on the shores of Lower Lindsey Lake may be in order. From the mat-step of your tent you may launch your canoe or kayak. When the sun begins to set, pull up a camp chair and sit back to enjoy the "fire on the lake" as the golden rays of the sun shimmer and dance over the liquid surface. If the mood strikes you, push the boat into the water, and with a few lazy strokes, paddle outward onto the lake. At the lake's center, away from pesky mosquitoes *(Culicinae)* and the hubbub of camp, you may drift away to the rhythms of current and wind.

Opening your eyes, you notice that the boat has drifted far up the lake and now it is your sense of sight that requires filling. Stretching before you the lake's surface shimmers and sparkles. The conifers stand upright on shore and upside down in their own reflection. The entire forest and lake recedes to the horizon with its variety of blue and green hues. Cast your eyes above the trees; the dominant presence of Fall Creek Mountain (7,490') bears observation. Eventually your reverie ends, and with a deep sigh of contentment, you dip the paddle into the lake and start the short but pleasant sojourn back to camp.

The Lake Paddle

Start your morning paddle by exploring the lake in a counter-clockwise direction. This approach will eliminate the constant glare coming off the surface that can wash out your view. The first item of interest may be the screen of aspens with leaves that appear to be in constant motion. After the sameness of the conifers, the bright bark and light green leaves of these deciduous trees adds a sparkle to the shoreline of the lake. Paddling westward you reach the site of the lake's dam and the site of the small footbridge that crosses over the spillway. Spilling forth in a controlled flow, Lindsey Creek tumbles its way downward, crossing Bowman Lake Road before joining the

All the campsites have a lakeside view.

Historical structures such as this one may be seen throughout the region.

waters of Texas Creek, 2.5 miles away.

Make your way around the lake to the southern shoreline where you can observe the grand stand of maturing pines whose presence dominates the scenery. If the sun is shining on the trunks of these giants, you admire the colorful contrast between the reddish bark of the trees against the neon chartreuse glow of Wolf Lichen/Staghorn Lichen *(Letharia vulpina)* that decorates entire limbs and partial sides of trunks. The trees thin onto a clearing where several campfire rings mark the past presence of campers. A hiking trail, whose head is at the dam, follows the shoreline and climbs onto the first ridge above the lake. Eventually the trail crosses an old logging road before making its way to Middle, Upper Lindsey and Culbertson lakes.

Enter the shaded area of the upper lake and you will see the craggy cliff of a rocky ridge. Bracken ferns grow on a protruding ledge near the waterline, while a matting of shrubs creates a mosaic of green on the upper wall. A lone aspen, whose roots have carved a niche in a crevice, spreads its branches outward. This deeply shaded zone hides shallow areas where dumped sediment from streams has built shifting contours of ever-changing lake bottom. Re-entering the sun-dappled waters of the lake, you can spot the far campsites by the rise of smoke and the flash of bright colors marking the location of tents, gear and vehicles. From here it is but a short paddle back to your campsite.

Area References

Durham, David L. *Place-Names of California's Gold Country.* Clovis, CA: Quill Driver Books/Word Dancer Press, 2000. 369 pp.

Storer, Tracy I. & Robert L. Usinger, *Sierra Nevada Natural History.* Berkeley, CA: University of California Press, 1963. 374 pp.

PADDLE LOCATION 9

Middle Lindsey Lake

(Portage Required)

Difficulty: Except for the daily afternoon wind, for boaters of all skill levels

Trip Length: Due to the long drive and required portage, this lake should be planned as a multiple-day trip.

Portage: Length of portage is approximately 0.48 mile from gate to put-in above the dam. The portage route is a gradual climb on a private section of forest road. No major obstacles other than exposed cobbles.

Paddling Distances: (see map)

From the put-in, NW end of lake to take-out for portage to Upper Lindsey Lake: 0.35 mile

Season: Late spring through early fall.

Lake Size: 1,700' x 1,000'

Elevation: 6436'

County: Nevada

National Forest: Tahoe National Forest, Nevada City Ranger District (530) 265-4531)

Maps: USGS 7.5 Minute Topographical Section: Granitville, Calif.

Adjoining Section: English Mtn. Calif.

National Forest Service Map: Tahoe National Forest

Road Maps: Compass Maps Inc.: Nevada & Sierra Counties; Nevada-Sierra Counties Street and Road Atlas

American Auto Assn. (AAA) Maps: Northern California/Bay & Mountain sections

Access: (See Paddle Location 8: Lower Lindsey Lake, for driving access)

Portage Access: Start your portage on the opposite side of the green gate located at the upper end of the road that passes through the campsites of Lower Lindsey Lake. The road starts off on an incline and levels off a short distance above. Take your time and take breaks as needed. I make my first break at the two mature Jeffrey pines located at the top of the first uphill pitch. Eventually you will spy the dam on the right as you round the bend of your last short uphill spurt. Pass the dam site and the small grove of conifers. Use the grassy clearing as your put-in. There are no rocks to scrape the boat and you have a clear section of lake to place the boat in prior to packing.

Heads Up:

- 4/10ths of a mile portage on a gated forest road.
- Exceptional views of Fall Creek Mountain and surrounding peaks.
- You will, in all likelihood, be the only paddler on the lake.
- Great campsites to paddle to.
- Dispersed camping only, although there are still fire rings at the former campground located on the north end of the lake (see map).

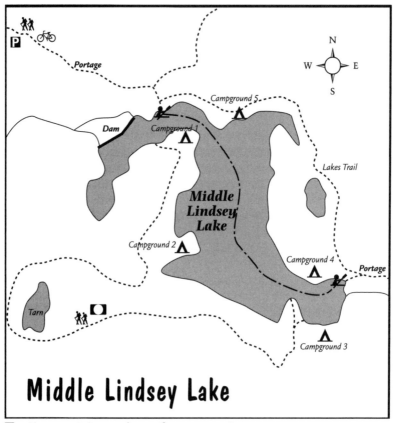

Middle Lindsey Lake

- ■ Fire permit is mandatory for any camping.
- ■ Bear country: pack and camp smart.
- ■ In spring, the wildflowers are gorgeous.
- ■ Additional portages to nearby lakes.
- ■ Hiking & mountain biking trails nearby.

Description: All good lakes come to those who are willing to portage to them! These next three Paddle locations—Middle Lindsey, Upper Lindsey Lake and Culbertson Lake—require portages of increasing difficulty prior to paddling on them. The portage to Middle Lindsey Lake is along a section of Forest Service road that is still in use by government and private residents. As a result, the road is in good condition with only minor obstacles for those paddlers using a boat cart. Upon arrival at the put-in, just before you paddle off, step carefully into the small grove of pines growing along the lake's edge between your put-in and the dam. Look down for rusty-red stems whose tops contain urn-shaped white flowers. These are Pinedrops *(Pterospora andromeda)*. They may reach a height of 2 to 3 feet. If you examine their stems, you will notice that they have no green coloration. These plants, like the bright red Snow Plant *(Sarcodes sanguinea)* you saw growing along the portage trail, cannot obtain their nourishment through photosynthesis. Instead, they live off the organic matter found in the litter of the forest floor, helped in part, by the symbiotic relationship of the fungi that coats their roots. On your path back to your boat, look down at your feet and spot the small delicate yellow *"B-flowers"* growing at ground level surrounding the grassy expanse near the put-in. They are often called *Belly flowers* because . . .they require getting down on your belly to examine them. These particular members of the "belly" family are Mountain Violets, *(Viola purpurea)*.

You are now ready to depart from the shore and begin your paddle. Point your bow toward the dam and enter the quiet water of the cove located just past the dam's concrete apron. The stillness of the water produces a picture perfect reflection on the lake's surface of the surrounding forest. Suddenly, a large bird startles you as it streaks silently but rapidly across the water. From a brief glimpse of the bird's shape and the color of the feathers, you perceive it to be an immature Bald Eagle *(Haliaetus leucocephalus)*. Small bullhead, probably the Black Bullhead *(Ictalurus melas),* identifiable by its small size, black back, and dark lower barbells dart ahead of the boat. This section of the lake is not only protected from the wind, but is shallow and therefore warmer than the main body of the lake. These factors contribute to the varieties of water plants and aquatic life that flourish within the cove. Just before you reach the end of the cove, you will spot a floating "life raft" consisting of a fallen tree trunk. Flourishing within and on top of this decomposing pile of

Looking north from Middle Lindsey Lake toward Bowman Mountain (7,386').

Break time on the portage road to Upper Lindsey lakes.

humus is a myriad of plants, ferns, flowers, moss and insects. Paddle your way around the shaded south shore and round the tip of the tree-lined mouth leading onto the main body of the lake. Just outside the entrance to the small cove you paddled out of, this part of the mainland jutting out into the lake contains a nice forested campsite (Campsite #1 on map). If you take out and inspect the area, look for emerging fairy rings of Fluted White Helvella mushrooms *(Helvella crispa)* growing through the pine duff.

Across the narrow entrance all along the eastern shoreline sits the former campground for Middle Lindsey Lake (Campsite #5 on map). Duff-covered iron fire rings sit unused in old camping sites scattered throughout the pine forest. Mosquitoes and other winged insects buzz and attempt to make you their next meal. Paddling past the narrow entrance to the cove by the dam, you now enter the main body of Middle Lindsey Lake. From here you have a choice to either cross over to the east side of the lake or follow the sunlit southwest shoreline. Either side has ample sights and places to explore, and it is only your whim that dictates the direction of your boat's bow. No matter the choice, a broad panorama of Sierra scenery begins to unfold. Jutting skyward, the multi-hued rocky slopes of Fall Creek Mountain (7,490') and its adjacent ridgeline dominate the skyline. If you are camping here at the lake overnight, be sure to have your evening coffee or tea in your boat, floating quietly at this spot, watching the sun's last rays touch the face of the mountain. *(See Paddle Tips for paddling at night.)*

Paddle past the bleached trunk of the downed fir resting in the water. If you are seeking a campsite on this side of the lake, then follow the shoreline as it faces south. Look for a shallow area in a very small cove to take out at and secure your boat. When you step past the shore into the tree line, look for a clearing containing a stone fire ring. This small campsite is the best site on this side of the lake (Campsite #2 on map). Running roughly parallel with the lake is a path that leads to a meadow, then a small tarn, before eventually connecting to the shoreline trail of Lower Lindsey Lake.

If you are paddling this area in spring, take the time to hike the short distance to the meadow. Upon entering the clearing you will be delighted to see hundreds of blooming Mountain Mules Ears (*Wyethia mollis*), Common Sun Flowers *(Helianthus annus)* and Brewer's Lupine (*Lupinus breweri*). Interspersed amongst these wildflowers and growing closer to the ground are clusters of Applegate's Paintbrush *(Castilleja applegatei)*. Leave the meadow behind and continue on the trail, and you soon come to the tree-shaded shoreline of another small mountain tarn. Find a place to sit and soon you will hear and see a variety of birds as they locate their food sources. The loud scolding-like chatter coming from the heights of a tall conifer will identify the presence of a Chickaree or Douglas Squirrel *(Tamiasciurus douglasii)*. If you look about you, you will soon find the litter of freshly cut scales of pinecones. These piles are characteristic of a squirrel's work.

Back at your boat, continue to follow the shoreline and paddle under the steep cliff face dominating the southwest end of the lake. Paddle your boat as close to the rock wall as possible. The dark blue color of Blue Penstemon *(Penstemon laetus)*, and the delicate creamy white petals of the Mariposa Lily *(Calochortus leichtlinii)* will catch your eye as the boat glides by. Growing in the crevices near the water's edge are delicate miniature ferns, and patches of moss.

Eventually you will round the face of the cliff and enter the upper end of the lake. Where the lake narrows—on either side of the rocky points—are suitable campsites. The one on the south side (to your right, Campsite #3), is rather small suitable for no more than two people. A larger camping area is found on the northeast point (Campsite #4). Although the smaller point is cozy and wind protected, in July at the height of the mosquito season the lack of a breeze invites swarms of hungry skeeters. During the day, however, this spot makes a perfect location for picnicking or swimming.

As an additional bonus, hike up the creek drainage to the expansive terrace that you saw earlier when paddling past the cliff wall.* From the top of the terrace you may enjoy the panoramic views of Middle Lindsey Lake, the portage and sight of Upper Lindsey, a glimpse of the forested Lower Lindsey Lake and also the distant canyons of the South and Middle Forks of the Yuba River. When you are standing on the lip of the terrace looking southeast toward Upper Lindsey Lake, notice the banded layers of gray and white rock that make up the base of Fall Creek Mountain's Ridgeline. This is the same feature described in greater detail in the Culbertson Lake Paddle Location. For those of you not portaging on to either Upper Lindsey Lake or Culbertson Lake, you may still hike into the area via a trail that may be picked

Your put-in for Middle Lindsey Lake has a wide, grassy area for loading your gear.

to the right of Upper Lindsey Lake Dam. (See map & Paddle Location 10). (*Note: If you are interested in a longer hike, use the 7.5 Minute Granitville Quadrangle to complete the short (0.78 mile) hike suggested in this guidebook.*)

This end of the lake culminates in an oval cove surrounded by willows *(Genus Salix)*, manzanita, and a few clusters of Jeffrey Pine. The shallow area covered by a dense growth of Yellow Pond Lilies *(Nymphaea polysepala)* also marks the location of the willow-covered mouth of Lindsey Creek. Located just to the right of Campsite #4, in a very small cove and at the base of a mature Jeffrey Pine is the take-out/put-in for the portage to Upper Lindsey Lake (see map).

If you are still seeking a campsite, the cleared area at the base of the knoll and marked on the map as Campsite #4, contains a fairly large site suitable for two or more couples. The take-out is not as easy as the other sites, however, this location keeps the mosquito hordes to a minimum without sacrificing the view. From here you may hike the former road (now trail) to Upper Lindsey Lake and Culbertson Lake.

Area References
*Blackwell, Laird, R. *Wildflowers of the Sierra Nevada and the Central Valley.* Edmonton, AB: Canada: Lone Pine Publishing. 1999. 288 pp.

Carville, Julie Stauffer, *Hiking Tahoe's Wildflower Trails*. Edmonton, ALB: Canada, Lonepine Publishing. 1997 edition. 350 pp.

Dalrymple, Byron, *Sportsman's Guide to Game Fish*. New York, NY: Outdoor Life Books-The World Publishing Company. 1968. 480 pp.

Horn, Elizabeth L., *Sierra Nevada Wildflowers*. Missoula, MT: Mountain Press Publishing Company. 1998. 214 pp.

Whitney, Stephen, *Western Forests A National Audubon Society Nature Guide*. New York, NY: Alfred A. Knopf, Inc. 9th Printing, 1997. 670 pp.

Old age, lightning or maybe the wind toppled this pine. Now it serves as a dramatic foreground to Middle Lindsey Lake.

PADDLE TIP

Lighting the way for a paddle at night

Sometimes, to fully appreciate a lake and its setting (to watch a moonrise, for example) you need to put the boat in the water under a dark star-lit sky. With a little forethought and preparation, this activity will enhance your vacation memories. Conducting a night paddle on one of the Sierra Lakes described in this volume is different from doing a similar exercise on busy lakes such as Tahoe or Donner. Most certainly, unlike Tahoe, you will be the only boat on the water, and be the only campsite on the shore. At first, this seems rather romantic, however, at night with no visible references a romantic paddle may turn into a frightening experience.

Here then, are a few tips that will help keep that night paddle or float on the "bright side" rather than the "dark side" (puns intended).

Preparation At Home

Back home, when packing for the trip, purchase several "glow sticks"-- flexible plastic tubes containing chemicals and a glass vial. They were initially designed for military requirements but have been adapted into all walks of civilian life. When you bend the tube it breaks the vial. By shaking the contents it creates a reaction that produces a bright glow. The glow lasts for several hours, depending on the outside temperature and the duration listed on the stick. What's neat about these sticks is that the light is not affected by water, they produce no heat, and the sticks come in a variety of colors and sizes. The sticks may be purchased at almost any sporting goods, military surplus, hardware, or paddle sports retail store (See Appendix). Almost all these glow sticks are designed with a hole either on one or both ends. Purchase and pack a length of thin cord or plastic tie-straps to tie off the sticks when they are ready to use.

If you haven't purchased one already, an essential piece of gear useful for boating and camping is the battery-powered headlamp. The lamp itself is mounted on an expandable band that fits on your head or headgear; the battery pack is located either behind the lamp or the backside of the band. This light source frees your hands and shines wherever you are looking. Recently, they have been improved by the addition of longer lasting, higher intensity lithium battery packs, and better-made bulbs. Purchase some reflective tape, then stick or sew it on your boat, paddle, PFD (Personal Floatation Device) and other essential gear. Any light shined on taped gear will of course, be reflected back. You will thank yourself for taking the time to accomplish this task when attempting to locate a critical piece of gear lying about at night. A piece of reflective tape placed either on a person's PFD, headgear or paddle eliminates any unfortunate accidents such as smacking your partner with a misplaced swing of the paddle. A good source for reflective tape is a local surveying store or marine hardware store.

Preparation & Usage In Camp

Sometime in the late afternoon, but before dusk, start your preparation for the forthcoming night paddle. If you haven't already done so, go ahead and tape your gear. Next tie off several of the glow sticks, but as yet, do not "break" them. Tie them either on tree limbs, nearby trees, or rocks.

You want to create a visible perimeter that marks the location of your campsite and put-in/take-out from the water. Here is where the different color schemes really work well. One color outlines the camp and the other color guides you back to your beach.

Have your headlamps or flashlights ready. Be sure to check that they work and that you have extra batteries and bulbs handy. I place mine in a small water-proof (dry) bag, reflective tape it, then buckle it either to a thwart (if in a canoe) or on the bungee cord on the foredeck of my kayak. Tie down on the rear deck or thwart (so you won't be blinded by the light) one glow stick. If there is a desig-nated leader in the group or if someone is carrying all the food and beverage, have them secure a different-colored light stick. While it is still daylight, become fa-miliar with the terrain surrounding your camp. At night only muted silhouettes of the trees and rock features will be visible; subsequently, pay attention to any dis-tinctive shape or size of a particular tree or cluster of trees, rocky knob or pile of boulders.

Those Little Things

Now that you have covered all the important safety items, take stock of the com-fort items that will enhance your time on the water. A small thermos with one or more cups, a snack or two, jacket, light- or long-sleeved shirt for warmth and mosquito protection, hat with ear covers, and a set of binoculars to view the moon and other celestial objects.

If you plan on viewing a rising full moon, it helps tremendously to know ahead of time the rising whereabouts of that globular object. Besides, it gives you a certain panache to point ahead of time and say: "Yep, the full moon should rise right over there just to the left of that ridge." (It helps if you are also correct in your prediction.) To make that happen, consult either your local paper under the weather section, or purchase an inexpensive tide log. They will list the type of moon, wax-ing (growing larger) or waning (decreasing), and moonrise and moonset times.

On The Water

Secure your camp. (You do not want to return to a camp party of bears, raccoons or other rodents). Set off the glow sticks and check your boat for all essential gear. Cast off and softly paddle outward onto the center of the lake—or area of clear visibility. Use your headlamps sparingly or at best, not at all. Allow your eyes to become accustomed to the growing darkness. Soon you will be able to "see" all the essential gear secured in your boat. Before you drift too far, look to see where the perimeter of glow sticks is in relation to your location. Locate those silhouetted terrain features. You are now ready for some fun!

If you are in a group, you may want to raft all the boats together by a strap or rope. If you do so, use D-rings or other quick release mechanisms. Do not tie the boats; knots may become deadly if an accident occurs and separation becomes warranted. Know which individual(s) boats have the ends of the strap. Again, if in a group, now is also a good time to "break" those glow sticks attached to the back of the boats. Instead of paddling, allow the boat or boats to drift. Use your paddles sparingly to set a course and keep away from obstacles or the shore. If you are on the water on a calm night with no moon, be prepared to feel a little vertigo when distinguishing the horizon line between the lake and night sky. Other than that, sit or kneel back, open your eyes, breathe deeply and become one with the majesty of night.

References

Dowd, John, *Sea Kayaking A Manual for Long-Distance Touring*. Vancouver, BC: Greystone Books (Douglas & McIntyre) & Seattle, WA: University of Washington Press, revised edition, 1997. 264 pp.

Hart, John, *Walking Softly in the Wilderness: The Sierra Club Guide to Backpacking*. San Francisco, CA: Sierra Club Books, 3rd Ed., 1998. 478 pp.

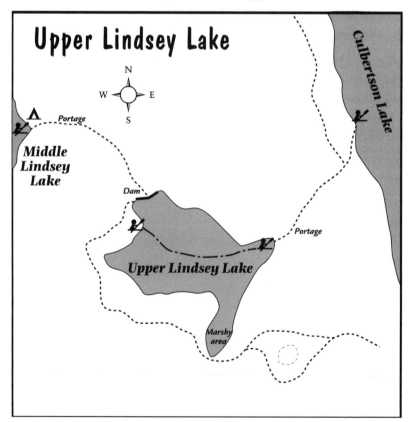

PADDLE LOCATION 10

Upper Lindsey Lake

(Portage Required)

Difficulty: With the exception of the strenuous portage to the lake, for paddlers of all skill levels

Trip Length: Given the time and effort it takes to portage to the lake, this paddle should be planned as an overnight campout.

Portage: A short 1/10th mile but steep carry. The cobble-strewn ground precludes the use of a cart. Your put-in is reached by carrying the boat across the top of the dam (it is wide enough) and into the small cove to the right of the dam.

Paddling Distances:

The paddle from the dam to your take-out for the portage to Culbertson Lake is 0.11 mile.

Season: Late spring when the snow has melted off the portage trail through early fall. The optimum time however would be in the late spring through early summer before the lake level drops.

Lake Size: 500' x 300'

Elevation: 6,546'

Historical Background: A date on the dam of October 21, 1954 pertains to the last repair on this dam. The entire system of lakes was enlarged in the last century as a source of water for hydraulic mining. When this form of mining became illegal, the water became the source of hydroelectric power and drinking water for Nevada City and the outlying foothill communities. Nevada Irrigation District (NID), and to a lesser extent, Pacific Gas & Electric (PG&E) share responsibility for the running and repair of the reservoirs.

County: Nevada

National Forest: Tahoe National Forest, Nevada City Ranger District: (530) 265-4531

Maps: USGS 7.5 Minute Topographical Section: Granitville

Adjoining Section: English Mountain

National Forest Service Map: Tahoe National Forest

Road Maps: Compass Maps Inc.: Nevada & Sierra Counties; Nevada-Sierra Counties Street and Road Atlas

American Auto Assn. (AAA) Maps: Northern California/Bay & Mountain sections

Access: (See Paddle Location 8 for the driving access to the start of the portage & Paddle Location 9 for the first half of the portage.) To reach Upper Lindsey Lake from Middle Lindsey Lake, take out at the base of the mature Jeffrey Pine tree located on the far northeastern end of Middle Lindsey Lake. This take-out sits across the lake and to the right of the campsite listed on the map as campsite #3. To reach your take-out, paddle around the small rocky point visible across from campsite #3. On the map, included in the guidebook, it is the point with campsite #4. Once you have rounded this point, you will see several pines growing in close proximity to each other.

There is an almost Zen-like stillness drifting on the surface before the wind picks up on Upper Lindsey Lake.

Aim your boat toward the large Jeffrey Pine growing closest to the shoreline. You should be in a small brush-sheltered cove. Take out on the gravel beach, where the slope is overgrown with a cover of bracken ferns. To the left of this pine tree is a large boulder whose base is partially obscured by ferns. I use the boulder as a reference to help locate my boat cart that I hide in the ferns. If you look to the right of the pine, you will spot the narrow trail leading upward toward the top of this small knoll. Use this trail to portage your boat and gear to the top of the knoll. At the top, follow the visible road cut to the right. It will turn into a short but steep and rocky path to the site of Upper Lindsey Lake. Look for the small rock-faced dam with a stream flowing from its base. Walk your boat across the dam, and put-in at the small grass beach located at the upper right corner of the dam.

Heads Up:
- Definitely, you will be the only boat on the lake.
- Wilderness Permit is mandatory for any overnight camping.
- Best campsite is located in a draw to the right of the dam.
- Bear country: pack & camp smart.
- The spring wildflowers are incredible!
- Great opportunities for hikes to nearby lakes and high country.
- Explore the marsh hidden in the southeast pocket of the lake.

Description: Carry the boat across the dam and "plop" it into the lake. Hopefully you have attempted this portage in the spring and have literally walked through a field of assorted wildflowers growing at the base of the dam. *(See Appendix IV: The Wildflower List, at end of this volume).* Overlooking the lake, aspen quiver in the growing breeze and the scent of pine permeates the air.

Highlighted by the rays of the morning sun, a lone boulder stands out like a beacon in the center of the lake. A blended mass of swirls, tilted layers and a mélange of assorted rock types join to form the line of ridges that culminates with the striking form of Fall Creek Mountain (7,490').

Leave your gear on the shore, enter your boat and strike out toward the center of this small picturesque lake. The lake is rather shallow in most places. The deepest spots seem to be close to the southeast end. Except for the immediate area near the dam, a thick cover of brush covers the remaining shoreline. Paddling into the small northeast arm of the lake it becomes difficult to locate the take-out site for the portage to Culbertson Lake. After searching the brushy shore, you'll finally spot the small clearing cut through the thick screen of deciduous shrubbery.

Today, however, your interest lies in exploring this small high country lake. Letting the boat drift out toward the sunlit boulder that dominates the center of the lake, you spot the carpet of green sedges growing around the boulder's base. From here you have a clear view of the lake, the dam and a mixed grove of fir and Lodgepole Pine. As you face the dam, look to your left and spot the entrance leading into the marshy area of the lake. From the shore, this part of the lake is hidden by brush.

Rounding the bend of brush that obscures the view of the marsh, look at the base of the brush that grows out from the shoreline. You should spot the rusting eyebolts and thick cable that was utilized during the construction and widening of this reservoir. If you hike in to here from Culbertson Lake, you will see the former road cut that sits just on the other side of the brush from where you are paddling.

The beds of sedges begin to thicken as your boat's bow progresses through the lush green carpet. If you continue on, eventually your boat will either ground against the mud or become held by the thick mass of sedges. Back paddle into a shady cover with an open view into the marsh. Now is a good time to take out your binoculars or fit a telephoto lens onto your camera. When things settle down, be ready for some excellent birding . . .not to mention the butterfly viewing. Back at the main body of the lake, in the late afternoon, the shallow water warms to a comfortable temperature and the lake becomes a delight to swim in. When you re-enter the main lake from the marsh, just to the left of the dam is a brush-protected clearing. Here the water is deep enough to dive in and you are well protected from the wind.

If you're camping here in late spring or summer, be sure to look for the family of mergansers that raise their young on the lake. These birds are shy and your presence will cause them to retreat into the thick brush along the lake's edge. If you have the patience or are willing to return after your paddle,

This is the roughest 1/10th of a mile on the entire portage.

locate a spot with a clear view of the lake. Bring binoculars or a camera with a telephoto lens. When the female merganser feels the area is safe, she will bring out her young. You will then be treated to a fine show of the mother instructing her young how to locate, dive and catch their meal of small fish.

Area References

Blackwell, Laird R., *Wildflowers of the Sierra Nevada and the Central Valley.* Edmonton, AB: Lone Pine Publishing, 1999. 288 pp.

Horn Elizabeth, *Sierra Nevada Wildflowers.* Missoula, MT: Mountain Press Publishing Company, 1998. 215 pp.

Wiese, Karen, *Sierra Nevada Wildflowers A Falcon Guide.* Helena, MT: Falcon Publishing, Inc., 2000. 187 pp.

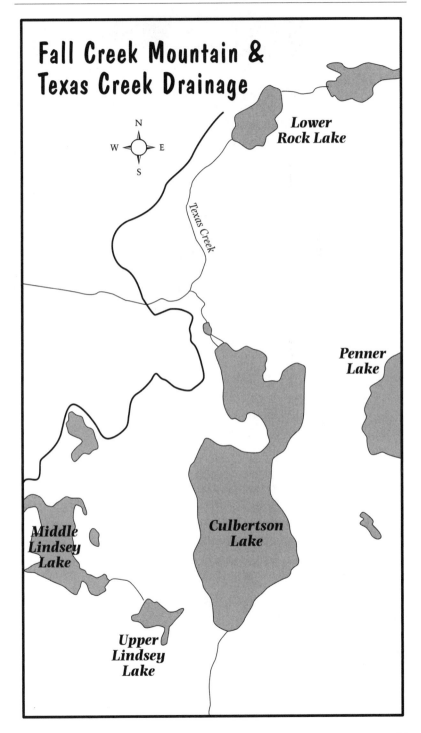

Fall Creek Mountain & Texas Creek Drainage

N
W — E
S

Texas Creek

Lower Rock Lake

Penner Lake

Middle Lindsey Lake

Culbertson Lake

Upper Lindsey Lake

Area 4

Fall Creek Mountain
& Texas Creek Drainage

PADDLE LOCATION 11
Culbertson Lake

(Portage Required)

Difficulty: With the exception of the strenuous portage, for all skill levels.

Trip Length: Given the time and effort it takes to portage to the lake, this paddle should be planned as an overnight campout.

Portage: 0.09 mile from the finger channel of Upper Lindsey Lake to the clearing visible off-trail paralleling Culbertson Lake. The most difficult part to this segment of the portage is taking-out among the brush in the finger channel of Upper Lindsey Lake. The thickness of the brush hinders unloading and loading. Once this task is accomplished, however, the trail to Culbertson Lake put-in is easy to follow. A short distance after you have begun your descent from the top of the small knoll separating upper Lindsey Lake from Culbertson Lake, look for a clearing to the right of the trail. The clearing slopes downward to the bank where pine trees are growing. A pathway is visible cutting through the edge of the bank and leading to the small level beach below. This beach is your put-in and take-out.

Paddling Distances:

From the put-in to: campsite, South end of lake: 0.23 mile;

The lower end of the lake: 0.57 mile;

From the put-in to the tip separating lower and upper lake: 0.33 mile;

From lower lake to the campsite at south end of upper lake: 0.72 mile (following shoreline clockwise)

Lake Size: 3550' x 1300'

Elevation: 6,442'

Historical Background: Culbertson Lake was named after J. H. Culbertson, the builder of the original dam in the early 1850's.

County: Nevada

National Forest: Tahoe National Forest, Nevada City Ranger District (530) 265-4531

Maps: USGS 7.5 Minute Topographical Section: English Mountain

Adjoining Section: Graniteville

National Forest Service Map: Tahoe National Forest

Road Maps: Compass Maps Inc.: Nevada and Sierra Counties; Nevada-Sierra Counties Street and Road Atlas

American Auto Assn. (AAA) Maps: Northern California/Bay & Mountain sections

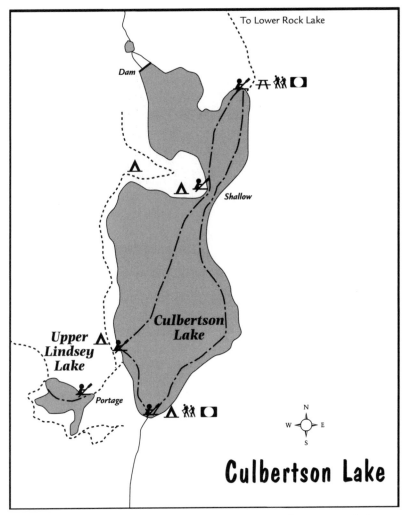

To Lower Rock Lake

Dam

Shallow

Culbertson Lake

Upper
Lindsey
Lake

Portage

Culbertson Lake

Access: (See Paddle Location 8 for driving access to the portage site)
The Boat Portage (beginning at Lower Lindsey Lake):
Start your portage on the opposite side of the green gate located at the upper end of the road that passes through the campsites of Lower Lindsey Lake. The road starts off on an incline and levels off a short distance above. Take your time and take breaks as needed. I make my first break at the two mature Jeffrey pines located at the top of the first uphill pitch.

Middle Lindsey Lake Paddle and Portage:
Eventually you will site the dam on the right as you round the bend of your last short uphill spurt. Pass the dam site and the small grove of conifers. Use the grassy clearing as your put-in. There are no rocks to scrape the boat and

Your first view of Culbertson Lake from the portage trail is breathtaking.

you have a clear section of lake to place the boat in prior to packing.

Unless you are planning to spend the day at Middle Lindsey or camp here overnight, steer your boat through the narrow passage leading out to the main body of the lake. Paddle toward the base of the left ridge that makes up a part of the mass of Fall Creek Mountain. To reach your take-out for the second portage to Upper Lindsey Lake, paddle around the small rocky point visible ahead and to your left. On the map, included in the guidebook, it is the point with campsite # 4. Once you have rounded this point, you will see several pines growing in close proximity to each other. Aim your boat toward the large Jeffrey Pine growing closest to the shoreline. You should be in a small brush sheltered cove. Take out on the gravel beach where the slope is overgrown with a cover of bracken ferns. To the left of this pine tree is a large boulder whose base is partially obscured by ferns. I use the boulder as a reference to help locate my boat cart that I hide among the ferns. If you look to the right of the pine, you will spot the narrow trail leading upward toward the top of this small knoll.

Portage To Upper Lindsey Lake:
Use this trail to portage your boat and gear to the top of the knoll. At the top, follow the visible road cut to the right. It will turn into a short but steep and rocky path to the site of Upper Lindsey Lake. Look for the small rock faced dam with a stream flowing from its base. Walk your boat across the dam, and put-in at the small grass beach located at the upper right corner of the dam.

Upper Lindsey Lake Paddle and Portage:

Paddle across this short lake, staying to the left of the granite boulder sitting in the water at the upper end of the lake. Enter the small finger channel to the left of the boulder and look to your right for a small clearing hacked into the brush. You may wish to bring a pair of pruning shears to clip any new growth blocking the take-out.

Portage To Culbertson Lake:

Lying behind this screen of brush is a narrow trail running parallel to the finger channel. Follow it north (left) through the carpet of bracken ferns to where it disappears over a tree-covered knoll for a distance of approximately 80 yards. At the top of this knoll you will have your first view of Culbertson Lake. Continue down the trail for an additional 100 yards to where the trail comes closest to the shoreline of the lake. Break trail to the right. Make your way down to the small beach visible through the pines growing on the bank above the shoreline. This small but level section of shoreline is your put-in and take-out.

Heads Up:

- A rugged portage is required to reach this lake.
- Carry pruning shears to clear new brush at take-out, Upper Lindsey Lake.
- Dispersed camping only.
- Campfire permits are mandatory.
- Bear country: pack and camp smart.
- In case of emergency, there are two employee residencies located at the upper end of the lake, adjacent to the dam.
- Excellent hiking on various trails located nearby.
- Superb birding and wildflower viewing.
- The fishing is great, especially with the use of a canoe or kayak.
- The lake's setting, at the base of the 500'+ multi-hued flank of a ridgeline, is nothing short of spectacular.
- With the exception of passing hikers, you will have the lake to yourself.
- Yours will be the only canoe or kayak on the lake.
- Bragging rights follow upon completion of trip.

Description: After all that toil, sweat and the sore muscles to boot, you stand on the knoll overlooking the setting for Culbertson Lake. The lake's dark blue surface contrasts sharply against the salmon-colored wall of the imposing ridgeline that dominates the skyline. Parallel lines of green mark areas of vegetation that have taken a hold in the fractures crisscrossing the length of the ridge. The mass that makes up the sidewall is so high that mature stands of conifers appear as shrubs growing along the flank of the ridge. On your side of the shore, similar stands of pine, fir and cedar rise to majestic heights obscuring the view down lake. Check the time: it is 8:30 in the morning, but not a whisper from a human voice or a boat on the water . . .today, this lake belongs to you! You catch your breath and fill your lungs with the scent of wildflowers and pine. Hefting your end of the boat, you spot the small clearing under the branches of a small grove of pine, and cautiously step off the trail. Descending the slope, you leave behind a gathering plume of dust and tumbling rocks. A short time later, you reach the lip of the bank overlooking the lake. Below you is the exposed small beach where you place your boat and prepare to reload your gear. You share some water and a snack with your partner, laugh at a shared joke, place your paddles in the water, and so . . .your day begins!

Upper Lake: Southern and Eastern Shorelines

Before exploring the lake and its shore, you first want to locate a campsite. Nestled under a grove of tall conifer at the south end of the lake is a suitable campsite. Following the shoreline, you pass a brushy patch of rock. The shoreline angles into a soft curve broken by the growth of a thick mass of brush. The sound of rushing water coming from within indicates a stream whose mouth is hidden by the screen of vegetation. A clearing lies immediately past this hidden stream; in its center is a small grove of living and dead conifers. A fire ring with adjacent log benches marks the location of your campsite.

As you paddle your boat closer into the cove, you notice the presence of the dominant rock wall that rises in the background. The signature curve of the wall gives it the appearance of an amphitheater. This geologic feature shows all the characteristics of a cirque, the former headwall of a mountain glacier. Cutting the center of the rock bowl into two dissimilar halves, a streambed slices downward in a steep gradient before taking on a less precipitous course as it enters the lake. Where the gradient is less steep, piles of boulders varying in size from a basketball to a Volkswagen lie in repose. Just before you beach your boat, the talus pile becomes hidden within the growth of lush greenery.

Up till now, you have faced the scenery that makes up the cirque and nearby vegetation. Turning around to face the lake, the panorama seems to stretch endlessly onward. You set up camp and flip a coin to determine if it is the lake or the cirque that will be explored first. The paddle wins and soon you are off following the shoreline alongside the shear cliffs. The croak of a raven (Corvus corax) and the tumbling sound of a small rock fall draw your attention to the side of the cliff where the edge of the talus pile sits. You spot movement amongst the rocks and, allowing the boat to drift, dig out the binoculars.

View of upper lake and ridgeline.

Standing out in clear relief is a small herd of Mule Deer *(Odocoileus hemionus californicus)*. Their light summer coats provide excellent camouflage against the backdrop of rock. This small group consists of several females and one juvenile. They slowly make their way along a faint trail that follows a ledge leading to a seep and a brushy plateau. To reach the seep, they must a leap across a small chasm. All the adults make the jump before proceeding onward to the water. A youngster, however, hesitates and frantically attempts to find another means of crossing. Its faint cries are carried down by the breeze. Just before it panics and leaps off-trail onto the talus below, one of the females appears and calls out to the young deer. Again the youngster attempts to make the leap but hesitates at the last second. Twice more this scenario is carried out before the female, in exasperation, leaps across and deftly works her way behind the young fawn. Brooking no nonsense from the youngster, she places her head between its hindquarters and with a rapid uplift, jerks it forward. The fawn's front legs first act as brakes, then begin to move rapidly forward as it propels itself across to land in a dust-blooming heap on the other side. Quickly the fawn scrambles up, shakes itself clean, and scampers off. Satisfied with her results, the female gracefully leaps back across. She passes the fawn, and without a backward glance, disappears behind a screen of brush. Although this entire occurrence lasted only ten to fifteen minutes, you feel as if it went on for hours.

Feeling extremely fortunate to have witnessed these creatures, you proceed onward with a heightened awareness of the surrounding terrain. Your boat has slowly drifted, carried along by the current and pushed by the breeze. You find yourself in the center of this upper section of the lake. Looking downward past the dark blue surface, the color shifts to an emerald green of the depths below. Overhead, contrails from passing aircraft slash across the cobalt sky. Their presence reminds you of the world you have temporarily, and with great physical hardship, chosen to leave behind.

As the breeze picks up, you begin to paddle toward the towering wall of rock and the shoreline you wish to explore. As your boat draws near, the opaque depths become clear and visibility increases to where you can spot the tops of huge boulders, the preserved trunks of long-dead conifers, and the slow undulations of big fish. Again you stop paddling and eagerly attempt to get a better view of the fish. To do so however, requires re-positioning your boat so the sun's reflection illuminates rather than washes out your view below. The fish meanwhile, don't wish to cooperate. They slowly move away, staying just ahead of the boat to captivate you with their presence, but not long enough to study their form.

This is just as well, for a wall of stone with its brushy shoreline looms large off your bow. You now begin to study the dominant presence of the rock wall that makes up the entire eastern shoreline. In addition to the rock's shear mass, its presence displays Nature's handiwork. Initially, this mass of rock was formed deep beneath the surface. Tectonic forces such as earthquakes and volcanism played a role in the initial formation and composition of the rock. The present shaping however, had to wait until the arrival of the Ice Age. The glaciers that followed carved their way through the original river valley by scraping and polishing their way downstream. Eventually, the planet began to warm, causing the glaciers to retreat and finally disappear. The after-effects of the glacier's handiwork however, remain to this day. What originally was a narrow valley cut by small streams now becomes a wide basin with walls of polished rock. Scattered about like a bag of spilled marbles, loose boulders of every size, shape, color and composition litter the breadth of the region. Piles of graded topsoil form ridge lines where before there was level ground. Depressions filled with water from melting ice formed small lakes such as the original Culbertson Lake.

Today, stands of pine, cedar, and juniper grow from crevices and leveled sections where soil has accumulated. Man has dammed these small glacial lakes and created deep reservoirs, but the grandeur of the ridgeline still remains. As you paddle along the flank of the wall where it disappears beneath the waters of the lake, take note of lichen *(Family Usnaceae, possibly phaea)* growing on the rock. The walls are covered with abstract patterns in yellow, orange, black and brown.

This side of the lake with its imposing rock wall contrasts sharply with the opposite shore, where the trees of the forest dominate the landscape. Instead of rock layers plunging into the depths of the lake, shallow beaches give way to brushy undergrowth and stands of conifer. Clearings of various sizes provide excellent campsites.

The Inlet

The expanse of Culbertson Lake suddenly diminishes into a narrow passageway that connects this larger body of the upper lake with the smaller and more intimate cove of the lower lake. Unfortunately, sitting beside the dam are two residences that belong to PG&E (Pacific Gas And Electric Company). Although their presence intrudes onto this wilderness- like setting, the distance between them and your campsite located on the opposite end of the lake allows you to almost forget their existence. In addition, the forested former moraine field that almost divides the two lakes acts as a natural barrier between you and the houses.

As you pass through the narrow inlet into lower Culbertson Lake, be wary of partially submerged boulders and edges of tree trunks that may scrape your boat's hull. Stay to the right following the rock wall as you pass through this inlet. When I first paddled here, the presence of the iron fire rings now partially submerged and the scattered rock suggested that this opening might be man-made. This possibility is very likely considering the history of the region. When early engineers such as B. Faucherie first scouted these lakes, they saw the possibility of enlarging then connecting them by means of tunnels, pipelines and flumes. Today this little-known engineering feat still shuttles water from reservoir to reservoir before piping it down to the residents of Nevada City, Grass Valley and outlying foothill communities. Unfortunately, very little has been written about the construction of these projects, only about their initial purpose: hydraulic mining operations.

Lower Lake: The Cove

Upon passing through the inlet, the lake opens once again, but on a smaller scale, into a series of small coves. To your left and facing north sits the lip of the concrete Culbertson Lake Dam. Built into the trees, and visible to the left of the dam are two company houses. I ignored this section of shoreline along the dam with its housing area and instead paddled into the small cove whose entrance is dominated by the presence of an enormous quartzite boulder. This imposing chunk of rock no doubt rolled down to here from its original placement in the strata of the adjoining ridgeline. Approximately thirty feet from shore, I had to paddle carefully to avoid the emerging rocks and other debris. All along the shoreline were piles of driftwood and huge logs washed in by the wind-generated waves. Boulders of various sizes lay scattered about. No doubt they rolled down from the flank of the same steep ridge whose presence was discussed earlier.

Stepping out I had to carefully place my feet so as to not crush the carpets of small yellow "belly flowers" growing the length of the shoreline. Upon close examination, I guessed that these flowers were some type of buttercup. Weaving my way through the obstacles of bleached logs and stray boulders, I made my way inland. A trail led through the brush and came out onto the

The approach to your campsite at the base of a cirque on the lake's southwest end.

bare granite of the first small knoll rising beyond the shoreline. These were the same group of knolls that I saw from my canoe during my approach into the cove. I made my way effortlessly to the top of the first knoll, paused, and took in the view. Partially obscuring the rocky terrain grew mats of Pinemat Manzanita *(Arctosaphylos nevadensis)*. Growing in stands or standing apart were Jeffrey Pines, Ponderosa or Yellow Pine, Lodgepole Pine, Sugar Pine *(Pinus la mbertiana)* and the pungently aromatic Western Juniper *(Juniperus occidentalis)*.

Picking my way carefully through the narrow openings between the manzanita, I worked my way to the top of the third and highest knoll. From here you can gaze at the lake on one side and down onto the forest-covered canyon of Texas Creek stretching outward to the northwest. Perceiving some movement at the corner of my eye, I slowly looked into the belt of pine growing on the edge of the embankment. Cautiously, and ever so slowly a female Mule Deer *(O. hemionus)*, silently stepped out from the cover of the trees. Her summer coat was a pale yellow, almost the color of straw. Although she had not spotted me at first, she detected a strange presence in her territory. My foot jarred or scratched the bare rock, and instantly her ears rose and zeroed in to my whereabouts. Her large ears clearly indicated why this species of deer are given the name "mule." Their ears are comparatively larger than any other family of deer. Once the deer bounded off, I again turned to study the three knolls aligned below me. From their shape and configuration, I surmised that they had the characteristics of a glacial terrain feature known as a *Roche moutonnee* or sheep rock. Their unique characteristic shape reminded early geologists, particularly the French, of a stylish wig as well as of the backs of unshorn sheep when viewed in profile. By definition, a roche moutonee is an elongated hill of bedrock shaped by a glacier. The long axis of the hill is oriented in the direction of the ice movement. The upstream side is smooth but striated; on the other hand, the downstream end is steep, rocky and fractured.

As you hike progressively to the top of each feature, you will obtain an emerging view of the lake, with its imposing ridgeline as well as the forested slopes of the Texas Creek Drainage. Back at my canoe, I quickly stored my gear and continued with the exploration of this end of the lake. With consideration to the families living in the housing area, I skipped the beach adjacent to the dam and the houses, and paddled toward the shoreline that marked the northern edge of the previously mentioned moraine field. Skimming along the shore I noted several camping sites that may be used when the houses are vacant.

Upper Lake: North Shore

I traced my passage back through the inlet and followed the southern edge of the same moraine field now located within the boundary of Upper Lake. Once again, as I cruised the shoreline several campsites caught my attention. These sites were located along the shore; I wondered if any additional sites existed beyond the belt of vegetation that screened the interior of the former moraine field. Where the finger-like field joins the main shoreline, I beached my canoe and hiked inland. Sure enough, located in a clearing that extends almost the length of the protruding field, one site after another may be utilized for camping purposes. As I walked past each clearing, I noted several former fire rings and other evidence of past campers. Obviously, the accessibility of the area with its short hike to either side of the lake and the grand view of Upper Lake make this entire peninsula a favorite for overnight stays.

Continuing to follow the now-northwestern shoreline, I spotted the same trail that I used as part of my portage from Upper Lindsey Lake to Culbertson Lake. I located a small gravel beach and secured my canoe. Here along the shoreline, the terrain is fairly level and each campsite has a small but lovely gravel beach. Surprisingly, when I went for a swim, the water was brisk but not discomforting.

The clarity of the water is astounding. Standing on the shore, I could easily view the entire length of the bottom in either direction. Occasionally, a trout would cruise slowly by, spot my movements, and dart into the more opaque depths. Wading out, the bottom consisted of gravel with no silt or mud. This made for easy and secure footing, not to mention any swirls of silt to hide the bottom with each step. After the short but refreshing swim, I continued to hike the trail back toward the high ground that leads toward the same ridge that separates Culbertson Lake from Upper Lindsey Lake.

Hiking through the conifer forest I noted that the area was covered with pines and cedars. It was evident that logging had taken place here at one time. However, growing here and there were individual second-growth giants whose broad girth and tall trunks established a certain presence that the other smaller trees did not have. Glowing with a neon intensity, chartreuse lichen add their special coloration to the predominate shades of green and brown. At one time, this species of lichen called Staghorn or Wolf *(Letharia vulpine)* was boiled in water by certain California tribes, to produce a yellow dye for their baskets.

The trail was readily visible and easy to follow. As with the clearings along the ridge of the moraine field, campsites of various size along with their fire-rings dotted the shoreline along the trail. Hiking further on the trail, I cleared the forest and began to ascend into a grassy clearing. Growing on either side of the trail was a dense matt of purple colored Bush Lupine *(Lupinus albifrons)*. Beyond this clearing stood another small grove of conifers and then the familiar section of trail that served as part of the portage between the two lakes was partially visible through the trees.

Retracing my steps, I soon made my way back to the canoe and proceeded to follow the remainder of the shoreline before completing my circumnavigation of the lake. By now the sun began to set and a golden glow lit the rock walls of the precipitous slope of the ridge located across the lake. Feeling a chill in the air, and that satisfied feeling of accomplishment, I continued with my slow paddle back to camp.

Area References

Cahalane, Victor H., *Mammals of North America*. New York, NY: The Macmillan Company. Fifth Printing, 1964. 682 pp.

Durham, David L. *Place-Names of California's Gold Country*. Clovis, CA: Quill Driver Books/ Word Dancer Press. 2000. 369 pp.

Guyton, Bill, *Glaciers of California*. Berkeley, CA: University of California Press. 1998. pg. 48.

Hundley, Norris Jr., *The Great Thirst Californians And Water, 1770s-1990s*. Berkeley, CA: University of California Press, 1992.551 pp. (pgs. 73-77)

IN THE EDDY

The Hike

Behind my campsite, hidden behind the screen of dead timber, dense brush and talus, is a trail. This trail follows a small streambed that leads to a clearing located above the marsh area of Upper Lindsey Lake. From there the trail splits into two directions. One section follows the southwest shoreline of Upper Lindsey Lake where it terminates at Upper Lindsey Lake Dam. The other half crosses the streambed and becomes part of an old road-cut that probably was part of a service road between the Lindsey Lakes and Culbertson Lake. Protected by the high walls of the cliff and the stands of conifers with their dense under-story of brush, multitudes of wildflower communities abound.

To reach the trail and hike along its path, I first had to boulder hop along the pile of colorful blocks of various rock types lying about. Shimmers of heat radiated off the high rock wall of the cliff. At my feet, sunlight sparkled off the many crystals that formed in the various rocks wedged in the streambed.

A short time later, I hopped off the last boulder and stepped into the cool shade courtesy of the pines growing along the stream bank. From this shaded arbor I could see the trail as it led off toward the streambed flowing from the marshy area of Upper Lindsey Lake. To my delight, the ground was dotted with colors of various hue and intensity. Reds and yellows from paintbrush *(Family Castilleia)*, the blue of the lupine *(Family Leguminosae)* and other blooms, combined with bright yellow blossoms from Mules Ears *(Wyethia mollis)*, all wavered sluggishly with the breeze.

Everywhere, a photograph waited to be taken! Slowly, I photographed my way through the gap separating the two lakes. Following the trail of blooming wildflowers I arrived at the base of the cliff where the trail turned to the southwest. Ahead of me was a clearing bordered on my right by the brushy shoreline of the marsh. The left boundary was predominantly rock, but not just ordinary rock. Layers upon layers of various minerals were set in folds and bends not unlike the swirled layers of a cake—only this "cake" ran for several hundred yards and was hundreds of feet high. At the base of these layers was an even stranger geologic sight. A mélange of rust-colored veins of crystallized minerals ran amok in a profusion of swirls and streaks within their matrix of schist. The scene resembled a cube of butter squeezed in your palm.

Obviously, some incredibly dynamic geological forces have been at work on these rock layers. Scrambling to the top of a ledge located approximately twenty feet above me I was able to have an unrestricted view of the meadow, and the overgrown portion of Upper Lindsey Lake. From this vantage point I could make out Upper Lindsey Lake dam and the put-in. I realized that I was standing on a bench of the same rock whose unique layers captivated me when I was viewing them from the dam.

Studying the outline of the lake I could spot the trail as it wound its way around both sides of the lake. Remembering the rusting cable when paddling

"A melange of rust-colored veins of crystallized minerals ran amok in a profusion of swirls and streaks . . . ."

the marshy area of the lake, I noted that a portion of the trail ran through the area where the cable lay. Maybe I could understand the purpose of the cable by hiking this portion of the trail.

Sliding down the scree of rocky rubble, I followed the trail back through the flower-covered meadow and rounded the shoreline of the lake. It wasn't difficult to figure out why the cable was resting in the lake. The "trail" I was on at one time served as a road connecting Upper Lindsey Lake to Upper Culbertson Lake. The proof of this was in the neatly preserved, carved road-cut and a small portion of the packed roadbed located in a natural saddle between the two lakes. Standing in the center of the cut, I could see the remnants of the old road as it disappeared down the bank of Upper Lindsey Lake and into the water. Remembering the strange disappearance of the old road across the lake above Upper Lindsey Lake dam, I surmised that possibly this portion of the former road at one time joined the old road across Upper Lindsey Lake. My best guess is that it is probably an old service road during construction of the reservoirs. My curiosity satisfied, I proceeded back on the former road, now trail, toward my campsite located beyond the meadow and below this picturesque saddle.

Sources

Storer, Tracy I. & Robert L. Usinger, *Sierra Nevada Natural History.* Berkeley, CA: University of California Press, 1963. 374 pp.

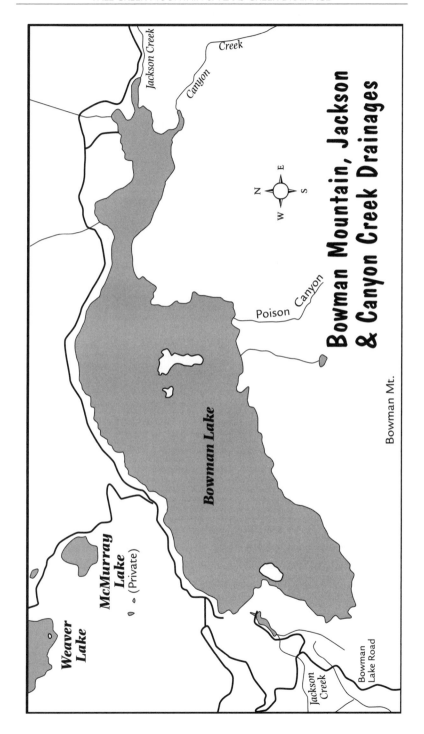

Bowman Mountain, Jackson
& Canyon Creek Drainages

Area 5

Bowman Mountain & Jackson, Canyon Creek Drainages

PADDLE LOCATION 12-A
Lower Bowman Lake

Difficulty: All skill levels may enjoy Bowman Reservoir. All paddlers should pay attention to the wind. The presence or absence of wind will determine what area you wish (or can) paddle to.

Lake Size: 68,510 acre feet/6.84 miles of shoreline

Elevation: 5,500'

Trip Length: The reservoir itself may be paddled as a day paddle.

Season: Best paddling is in the spring when the snow has melted off the road. The reservoir is open through the summer and into the fall, until sufficient snowfall closes the road.

Historical Background: The original dam was built in 1868, raised in 1872, and again in 1876. The present dam was constructed on the sight of the first dam using granite from the original dam and nearby quarries. The modern dam was dedicated on July 1, 1927. Bowman Dam was named for James F. Bowman, an early settler from Scotland, who came to the area in the early 1860's. You passed a former cabin site belonging to his ranch holdings, driving up on Bowman Lake Road/Forest Road 18. (Look for a wooden sign located on the right before you cross Canyon Creek.) The main ranch was built near Poison Canyon on the southeast side of present day Bowman Lake. At the time of his settlement the lake was called Little Bowman Lake. When the two lakes combined into present day Bowman Lake, the lake covered the original ranch site. Originally the purpose of the dam was to provide water pressure for hydraulic mining. Operation of the dam is now controlled by the Nevada Irrigation District as a principal source of water for the county. The present dam consists of two sections: the main dam visible from Bowman Lake Road; and a smaller dam located behind the large island, south of the main dam.

Paddle Distances: Lower Reservoir (see map): From the primary launch site to: Yellow Metal Mine site (direct route): 0.56 mile; The island: 0.90 mile; Wagon road site: 1.35 miles; Yellow Metal Mine site: 2.20 miles; Poison Canyon by way of the islands: 1.82 miles

County: Nevada

National Forest: Tahoe National Forest, Nevada City Ranger District (530) 265-4531

Maps: USGS 7.5' Topographical Sections: Graniteville Quadrangle and English Mtn. Quadrangle

National Forest Map: Tahoe National Forest Service Map
Road Map: Compass Maps Inc.: Nevada and Sierra Counties; Nevada–Sierra Counties Street and Road Atlas
American Auto Assn. (AAA) Maps: Northern California/Bay and Mountain sections

Access: Take Interstate 80 East, drive past Yuba Gap and Crystal Lake Road turnoff. Exit right onto Highway 20 west. Continue on Hwy. 20 for 4.0 miles. Turn right on Bowman Lake Road (Forest Service Rd.: 18N18). Follow the road for 16 miles to Bowman Reservoir. *(Note: At mile marker 10.5 the pavement ends and a rough, corrugated cobble strewn road begins. Although these last 5.5 miles are recommended for high clearance vehicles [4x4 is not necessary], I have seen everything from Honda Civics to 30-foot motor homes negotiating this road.)*

Heads Up:
■ Only small-motorized craft and paddle craft are allowed.
■ No crowds.
■ Spectacular scenery, historical sites and waterfalls to explore.
■ Centrally located to other lakes.

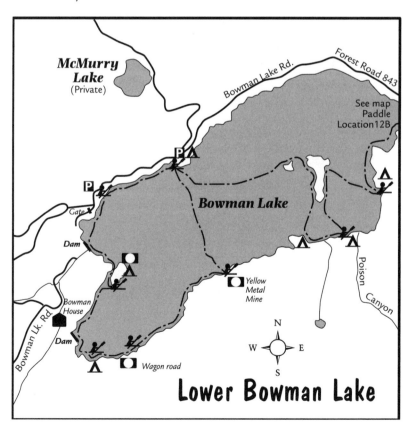

The last uphill section of the drive before reaching the lake.

■ Campfire permit is required for any overnight camping.

■ Dispersed camping is allowed throughout the area.

■ The closest Forest Service Campground containing vault toilets and an unimproved crushed rock boat ramp is located at the upper end of Bowman Reservoir (see map).

■ The closest stores are: at the entrance to Kelly Lake private camp ground off Crystal Lake Road, and the service center in Nyack.

■ Bring your own water / water purifier.

■ Bear Habitat: pack and camp smartly.

■ No other services or phone. Emergency aid may be obtained from the Bowman Dam facilities (if occupied) located beneath the dam site.

Description: Bowman Reservoir offers a cornucopia of delights to those paddlers willing to endure the hardscrabble road leading into the reservoir. To paddlers new to the Grouse Ridge region, the primary access road—Bowman Lake Road/Forest Road 18—may deceive you unless you are willing to road test your vehicle. The road begins as a typical paved two-lane backcountry road, but beginning at mile marker 10 1/2 (at the Texas Creek crossing), the last 5.5 miles of road deteriorates rapidly into a cobble-strewn washboard track. When you have crested the last ridge leading into the reservoir and bounced up and down on the final cobble, the first view of the reservoir, shimmering in its bowl of glacier-sculpted rock, will make-up for the grueling drive. From this vantage point (see map) you will notice that the primary road continues paralleling the reservoir, and an access road leading down to the reservoir is to your right. This short road leads to a boat launch located below the main road and to your left. To the right of this road is another road that leads to facilities at the dam site. It is usually gated off only a short distance below. I do not recommend using this first access road because the turnaround at the boat launch is muddy and rock strewn. Additionally, thoughtless campers using the only level area that comprises the turnaround usually block it off. Instead, continue your way on the main road for another one-half mile until you come to the road junction (McMurray Lake Road) that enters from the left, and leads to McMurray and Weaver Lakes (described in Paddle Location 13). To the right of this junction is a pullout with a steep access leading to a group of level areas containing several camper made fire rings. Unless you have a high-clearance vehicle, I recommend that you use the pullout next to the primary road to park in for the unloading of boats and gear. From this vantage point, you have an excellent view of the reservoir and the destination points to which you will be paddling.

Located directly across the lake, the talus pile of yellowish rock piled around a stand of tall conifers marks the location of Yellow Metal Mine, coincidentally, one of the places you may explore on this lake. Down-lake toward the southwest, are the main island and dam. Both are conveniently accessible as day paddles from this put-in. To reach the upper lake and the waterfalls, you may use this put-in site but be prepared for a longer paddle and a headwind on your return. Because of this, I have divided the description of the paddles as those located on the lower lake from the ones on upper lake.

Getting ready to paddle Lower Bowman Lake.

LOWER LAKE
(Paddle To Yellow Metal Mine)

Portage your boats and gear down the cobble-strewn road to a small cove that faces southwest toward the dam. Adjacent to the scrapped slope of barren rock is a small patch of coarse sand—the ideal spot to set your boat. Before heading out toward the mine site, take the time to become familiar with the landscape surrounding the mine as viewed from this part of the lake. It is not coincidental that a mine is located within this area. Unlike the geologic setting for most Sierran lakes, nestled in granitic basins, Bowman Lake sits in a belt of former bedrock composed of complex metamorphic, metasedimentary and igneous rocks. This entire assemblage arrived via the movement produced by plate tectonics and "attached" itself to the former margins of the earlier continent. These floating assemblages of varied rock are called *island arcs*. When they attach themselves to continental margins they form new *terranes*—"a homonym that refers not merely to surface configurations but to a full three-dimensional piece of the earth's crust."* (For a better understanding of how these terranes occurred and the geologic histories of the region, see the books listed in the Area References section at the end of the chapter).

Gold and other important minerals were deposited within the rocks that make up some of these terranes. Eventually, these minerals were exposed at or near the surface, primarily as a result of moving water and ice. With the discovery of gold in California, it didn't take long for miners to seek out the exposed rock outcrop such as the one bordering the lake. The mine itself is nestled at the base of Bowman Mountain, elevation: 7,386'. To the far left looking up the lake, a reddish colored ridge is Red Hill, elevation: 7,060'.

The belts of conifers growing down the flank of Bowman Mountain are primarily Jeffrey Pine, Lodgepole Pine, and Incense Cedar. Bands of Pinemat Manzanita *(Arctostaphylos nevadensis)* and other assorted shrubs surround the stands of conifers. As you view the mine's location, keep in mind that the mine and its facilities were built prior to the formation of the reservoir. This will become evident when paddling along the shoreline that contains the remnant of an old wagon road constructed to bring in equipment to the mine and carry out heavy loads of ore.

Paddling Out

Upon launching from the cove, if you are fortunate to be on the water before any wind, the paddle is straightforward across the lake to the mine site. However, if there is a strong wind, it will usually blow from the Southwest, and the direction of the dam. Before beginning your crossing, study the wind pattern. Usually the wind here blows in gusts. Time your start to a lull in the wind, and once on the water, look for the telltale ruffling of the lake's sur-

Approaching our first destination, the big island near the dam.

face. The approach of this visible surface shimmer indicates an arrival of a fresh wind gust.

For a safer but longer approach, I recommend that you begin by paddling into the wind using the island located near the dam, as your reference point. Paddle toward the island, passing your original destination of the mine and slowly begin a left loop that will place you on a downwind tack to the site. Although this approach is longer, you will not have to broach (paddle broadside) to the wind and subsequent chop formed on the wind swept lake. Furthermore, you will not subject yourself to the potential danger of capsizing your boat when hit by a surprise gust or errant wave.

To locate the mine site, first look for the exposed hogback ridge of bare rock that juts from the base of Bowman Mountain and forms a rocky point at the water's edge. Located to the right and at the base of this ridge is a small grove of conifers. Scattered above the grove are piles of yellow-orange or rusty colored waste rock (rock removed from underground mine workings). As you paddle closer, you will spot the wooden frame of the ten stamp mill used in the crushing of ore-bearing rock.

When the water level recedes in the spring, keep an eye open for pieces of old metal lying barely submerged near the shore. Unfortunately, there is no beach to take out on, only sharp-edged rocks and boulders dominate the water's edge. Upon stepping out of your boat, be sure to remove it completely from the water or the prevailing wind will batter it against the rocky beach.

Hike to Yellow Metal Mine
(See In the Eddy)

The Island and Bowman Dam Sites

The location of the road junction as your put-in provides the paddler with easy day access as well as an excellent early departure for all places of interest surrounding upper reaches of Bowman Reservoir. To reach the island, I recommend that you paddle along the northern shoreline until you reach the boat ramp. From the ramp, strike out for the main dam site and follow its line until you reach the narrow channel separating the island from the main shore.

Approaching the dam may start a slight tingle on your skin or produce goose bumps, particularly when your boat is only a few feet from the concrete abutments of the dam. If you have made your approach this close, however, take the time to study the dam's details as you glide by. Look for odd pieces of octagonal iron sticking out of the concrete: these are rem-

The bleached area shows the high-water level.

nants of the drill bits used in the construction of the dam. Why these iron bits were placed in these settings makes for a good engineering point to ponder.

The Island

Skirt past the dam, enter the narrow channel and cross over to the island only a short paddling distance from the dam. As you make your approach to the island, take a close look at the island's rock walls. You will notice the bleached water line that indicates where the high water reaches when the reservoir is full. If the water level is low enough, you should clearly see oval-shaped, darker colored rock imbedded within the matrix of the parent rock. These odd bits of imbedded stray rock are called inclusions and they may range from several inches to a few feet across. Most of them are chunks of basalt (an igneous rock type) with the occasional chunk of metamorphic (changed rock) rock thrown in to flavor the mélange. Their presence is an indicator of the dynamic forces that occurred in the creation of the bedrock and in particular the formation of the Sierra Nevada Mountain Range.

The best put-in to explore the island is a small inlet located on the southwest side facing the channel. Step out of the boat and look for a faint trail leading up to the top. A small level gravel bench is located above where the boats are beached. This is an ideal spot to use as a campsite for those wishing to stay overnight. Continuing upward you will pass the few stunted conifers growing on the island. Besides the firs several pines also make their home on this windswept island. The bleached snag of a long-dead tree stands as a nesting site for birds that have drilled cavities into its trunk. Patches of Pinemat Manzanita help anchor the thin crust of soil and provide it with nutrients. In the spring, you will spot the occasional wildflower showing its colors in the rocky niches.

If the sun's angle is just right, you will view a glistening shimmer off the surface of the bare rock. This glacial polish was created by the action of former glaciers that once dominated the region. If you examine the surface carefully, you will notice grooves and scratches etched into the bedrock. These were formed by the many pieces of gravel, rock and even the ice itself as glacier's weight passed over the parent rock. Today the deeper grooves provide a valuable service—first, as a collector for the build-up of soil, subsequently, as a haven for the growth of young plants and even tree seedlings. Before leaving, don't forget to hike to the top of the domed height of the island. Your reward—a magnificent view of the reservoir and surrounding basin.

The South Shore
(Bowman Dam sites)

To explore the area around the dam, paddle across the narrow channel to

View of the big island and lower Bowman Lake.

the small cove that faces south, visible directly across from the island put-in. Once out of the boat, look for a small clearing just above the scrape zone south of the cove. This narrow trail intersects a former construction road that leads from the dam to the rocky heights above the dam itself. As you hike up the former road, you will pass through a stand of second growth Jeffrey pines. If the day is warm, walk up to a tree and inhale the aroma of the bark. Breath deeply of the resins that seep out of the grooves in the bark of the tree.

In her delightful book: *Graced by Pines,* Alexandra Murphy explains the cause of your surprise: "Some days the pines smell like vanilla, or other days like butterscotch [or even pineapple]. Sometimes they hardly smell at all. Their scent comes from volatile oils, called terpenes, in the pines' resin. Because the amount of terpenes released increases as the resin heats up, the trees smell strongest on a warm sunny day."

When you reach the top, just before you start down the flagstone steps that lead into the former quarry pit, look to your right for a representative of the Cypress tree family. This single Sierra Juniper/Western Juniper is a lonesome visitor from the nearby windswept granite ridges. From this high vantage point, you have a clear view of Canyon Creek Gorge and the glacial broadened Canyon Creek Canyon. If you hike to the edge facing the gorge, look down and you should spot several well-constructed buildings. These structures belong to the Nevada Irrigation District, the company that owns the majority of the reservoirs located within the Grouse Ridge Region, and their associated dams. On your return hike, you will have an unsurpassed view of the entire length of Bowman Lake and the conifer crowned island you recently visited.

Continue your paddle through the channel and you will pass a wall of rock. The water line separates the lower bleached section from the lichen-covered and stained upper section. Look for vertical stain lines leading down the rocky wall. These lines mark the location of thin waterfalls that flow during the spring snowmelts and after a heavy rainfall. The lower bleached surface clearly shows many of the inclusions described passing the island.

Once you have paddled past the rock wall, located high above and to the right of the smaller dam, you will notice some whitish cap rock. This is a pile of surplus cement that was dumped sometime during the construction of the dam. Paddling past the small dam you will enter a lovely cove blocked from the wind and shaded by the trees of the forest growing near the lake's edge. Here is a nice spot to put in, take a break, and enjoy the view of the lake.

Just around the south point of this same cove is an excellent campsite with a northern exposure. The site contains an already built fire ring and a level area that will easily accommodate two tents. To find it, look for two mature Jeffrey pines growing above the small bench created by the scraping of the shoreline. When I was exploring the site, I came across a standing snag in a small clearing above the campsite. On it were several large fungi called Red-belted Polypores *(Fomitopsis pinicola)*. This type of fungus, similar to shelf fungus, causes decay in many conifers and hardwood trees.

The Wagon Road

The destination to the old wagon road bed is a close encounter on this end of the lake with a historical site that dates back to the gold hunting years of the last century. Having the use of the 7.5 Minute Graniteville Quadrangle will greatly facilitate the spotting of the rock-walled support bed of the former wagon road. Using your topographical map sheet, look for the first small cove located due east of the most southern edge of the lake. It is the first cove east of the numeral 8, (which denotes that particular *"section"* on the map).

From the water, as you paddle following the shoreline, look for a small clearing that contains many large boulders and rock debris. This jumble of rock is the talus pile from the construction of the road, and rock fall from the above unstable slope. Immediately to the left of the clearing, just above the scrape zone and partially hidden in the shade of the trees, is a short stack of rocks that angle upward in the direction of the clearing. This stack of stones is a fine example of dry stacked rock used as cribbing in support of the road-bed. You will also note that the present road ends at the scrape zone of the reservoir. When the road was originally built, it extended downward following the pre-scrapped contour of the land. This is a great example of a field observation that allows one to make an educated guess as to the general age of the road and subsequently, the mine itself.

Hike up the old roadbed and you will come to an interesting piece of machinery partially buried by debris (see In The Eddy, pg. 124). Standing on the level section of roadbed above the hoisting wheel, look at the road as it bends to the left. You may follow it for a short distance before it disappears in a tangle of trees and brush. I suspect that it dropped down following the slope of the former pre-scrapped surface before crossing the channel of the now submerged Jackson Creek.

From the cove containing the wagon road it is a short paddle following the shoreline to the cobble beach and the site of Yellow Metal Mine. You may then choose to either complete the loop by paddling across the lake to your put-in, or continue east along the shore to Poison Canyon and the upper reservoir.

The Islands and Poison Canyon

Stand on the bluff where you parked your vehicle and look to your left. You will notice two islands lying close to the water in the foreground of Red Hill. When the reservoir is full, these two islands maintain an easily accessible shoreline. From any of these beaches you may secure your boat and explore the islands. Located directly behind the islands and flanking the slopes of Red Hill is a large cove that contains a huge expanse of level beach and a forested interior with many places to camp.

Poison Canyon is the main drainage containing two creeks' runoff from the slopes of Bowman Mountain and Red Hill.

To reach this area of the reservoir, I recommend that you use the two islands as your reference point. From the islands you may plan your paddle based on whichever part of Poison Canyon shoreline interests you the most.

The Islands

The two islands with their low relief are used by Canada Geese (*Branta canadensis*) as a nesting area; consequently, if you are paddling to the island during springtime pay close attention to any nesting birds. Please do not attempt to land near them. Because the islands contain so little relief, the wind blows freely over their surface. Only on the larger island—with its rocky bluff and glens of trees—is there a respite from the wind. However, on a calm day the small cove on the leeward southeast side of the larger island contains a sheltered beach for swimming. As the reservoir draws down during the summer months, keep your eye out for shallow areas, where you may scrape your boat's hull on the emerging rocks.

The islands near upper lake.

Poison Canyon

From the islands, the view south of the cove that marks the shoreline to Poison Canyon is readily visible. If you are interested in camping overnight, two locations exist within a short paddle of each other. The first site is located on the southwest tip of the cove to the west of the small barren island immediately offshore of the southern tip. Don't be surprised if you share your site with a family of Canada Geese! The geese like to feed on the emerging grass and other plants in the area.

Follow the cove past the island and you'll arrive at the first of two stream mouths that empty into the reservoir. This first stream, which does not have a name, flows out of a small tarn lake hidden by a belt of conifers at the northern flank of Bowman Mountain. An indistinct trail follows the streambed to this picturesque lake.

Poison Canyon Creek

Continue past this first stream and your paddle will take you to the center of the cove and the location of the second stream mouth: Poison Canyon Creek. By late spring the location of the stream's outlet is hidden by an overgrowth of brush possibly willows and alders. A good reference to remember as a location point for Poison Creek is that the creek flows down from the forested saddle stretching between Red Hill and Bowman Mountain. Beach your boat to the right of the creek and follow the creek bed into the forest. Located in a grove of pine adjacent to the right bank of the creek is a shady clearing that has been converted into a comfortable campsite. If you use this campsite, please respect the effort that went into making this site so comfortable.

Located just above the camp a trail leads into the brush that surrounds the creek. In the late spring, wildflowers and the scent of Swamp Onions *(Allium validum)* will assail your senses with their garlic-like odor. Numerous other trails lead off into the forest and allow you to explore the conifer-covered slopes of Poison Canyon.

Area References

Gudde, Erwin G. *California Place Names: The Origin and Etymology of Current Geographical Names,* 4th ed., revised. Ed. William Bright. Berkeley, CA: University of California Press, 1998. 467 pp.

Hoover, Mildred Brooke, Hero Eugene Rensch; and Ethel Grace Rensch. *Historic Spots In California,* revised ed., 4th printing. Ed. Ruth Teiser. Stanford, CA: Stanford University Press, 1962. 411 pp.

*McPhee, John, *Assembling California.* New York, NY: Farrar, Straus and Giroux, 1993. 304 pp.

IN THE EDDY

A Paddle to Yellow Metal Mine

"The quartz miner had three principal tasks confronting him:
First, the mining of the ore; second, reducing it to powder;
and third, extracting the gold from the powdered rock.
. . . For actually getting out the ore, they depended upon
picks, hand drills and sledges, mildly assisted by black powder.

. . . For the pulverizing of their ore the quartz miners had
recourse to some form of stamp, . . .
The stamp. . .was a machine that delivered hammer-like blows.
. . . Its heavy pounder was lifted eight to twelve inches and then
released   to come crashing down on the ore.

His [the miner] remaining problem was to separate the gold
from the powdered rock with which it was mixed.
. . . Water and gravity and quicksilver, with its remarkable
amalgamating quality, were called into action in sluices,
riffle boards, shaking tables, and other such devices."

--John Walton Caughey, Gold Is The Cornerstone, *pgs. 253-255*

The crisp and clear Sierran air heightened everyone's senses as we viewed our destination from the rocky bluff above Bowman Reservoir. This reservoir is just one of many such artificial lakes that were created by 19th century engineers to supply a reliable source of water for ongoing hydraulic mining operations located in the Sierran foothills. Bowman Reservoir, one of the more accessible lakes, sits in a basin of similar lakes within the Yuba River Drainage. The drainage itself makes up the west-central portion of Tahoe National Forest (see map).

California State Parks Ranger, Chuck Scimeca, his wife, Pam, Bert and Pat Hall, volunteer docents at the South Yuba River State Park, (Bridgeport Covered Bridge Historical Site) and I were getting ready to paddle and document the historical remains of the Yellow Metal Mine. Although existence of the mine is common knowledge between residents of nearby communities, to our knowledge, no one has documented or recorded the site for historical purposes.

Eventually with loud groans and exaggerated grimaces, we portaged the canoes and gear down to the reservoir where I promised an easy-water access and a gravel beach. Much to my chagrin, not to mention a blot on my reputation as guide extraordinaire, the water level had been drawn down leaving my beach with the easy access high and dry. After some good-natured ribbing and searching, a rocky but gentle slope leading to a small cove was located nearby.

It wasn't long before the two canoes were loaded and their bows pointed in the direction of the opposite shore. With little to no wind, each canoe's bow cut the glassy smooth water leaving behind the rippled wake of their passage. When Bert and I caught a glimpse of the second canoe passing abreast of us, we both had a good chuckle. Sitting regal-like in the center was Pat, looking very much like "the Queen of the Nile."

Our first destination was the site of the old wagon road. This road was initially built for the purpose of bringing construction material and the heavy stamp mill to the mine site. Later, the road was used to haul out the crushed ore. It had snowed since my last time here, consequently, almost all the natural references and landmarks were covered in a mantle of white. A short cruise along the shoreline allowed me to spot the telltale angle of stone cribbing that marked the foundation of the road segment.

Beaching our boats, we waited until Bert finished making a videotape of the cribbing, then hiked up to the top of the road cut. Chuck and Pam were amazed at the excellent condition of the stone cribbing that provided the foundation for the roadbed. At the top of the cribbed roadbed sat a winch, partially buried in a pit dug to one side of the former road. Still attached to the drum was a cable with a metal harness and a long iron hook. The positioning of the winch at the top of the steep grade suggested a possible use of the hoisting wheel either for the purpose of assisting the ore wagons or, more than likely, in hauling timber. Everybody was delighted with the handsome craftsmanship of the spokes that supported a wheel of the winch. As we wandered about the area, it wasn't long before we came across old lumber and other artifacts that we recorded and left in place.

As a freshening breeze ruffled the surface of the reservoir, we soon climbed into our canoes for the paddle to the mine. Just before we rounded the point that marked the location of the mine, Bert pointed to an opening high on the cliff-face and partially hidden behind a grove of pines. Soon we spotted a second hole. In my previous trips to the site, I had surmised that only one mine entrance or adit

The take-out to the mine. Note the stamp mill in the background.

These stamps crushed the chunks of ore into smaller pieces needed for the refinement process.

(an adit is a horizontal opening to a mine but has only one entrance) was worked. The site of two additional entrances increased everybody's curiosity.

After stepping out of the canoes, we beached and secured the craft. Then, like children in a toy store, we "oohed and ahhed" at the sight of the standing stamp mill. Lying scattered about and below the mill, were other rusting pieces of interesting machinery. Now, Bert and Chuck were in their element!

"Here you go," said Bert pointing to what looked like an oversized iron hose nozzle. "This is a crusher for the ore. And up there"--pointing to what looked like a rusting threshing machine--"is all that's left of the shaker table." Bert went on to explain that once the ore rock was initially crushed in the first crusher (now lying under the stamp mill), it went through the stamps for a final crushing. The final step was a recovery process, where the gold and other important minerals were separated from the ground rock. Different metals sort themselves in a particular order and the shaker table made that happen.

Chuck located the iron frame that held the second set of stamps lying empty on the rocky beach. His excited voice brought all of us to gather around the iron relic. Stamped proudly within an embossed seal, on the top plate of the frame, were the name and origin of the manufacturer: MINERS FOUNDRY AND SUPPLY CO NEVADA CITY, CAL. We now had a local source from which we could trace and obtain information. The Miners Foundry And Supply Co. was a main manufacturer for all kinds of mining tools and machinery in and around the local gold fields. It would not be difficult to trace any bill of sale from the foundry to the mine.** Along with the mill casing, other artifacts of note lying about included: a steam boiler; a very early model gasoline engine; and an iron base plate with the lettering, UNITED IRON WORKS OAKLAND CAL.

As interesting as these relics were, they paled in comparison to the sight of the stamp mill! Still standing over the concrete foundation on which it was built, the bleached wooden framework with the remaining five stamps cast a powerful presence. The left battery is still in place, and its five two-piece heavy iron pistons are still connected to the shaft, which in turn, is connected to a cam.

Streaks of rust have bled over the concrete foundation. A pack rat has built its nest high in the crevice of the wooden hopper. The pulley wheel reclines on its side several feet away and the leather belt pulley has long since rotted or disappeared. Underneath the wooden framework lies the rock crusher with its vise-like crushing unit partially buried in the pine duff. The entire mill, when viewed from the rear, has a decided tilt to it. Despite such a forlorn appearance, by standing back and closing your eyes, you can imagine the noise and the shaking of the ground nearby as the stamps lifted in sequence to crush the ore.

Following a trail on the edge of the tailings, we hiked to the top of the rock pile that was built as a bed for a narrow-gauge track on which the ore carts shuttled their way to the stamp mill. The track, whose iron rails still remain, ran from one of the adits to the hopper bin. Following the tracks we soon came to a boulder buried entrance where the rails disappeared under the rubble. All that's visible of the former entrance are the tops of two joined cross beams.

We knew, however, that based on what we saw from the water there are still at least two more adits to record. Pam and Pat, exploring the pile of waste rock, soon noticed a rock wall and pathway leading upward along the side of the talus slope. Carefully negotiating the sharp and loose rocks, we made our way up the former path. At a "cut" in the ridge face, looking up, we spotted the opening of another adit. After a short scramble, Bert, Chuck and I stood on the talus-packed floor in front of the main adit's entrance.

Bert and Chuck quickly pointed out to me the remains of the quartz vein that probably guided the miner's decision to start their mine entrance at this particular spot. Picking up a choice piece of tailing, we examined it for clues as to the kind of ore inside the mine. Along with the quartz, traces of galena (lead), and iron pyrite (fool's gold) was bound in a matrix of yellowish rock. Just inside the immediate entrance of the adit, I examined the rock face. Still in place after these many years were drill holes for holding the dynamite! Not venturing any further into the shaft due to the fear of a rock fall or the presence of unsafe air, we videoed the area around the entrance, noted that the third adit was only an exploratory scrape to determine the direction of the vein. Finally we turned and began our long descent to the lake and our waiting canoes. As we paddled back across the lake, each one of us retained a special memory of the day's events and the added pleasure that a pictorial record of the mine will now exist for future historians.

Sources

Caughey, John Walton, *Gold Is the Cornerstone,* Berkeley, CA: University Of California Press, 1948. 321 pp.

Sagstetter, Beth & Bill, *The Mining Camps Speak,* Denver CO: Benchmark Publishing of Colorado, 1998. 283 pp.

Additional Information

*The mining claim was recorded on September 16, 1907 as a group claim under: Yellow Metal Group of Mines. 1500 linear feet of high-grade gold-quartz were mined from the site, for a total of: $2 million+. The mine was closed sometime around 1936. (Nev. Co. Recorders Office, Mining Claims Book 22, pg. 207. Cal. Div. of Mines and Geology, Bulletin 193: Gold Districts of California, 1970. pg. 53.)

**Research has since established that Miners Foundry And Supply had a contract with Yellow Metal Mine for the manufacture and delivery of a 10 stamp mill. The date of the contract was, October 9, 1909. (Nev. Co. Recorders Office, Mining Claims Book 22, pg. 207.)

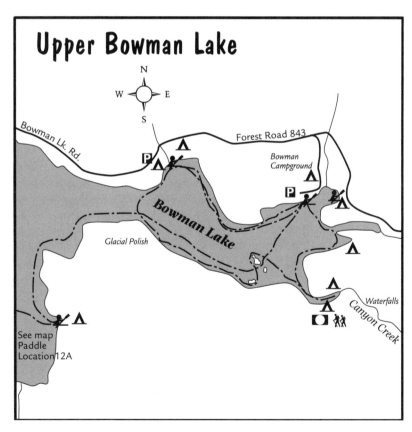

PADDLE LOCATION 12-B
Upper Bowman Lake

Difficulty: All skill levels
Upper Reservoir Size: Approximately ½ of a mile in length from the mouth of Jackson Creek to the Narrows, by ¾ of a mile wide.
Trip Length: A short day paddle.
Paddle Distances: (see map) Upper Reservoir:
From the Bowman Campground boat ramp to:
Take-out for waterfall hike: 0.82 mile;
Cove at entrance to channel: 0.51 mile;
Campsite with island view: 1.28 miles;
Poison Canyon campsite: 1.95 miles
Clockwise circular route between channel to the falls, the islands,   North shore-line and the boat ramp: 2.03 miles
Season: spring, when the snow has melted off the road. The reservoir is open through the summer and into the fall, until sufficient snowfall closes the road.
County: Nevada
National Forest: Tahoe National Forest, Nevada City Ranger District (530) 265-4531
Maps: USGS 7.5' Topographical Sections: Graniteville Quadrangle and English Mtn. Quadrangle
National Forest Map: Tahoe National Forest Service Map
Road Map: Compass Maps Inc.: Nevada and Sierra Counties; Nevada–Sierra Counties Street and Road Atlas
American Auto Assn. (AAA) Maps: Northern California/Bay and Mountain sections
Heads Up: (See Lower Bowman Lake, Paddle Location 12-A)

Access: The put-in for the upper half of Bowman Reservoir is reached by driving an additional two miles beyond the first put-in on the former Bowman Lake Road. According to the Tahoe Forest Service Map, Bowman Lake Road ends at Mile Marker 15. The road paralleling Bowman Reservoir is now Forest Road 843 on the Forest Service map, and Meadow Lake Road on the Compass Map. Turn right at the sign for Bowman Lake Campground and follow the road past the first few campsites and the cinder block toilet. When you arrive at the large level gravel parking area, look to your left for the ramp leading down to the water.

Description:
Canyon Creek (Pools and Waterfalls)
The paddle to the mouth of Canyon Creek is short and sweet. Once you have launched your boat from the ramp, you may either follow the shoreline on your left (easterly) or paddle directly across to the narrow inlet that enters the reservoir from the southeast. This inlet serves as the entrance to Canyon

On the road again, paralleling the lake to upper lake boat ramp.

Creek (see map).

If you select the scenic route, the first inlet east of you is the drowned channel of Jackson Creek. The tall mature conifers growing on the rocky ledge are Jeffrey Pines. As you pass through the narrow channel, look to your left and you will spot the trace of Meadow Lake Road as it winds its way to Jackson Creek Campground approximately 1/4 mile ahead. Between the road trace and the water is a large level area—this is the flood plain of Jackson Creek. After the runoff in the early spring, this area becomes a favorite camping site for fishermen and hunters. Later in the summer, families with tents and RVs are a common sight.

As you re-enter the reservoir, paddle around the southern point of Jackson Creek Channel and enter a small cove that is used by families of Canada Geese and the Common Merganser. It is not unusual to find several families of these birds feeding or guarding their newly hatched young in the protected shelter of coves. If you enter a cove containing any family, please do not paddle toward the birds. If they panic and disperse, one or more of the young may become separated from the group and fall victim to predators. Instead, back paddle and observe the birds from a distance. Leave enough room for the parents and brood to pass out of the cove.

Canyon Creek

Round the second point and enter the channel of Canyon Creek. On your left, tucked in the shelter of a boulder outcrop, is a fine large campsite complete with a private beach. Paddling a little further as you round the second bend, look to your right for another lovely two-person site suitable for camping. Eventually you will feel the tug of the current that marks the end of the reservoir and the beginning of the creek. From here on until you secure your boat, pay attention to channel in front of you where there are submerged boulders with tips that can scrape or hang your boat on a rock (see Paddle Tips).

Your take-out is determined by the shore containing the best beach to allow a "clean" exit from your boat. In the early spring when the water level is higher and the flow swifter, look for a quiet eddy to takeout. As summer progresses a gravel bar begins to appear on the north shore of the stream mouth. However, the trail to the falls is located on the south shore of the stream. If the stream flow is low, you may wade across, otherwise, bring a towline and tie your boat to a snag or boulder on the south shore.

Follow the stream away from its outlet into the reservoir and you will spot a narrow trail zigzagging through the cobbles and into the trees. The trail follows the dry bed of a secondary channel that appears on your right. Although the trail leads through some brush and trees, its pathway is easier than climbing over slick boulders of the main streambed.

This is the first pool you'll encounter in Canyon Creek before it merges with Upper Bowman Lake.

Scrambling over rocks for a better view of the upper falls.

Pools and Waterfalls

When you round the bend of Canyon Creek, you will first hear the sound of rushing water, and then spot the shimmer of cascading falls as they tumble from rocky ledges. Stepping out of the tree cover, your first sight of a deep-water pool being fed by a white frothed waterfall will take your breath away!

In the late summer, I brought Kim Perrino, and her friends Scot Schrum, Lothlorien Homet, and Cindy and Jim Long on a tour of the reservoir. We arrived at this site in the late afternoon after a full day exploring the lake. You can imagine the look of delight that appeared on their faces when they stood at the bank of the deep-water pool, with its mirror-like surface reflecting the forest's trees. It did not take long for all of us to drop our gear and plunge into the coolness of the inviting water. On the opposite (north) shore a large flat boulder warmed by the sun provided the perfect spot to sunbathe.

From the base of this large pool, a trail following the southwest edge of the rapids leads to the upper levels of pools and waterfalls. The second level contains a smaller pool or "tank" fed by two veils of gushing white water. The third and highest level is reached by ascending the block of glaciated rock located to your right (south) side. From this height, your view to the west of the descending staircase of rapids and pools, culminating with the distant view of the reservoir, is truly spectacular. Look south into the gorge from where the stream flows—additional pools and drops are discernible. If you were to follow this canyon stream for an additional 1/2 mile, you would arrive at its source: the base of Sawmill Lake Dam (See Paddle Location 14: Sawmill Lake).

As you appreciate the view and charm of this spectacular canyon, give thanks to the engineers of the Pacific Gas & Electric (PG & E) Company, and Nevada Irrigation District (NID). They used the natural gorge as an outflow from Sawmill Reservoir into Bowman Reservoir instead of a series of pipelines! Because of this engineering decision, Bowman Lake Canyon maintains a continual flow of water even during the low water months of late summer and fall.

The Islands and Shoreline of Upper Bowman Lake
The paddle to the small group of islands and the subsequent southern shoreline of upper Bowman Lake may be done either as a continuation from the falls or as a separate paddle. To make the time spent at Bowman more fulfilling, an early start will ensure adequate time to explore the islands and shoreline—you can then follow up with a late afternoon paddle to the falls. The western setting sun will bathe the area around the falls in a golden glow, and the anticipation of a swim in the deep pool will cap the day off nicely.

The size and shape of these shoreline islands changes as the reservoir's water level rises and falls. They are small and compact in the spring, with few if any landing sites, but are picturesque and provide a scenic backdrop for lunch or picnicking. As the season progresses, the islands seem to reshape themselves and develop new personalities. Beaches with small, but clear, pocket coves are just right for a swim or quick plunge; terraces composed of wild flowers and bunches of sedges grow to the water's edge. Small glens of shimmering aspen provide shade and glimmer with greenish light. As you paddle in and around each island, you will be surprised by the many encounters with families of ducks and geese that use these islands as nesting sites.

South Shore: Upper Bowman Lake
Upon leaving the islands, paddle toward the shoreline and note the change from the expansive views around the islands to the sudden somberness of the encroaching forest. The depth of the forest appears impressive, however this first impression is misleading. The belt of conifers that stands at the

View of Upper Bowman Lake and the main pool of Canyon Creek.

shoreline only appears to contain multitudes of trees growing back from the lakeshore. In reality, due to the mute light screened by the tree line and the background of dark-colored rock, the forest appears larger than it is.

If you venture out to explore this area, depending on the season, look for shade-loving wildflowers, many of which are saprophytes (obtaining food and nutrients from dead or decaying matter). One of the most colorful and rare of the forest's plants is the deep red Snow Plant *(Sarcodes sanguinea),* a member of the *Wintergreen Family.* Its bright red fleshy shoots rise up from the forest floor a foot or more in height. The plant is similar in appearance to asparagus stalks. Native Americans used to gather the Snow Plant and use it for food. Today, however, because of its beauty and relative rarity, California state law protects the Snow Plant from being picked or damaged. Another member of the wintergreen family that does not photosynthesize its own food is the Pinedrop *(Pterospora andromedea).* It appears as a reddish-brown sticky shoot (1-4') with many small white flowers hanging from tiny stalks. In the moist areas, particularly near the areas of runoff, look for emerging Corn Lilies *(Veratrum californicum)* with their characteristic tightly rolled leaves resembling cigars. It is important to be able to identify this plant because it bears a close resemblance to eastern skunk cabbage *(Symplocarpus)* that is edible. Corn Lilies, however, are extremely poisonous and should not be handled or eaten.

Growing off the rotting trunks of dead-standing snags and looking like overgrown warts, you will see fungus of every shape, size and color as you venture deeper into the forest. Upon reaching the base of the rock wall, you'll see that the dark stains discoloring the rock are algae. Growing in varying mosaics (but usually in a traditional circular pattern) are various forms of rock lichens *(Lecideaceae and others)*. Their colors range from fluorescent orange, sulfur yellow, and assorted shades of green, to the drab tones of gray and black. Although these lifeforms are commonly referred to as such, lichens are not true plants. They are the result of a *symbiotic relationship* between fungi and different types of algae. Of the three common types, the crust-like lichens called crustose, and the fleshier looking foliose are both known as pioneers—they grow on rocks and bare rocky surfaces.

Paddle quietly and listen to the forest sounds as you pass by the tree line. The constant swish of the trees as they rustle in the wind, the noisy screech of a Steller's Jay *(Cyanocitta stelleri)* followed by the angry "chirr" of a Chickaree (Douglas Squirrel) *(Tamiasciurus douglasii)*, the proud cry of the hawk circling overhead, and the constant lapping of wind-driven wavelets against the shore all speak eloquent volumes on the diversity of wilderness. Eventually, you will pass the conifer-covered cove and enter the main body of the upper lake. Here you will feel the full blast of the wind if it is blowing from down lake. If you are on the reservoir when the wind is not its usual dramatic self, you are indeed fortunate. With little to no wind to contend with, paddle alongside the bare rock wall of the southeastern shore.

The scarcity of a vegetative cover ensures that the barren flanks of the rock ridges will not conceal the work of former weathering on a grand scale. The exposed bedrock reveals all the signs of having been ground and polished by the work of ancient glaciers. The polish was formed by the combination of extreme pressure and the presence of fine-grained sediments mixed in the ice. As the glacier moved over the rock, pressure from its weight and the grit of the sediments polished the rock's surface. Larger and coarser sediments produced scratches and grooves instead of polish. These striations run anywhere from a few feet to hundreds of yards. The larger sections of rock, visible on the upper terraces, resembling stacked and tilted blocks are formed by another type of weathering process. The splitting away of layers of rock along cracks or joints in the bedrock is called exfoliation. Those shaded, wavy crevices visible all along the sides of the ridge are the joints from which layers of rock are being peeled away by the work of wind, water and ice. The results appear much like the exposed layers of an onion.

Much of this evidence is visible at eye level and only a few feet from the shore. A particularly fine section of shoreline displaying a variety of glacial weathering effects is located on the south side of the narrow channel. This is the same channel that I call "The Narrows" on the map; it connects the smaller section of the reservoir to the main lake body (see map).

If you plan to paddle through this narrow channel, look for a protected cove on the southwest end of the channel. This small cove is suitable for either a campsite or a break area. Once you have paddled through the narrow neck of the channel, you enter the leeward (away from the wind) section of the bay. Those islands described earlier act as a wind block, giving the paddler a little relief. If you decide to paddle to the nearest island from this side of the bay, be alert to shallow areas as you approach the islands. Many of these barely submerged rock outcrops remain undetected due to the combination of the sun's reflection and the wind's agitation of the lake's surface.

If you continue to follow the shoreline into the bay, you will enter a narrow inlet that contains a small seep. I suspect that this seep is an active stream during the spring runoff. As you enter this inlet, the shore on your left contains a lovely terrace suitable for camping. A narrow game trail leads from the steep rocky beach, passes through the brush growing above the scrape zone, and ends at the terrace. If you are feeling adventuresome, the shore on your right leads to a moderately steep knoll. Your reward for accomplishing this easy hike is a commanding view of the islands, the lake, and its forest-covered western basin. When you are ready for the return paddle, if the wind is up, you will have the satisfaction of knowing that it will be against your back.

Area References

Blackwell, Laird R. *Wildflowers of the Tahoe Sierra*. Redmond, WA: Lone Pine Publishing, 1997. 144 pp.

Gilligan, David. *The Secret Sierra*. Bishop, CA: Spotted Dog Press, Inc., 2000. 288 pp.

Moore, James G. *Exploring The Highest Sierra*. Stanford, CA: Stanford University Press, 2000. 427 pp.

National Geographic Society, *Birds of North America,* 2nd Ed., 8th printing. Washington DC: National Geographical Society, 1987. 464 pp.

Storer, Tracy I. & Robert L. Usinger, *Sierra Nevada Natural History*. Berkeley, CA: University of California Press, 1963. 374 pp.

PADDLE TIP

Transitioning from flat to moving water

When entering a drowned river channel, particularly during high runoff, be aware that you are leaving a flat-water environment and entering one of moving water. This mental shift is important because your response time to changing conditions must increase rapidly. Here are a few moving water conditions that you, the paddler, should be aware of; and subsequently, react to.

Current: The transition from tranquil paddling on the surface of a lake to where the lake becomes part of the dynamic flow of a stream or river, may be subtle or sudden. This book is written to describe quiet water conditions, therefore, any transition from still water to the first-felt tugs of current will occur slowly and increase subtly. This fact becomes particularly true when you approach the mouth of an in-flowing stream. Once you have felt the first persistent tug of current, maneuver your boat into the center of the channel. You are now in position to scout ahead and react to any obstacles or other hazards.

Eddies: In simple terms, an eddy is the movement of water in reverse to the river's flow. Since you are paddling against the current (the river's flow), encountering eddies may be of benefit to you. Eddies occur either behind obstacles or near the shoreline. Wherever an obstruction causes the water to pile up upstream of the obstacle, the level of water behind that obstacle is lower forcing the water to flow upstream to fill the depression.

Eddy line: Although this potential hazard will not be encountered in the conditions you will be paddling, the knowledge of its presence and cause will increase your ability to read moving water. An eddy occurs behind an obstacle, for a space of time the eddy and the main current flow next to each other but in opposite directions. Eventually, the eddy loses its strength and rejoins the main current. This fluid line of opposite flow is the eddy line. The hazard comes from not knowing of its presence and being ill prepared when the bow or stern of your boat is suddenly spun in the direction of the stronger flow. If you are in a canoe, a spill may soon follow.

Additional Sources

Ray, Slim, *The Canoe Handbook Techniques for Mastering the Sport of Canoeing,* Harrisburg, PA: Stackpole Books, 1992, 210 pp.
Still one of the best introductory guides for novice and "mossback" canoeists.

Wyatt, Mike, *The Basic Essentials of Sea Kayaking,* 2nd Ed. Merrtillville, IN: ICS Books, Inc., 1996.
Written for the beginner and novice kayaker. The author relates useful, solid information, but skips the jargon and technical stuff.

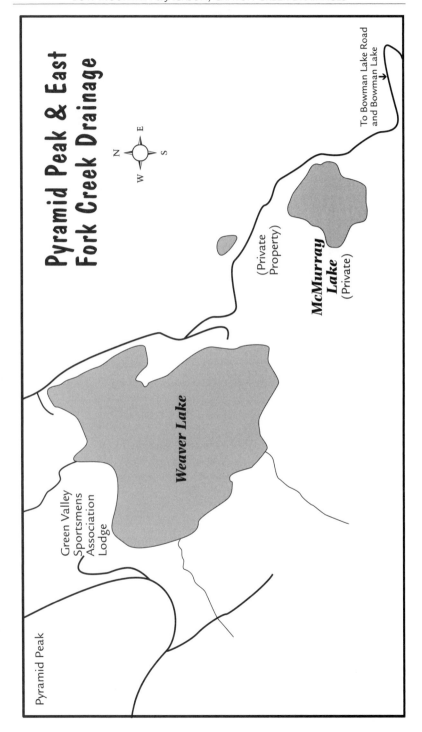

Pyramid Peak & East Fork Creek Drainage

N
W — E
S

To Bowman Lake Road and Bowman Lake

(Private Property)

McMurray Lake (Private)

Weaver Lake

Green Valley Sportsmens Association Lodge

Pyramid Peak

Area 6

Pyramid Peak
& East Fork Creek Drainage

PADDLE LOCATION 13

*Weaver & McMurray Lakes**

*Note: Access to McMurray Lake from the road is restricted due to private property that surrounds this portion of the lake. This restriction includes the former campground as well.

Difficulty: All skill levels may paddle Both Weaver and McMurray Lakes.
Trip Length: Both lakes are considered as day lakes, but because of the long driving time, plan on a multiple-day stay.
Lake Size: Weaver Lake: 1/2 mile long X 4/10th's mile wide; McMurray Lake: 1000' x 900'
Paddling Distances: (see map for routing)
From put-in to take-out at dam: 0.26 mile
From put-in to small cove South end of lake: 0.67 mile
From put-in to intermittent stream southeast shore: 0.84 mile
From put-in to campsite northeast shore: 1.09 mile
Elevation: Weaver Lake, 5,688'; McMurrray Lake, 5,832'
Season: Late spring through fall
Historical Background: Named for Dr. James Weaver who dammed the original lake in 1853. This reservoir, along with the water from the Middle Yuba River, fed the Memphis and Orleans Flume (also known as the Weaver Ditch). It transported a small volume of water to the mines at The Flats and Columbia Hill. Sometime after 1860, the ditch became a part of the Eureka Lake Company.*
County: Sierra
National Forest: Tahoe National Forest, Nevada City Ranger District (530) 265-4531
Maps: USGS 7.5 Minute Topographical Sections: Granitville
National Forest Service Map:
Road Maps: Compass Maps Inc.: Nevada and Sierra Counties; Nevada–Sierra Counties Street and Road Atlas
American Auto Assn. (AAA) Maps: Northern California/Bay and Mountain sections

Access: Take Interstate 80 East, drive past Yuba Gap and Crystal Lake Road turnoff. Exit right onto Highway 20 west. Continue on Hwy. 20 for 4.0 miles and turn right on Bowman Lake Road (Forest Service Rd. 18N18). Follow the road for 16 miles to Bowman Reservoir. *Note: At mile marker 10.5 the*

One of two lakeside primitive campsites at Weaver Lake.

pavement ends and a rough, corrugated cobble- strewn road begins. These last 5.5 miles are recommended for high clearance vehicles and 4W-drive is not necessary. HOW-EVER, a high clearance vehicle *is necessary* to negotiate the protruding cobbles, deep potholes and exposed roots located at the turn-off for McMurray Lake Road. From Bowman Lake Dam, drive another ½ mile to the turn-off for McMurray Lake Road (see map). Follow the road as it climbs up and over the ridge leading to McMurray Lake and then Weaver Lake. Unfortunately, The entire McMurray Lake front property adjacent to the road has been posted as private property. Your only access to the lake is by portaging through the forest located near the former campground. You will see the old camp-ground when you complete the climb over the ridge.

To reach Weaver Lake, continue past the campground and McMurray Lake, look for a steep downhill turn-off located on your left, approximately ¾ miles from south end of McMurray Lake. This first turn-off contains room for six or seven campsites, a vault toilet, and a primitive dirt boat launch. If the area is full, drive through the campsites and connect back onto McMurray Lake Road. Turn left and follow along the shore for ½ mile. A second smaller camping area sits on your left. If you are seeking privacy, instead of attempt-ing to camp at the lakeshore, seek any area on your right and make camp in a clearing away from the lake.

Heads Up:
- ■ Campfire permit mandatory.
- ■ Dispersed camping along lake's edge.

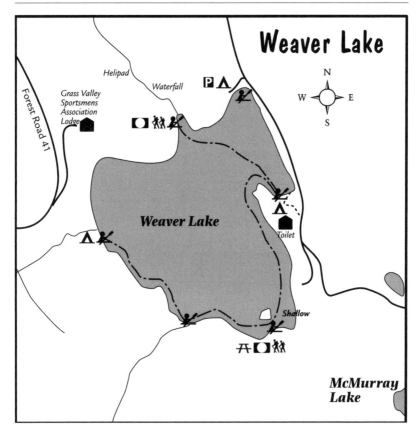

- Limited camping locations along shoreline. Those that are available are close to each other, limiting your privacy. One vault toilet located at each site. No other amenities available.
- Bring own water.
- Better camping located away from lake adjacent to the road facing east. Drive or portage paddle craft to lake.
- Bear Country: pack and camp smart.
- Several boat-in sites, see map.
- Incredible view of waterfall short hike from the dam.
- Several coves, one with an island, wind protected and excellent for swimming.

Description: Weaver Lake is a lovely lake sitting in a basin surrounded by a forest of conifers. Unfortunately, because of the terrain surrounding the lake, there are only a few areas level enough for suitable camping. This "problem," however, also works to your advantage by keeping the crowds away. The best camp sites and put-ins are located on opposite sides of the same cove that forms the northeast side of the lake. The area on the southeast side of the lake contains approximately five suitable sites and one wooden pit toilet. The parking is on a grade under a conifer canopy. If you are seeking privacy, or do not wish to negotiate the steep bank that leads to the lake's edge, then set up camp on the east side of the road that parallels the lake. I have noticed that these sites are more open allowing more sunlight and are far more clean than the heavily used shore sites. Leave your vehicle in these upper areas if you are planning to boat camp at the site depicted on the map. This prevents a congestion of vehicles for those people wishing to camp near the lake.

Once you are on the water, unless you are going to boat camp at the one small site located on the west end of the lake, I would recommend a leisurely paddle to the cove adjacent to the dam. If boat camping, secure the site early before venturing out to explore the lake. I don't depict this area, but if the one site has been taken, you may find a suitable camping site located on the small knoll that protrudes onto the lake between the dam and the lodge.

Before you leave the small wind-protected cove, notice the healthy growth vegetation on the bottom of the lake. This is the same waterweed called Elodea *(Anacharis canadensis)* whose presence is found in almost all Sierran lakes. Due to the water's clarity, drift slowly out toward the main lake and see if you can spot some of the trout and crayfish or crawdads *(genus: Pacifastacus)* hiding out amongst the weeds. This commonly seen crustacean provides a valuable service to the lake's ponds and rivers. The lowly crawdad is an active and highly proficient scavenger. While this feat seems rather dull, consider the problem of organic decay in the cold waters of the Sierran lakes. Thanks to the help of langostino, this miniature lobster keeps the lakes clean, clear and healthy. In addition, they are a main food source for a variety of fish, birds, and mammals . . . including humans. Like many other arthropods, the crayfish is able to regenerate lost limbs and sheds its outside skeleton as size increases.

All along the shore are sedges. When the sedges bloom in spring, the many seed-eating birds and mammals seek the small seed clusters. Up along the northeast bank, a stand of aspen appears to shiver with the passing of each breeze. Move out of the cove along the sunny northern shoreline and note the exposed rock formation eroding along the banks. Instead of the common granite, this entire section of the lake consists of igneous (volcanic) rock. You will come across the granite on the opposite western side of the lake. Growing in tall stands Ponderosa Pine mixes with Lodgepole Pine, a few Jeffrey Pine, Incense Cedar and the deciduous Black Oak. Clustering in thick mats around the trees are two different species of manzanita—the taller more robust bush-like Green Manzanita, with its pinkish bell-shaped flowers and smooth reddish bark, and the shorter scrubby Pinemat Manzanita.

When you round the point leading into the small cove containing the concrete dam, find a take-out spot and secure your boat. From here hike down the dammed creekbed to a waterfall located a short distance downstream. Before you trek down to the creekbed, note the shape of the bedrock around the dam. You are standing on a former lava flow. If you look closely at the exposed basalt, you will spot some of the material in parallel columns. This type of formation is given the term columnar jointing or prismatic jointing. The columns are formed as the lava contracts during the cooling process. The extent of this former flow becomes apparent as you follow the streambed. The stream has cut at least twenty feet into the solid basalt. Several hundred yards from the dam the stream drops as a ribbon fall hundreds of feet down onto the floor of Poorman Valley. The stream itself has become a hanging valley created by the erosional actions of a former glacier that carved its way through here eons ago. When the glacier melted, it exposed the sidewall of the former lava flow and consequently, left the stream high but not dry.

If you hike the trail that follows the ridgeline on the west side of the stream, you will come to a dramatic vantage point where you can clearly see the waterfall and the undercut basalt. The height of this flow is only partially revealed at this overlook. To gain a proper perspective on the extent of the flow, locate the lone black knob that forms part of the ridge on the left (west) side of the valley. This is Pyramid Peak (5,925'), a lone remnant of the former cap rock that made up the original top of the flow. If you have the time and energy, follow the same trail that crossed onto the streambed. It winds its way through the conifer forest below Pyramid Peak before ascending to the top of the peak.

Back at the cove where your boat has hopefully been secured, note the lovely yellow flowers of the Musk Monkeyflower *(Mimulus moschatus)*. Gently touch the leaves of this plant and you will feel the many white hairs that cover the plant. If you crush one of the leaves or place your nose near the plant, you will smell a musky odor that characterizes the plant's name. Also protruding from cracks and clefts in the basalt, the bright yellow-orange flower clusters of the Sulfur Flower, Sulfur Buckwheat *(Eriogonum umbellatum)* provide a colorful contrast against the black and gray of the basalt.

Round the tip of the shallow knoll protruding into the lake and look for a suitable clearing. This is the site for the alternative camp should the main site along the west shore be unavailable. Just beyond the screen of vegetation growing along the knob's shoreline, the emerging structures of the historical Grass Valley Sportsmens Club Inc. It was established in the late 19th century and has remained active to this day. A similar organization, the Grass Valley Rod and Gun Club, has its lodge on the shore of Fuller Lake *(see Paddle Location 1)*. As a matter of fact, during the last half of the 19th century, many of the lakes and sites of the Sierras became popular with local citizens seeking a rest from the daily toil. As a result, numerous hunting, fishing and nature clubs were formed at the more "accessible" locations.

Pass the landscaped area of the club and enter into the northern elbow of a shallow cove. Here the slope begins to steepen dramatically. Tall conifers, primarily Ponderosa and Sugar Pines obscure any views of the surrounding ridge. At approximately the center of the cove, look for a thick cover of brush. Listen for the sound of running water. This is the location of the stream that I have marked, but is not shown on the 1982 7.5 Minute Quad. A small sand and gravel beach will appear to the left (south) of the mouth of the brush-covered creek. Here, too, is the location of the boat-in campsite. The site will comfortably hold two maybe three, if tents are not utilized. A small fire ring has been constructed and is ready for use. During the day, you have a spectacular view of the lake and in the distance Quartz Hill Ridgeline (7,010'). The large glacier-widened valley visible to the left of the ridge belongs to Tom's Creek, a tributary of East Fork Creek, both of which are part of the Middle Fork Yuba River Drainage.

At night, star clusters that form part of the Milky Way stretch overhead

The campsites on the south end of the lake enjoy the comforts of an enclosed privy.

Overview of Weaver Lake with Pinoli Peak (7,297') to the left and Quartz Hill (7010') on the far right.

and are reflected on the still surface of the lake. The eastern exposure ensures a morning of light and warmth radiating on the camp. In your explorations around the stream, particularly in the summer, you will notice a three-to-five lobed leafy plant containing many flattened reddish berries. This is a Thimbleberry (*Rubus parviflorus*), an edible member of the Rose Family (*Rosaceae*).

Continue exploring the southwest shoreline and paddle past a small point jutting outward. Be wary of submerged and partially concealed rocks that form part of the point. Once you are past the point, the forest gives way to a granite rock wall descending into the lake. Another unmarked brush-filled stream (this one flows only through Spring) serves as the demarcation between the trees on one side and granite on the other. Continue paddling past the stream mouth until you spot a couple of conifers with a rope swing. They are located just above the entrance into the large cove containing the small conifer-covered island. A partially submerged shelf provides adequate footing for a take-out. This spot also has a narrow trail that leads to the top of the first bench marked on the map as the 5,800' contour. From here one may easily hike to the 6,000' bench and, if still motivated, scramble to the ridge top (6,522').

Be sure to memorize the landmarks surrounding the trail just as you clear the lip of the ledge leading to the first bench. Otherwise due to the degree of slope obscuring your take-out, you may lose the trail and be forced to scramble down the scree pile before regaining the trail. When Bert Hall and I hiked the area, we enjoyed our lunch under a mature Jeffrey Pine growing on the ledge that marked the 6,000' contour. From here the view was nothing short of spectacular. Not only do you have a clear sight of Weaver Lake and the surrounding forest, but in addition, you gain an unobstructed panorama of the terrain stretching from Pyramid Peak to Pinoli Peak (7,297') to Quartz Hill.

At the take-out the lake is very deep. From the deep water to a shallow mud bottom, the depth of the lake changes rapidly as you enter the cove. Bleached tree stumps mark the former shoreline and indicate how far the waters of the reservoir have risen.

Another dramatic change occurs in the terrain that forms the shoreline. Instead of steep granite walls, you are now surrounded by thick brush that hides a stream drainage. Lodgepole Pines intermix with willows, alders *(Genus Alnus)* and aspen. The light green mantle of sedges and smaller sections containing reddish floating leaves of a pond weed *(Genus Potamogeton)* mark the shallow areas within the cove.

The small island with its mantle of conifers and deciduous trees, adds to the beauty of the cove. Here in this shallow area, the water has a chance to warm, thus a grand swimming area is created. This has not gone unnoticed by landowners having property on the main shore located across the cove. They have strung a power line to the cove and placed a fuse box on one of the pines. I imagine that the nightlife here in the summer may become quiet lively.

The Grass Valley Sportsmen Club has existed since the last century and continues to remain active.

Upon leaving the cove, if you continue following the southern shoreline this area of the lake becomes private property as the official looking POSTED signs attest. The last time I paddled Weaver Lake in 2001, the cabin that had been along this section of shore has burned down. We shall see if a new cabin takes its place. Eventually, you round the last point before entering the cove you started from and are looking forward to the cold drinks sitting in the cooler in your vehicle.

Area References

*Personal communication with Mr. Hank Meals.

Palmer, Laurence E. & H. Seymore Fowler, *Fieldbook of Natural History Second Edition*. New York, NY: McGraw-Hill Book Company, 1975. pgs. 430 and 336.

Schoenherr, Allan A., *A Natural History of California*. Berkeley, CA: University of California Press, 1995 1st paperback ed. pgs. 579-580.

Horn, Elizabeth L., *Sierra Nevada Wildflowers*. Missoula, MT: Mountain Press Publishing Company, 1998. 215 pp.

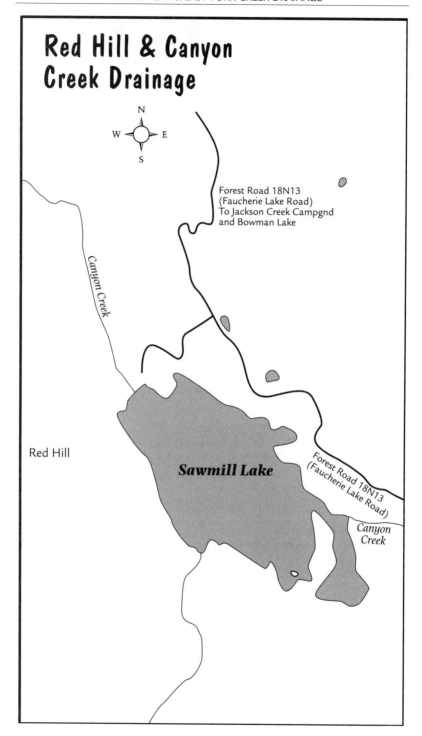

Red Hill & Canyon Creek Drainage

Forest Road 18N13
(Faucherie Lake Road)
To Jackson Creek Campgnd
and Bowman Lake

Canyon Creek

Red Hill

Sawmill Lake

Forest Road 18N13
(Faucherie Lake Road)

Canyon
Creek

Area 7

Red Hill & Canyon Creek Drainages

PADDLE LOCATION 14

Sawmill Lake

Difficulty: No major problems. Strong late afternoon gusting winds more of a nuisance rather than a safety factor.

Trip Length: Excellent day paddle, but the driving time makes this destination more enjoyable as a weekend trip.

Lake Size: 0.79 x 0.33 miles

Paddle Distances (see map): From the put-in/take-out northeast mid-center to:

Canyon Creek beach and campsites: 0.38 mile

Campsite and hike, upper lake cove: 0.61 mile

South Fork Canyon Creek waterfall and campsite: 0.42 mile

Take-out, North end of dam: 0.45 mile

Take-out, South end of dam and trailhead: 0.56 mile

Elevation: 5,863'

Season: In the Spring, when the snow melts off the road, to the first snows of fall.

County: Nevada

National Forest: Tahoe National Forest, (Nevada City Ranger District (530) 265-4531)

Maps: USGS 7.5' Topographical Sections: English Mtn., Calif. Quadrangle

National Forest Map: Tahoe National Forest Service Map

Road Map: Compass Maps, Inc.: Nevada and Sierra Counties

American Auto Assn. (AAA) Maps: Northern California/Bay and Mountain sections

Access: Take Interstate 80 East, drive past the exit for Yuba Gap, turn off onto Highway 20 west. Continue on Highway 20 for 4 miles and turn right on Bowman Lake Road (Forest Service Road: 18N18). Follow the road for 15 miles until 18N18 ends at the mile marker #15 at Bowman Reservoir. Continue on the same road, paralleling the reservoir, now designated as County Road 843 (Graniteville Road). The first turnoff for the lake will be posted on the right approximately 2 miles from Jackson Creek Campground. *Note: The drive to this section of the lake and dam is not suited for trailers or RV's.* In addition, the first sites visible at the turnoff do not have an adequate boat access. Additional sites that are more suitable for parking and boat launch are to be found along the main road that follows the lake (see map).

Heads Up:

■ Multiple use area. If you're not paddling, hiking and mountain biking provide alternative fun.

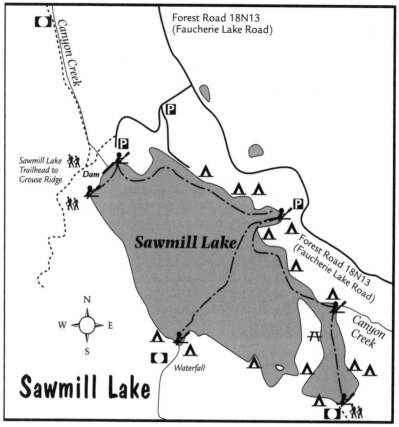

- Don't miss the hike to the pools and falls below the lake(see map).
- Campsites are plentiful especially for boat-in camping.
- Basic supplies available off Interstate 80 at the Country Store, Yuba Gap Exit to Crystal Lake Road; at the entrance to Kelly Lake.
- No formal campground dispersed camping only.
- Campfire permit required.
- Bear activity common, so pack and camp smart.
- Easy access to nearby lakes.

Description: There is so much to do at and around Sawmill Lake that a weekend will fly by before you realize it is time to pack up and go home. This is one of those locations where you can turn to other activities if paddling does not pan out. For those of you who enjoy hiking there is a whole selection of trails that may be accessed. Mountain bikes are perfect for negotiating the main Forest Service road and the outlying logging roads (see map).

The biggest problem to camping at Sawmill pertains to the quest for the perfect campsite. The only way to find a suitable site is by parking along side

To reach Sawmill and Faucherie lakes requires a stream crossing.

the main road and hiking through the screen of conifers until you find a site. From the many previous campers, there are several side roads leading to lakeside sites. The trick is to find and then claim one with a vehicle access. Otherwise, you will have to carry your gear through the forest to the lake. Even if you are boat camping, locating an easy vehicle access is desirable. Once this task is over however, you can relax and begin to enjoy the incredible beauty that surrounds you.

On a calm, sunny morning the rising sun paints the slope of Red Hill (7,060') a series of pastel reds, yellows and oranges. The nearby conifer forest is still dark but already you can hear the chirping of the birds. You can explore the lake and then hike to the top of a nearby ridge. From that peak you will have a splendid view of the day's paddle.

Cast off, round the point, bank to the left and proceed to paddle up lake, following close to the shore. I have learned that by sticking close to shore, you may quickly spot any wildlife, plants or interesting features that may require landing for a closer study. In addition, paddling close to shore takes you out of all but direct wind. This is a nice advantage, especially when you still have the entire day ahead of you and are conserving your energy.

A short distance from the put-in, you'll pass the remains of a couple of wooden structures leaning haphazardly from neglect. These are projects that were constructed some time ago by the Boy Scouts. This section of the lake is part of a Boy Scout Camp, but in the years I have been coming here I have not seen or heard any activity. As you hike through the trees near the lake looking for a suitable campsite, you may come across old pathways lined with rock. The Scouts constructed all of these trails. Some follow along the shoreline of the lake, while others lead from the lake, then meander through the trees before providing an exit onto the main Lake Faucherie Road.

Paddle past the former Scout projects and enter the narrow passageway that used to be the former channel of Canyon Creek. Upon passing through you may either turn left and enter Canyon Creek with its lovely gravel beach, or continue on into Upper Sawmill Lake. This section of the lake, although no larger than a good-sized pond, was formed from low ground when the modern dam increased the holding capacity of the lake. Many of the still-standing snags are burned remnants of the former forest that stood here prior to the lake. They now provide an aesthetic natural sculpture, not to mention their value as nesting and perching platforms to varieties of birds.

Although the upper lake is small, it is full of charm. In addition to the fascinating "ghost forest" standing in various shapes and sizes throughout the breadth of the lake, the water is incredibly clear. If you let your boat drift with the current, soon you will be able to observe fish swimming, crayfish (*Pacifastacus leniussulus*) carefully making their way over objects, and closer to shore, and frogs attempting to hide in the silty bottom.

Continue on and reach the end of this part of the lake. If you want to climb to the top of the ridge above the lake, find the grassy area with a small clearing beyond the shore and beach and secure your canoe. A well-built fire ring and log benches in the nearby clearing make this a perfect campsite. If you hike through the brush and conifers that line the shore you will come upon the base wall of the ridge. A small trail, either from animals or other hikers, leads through the manzanita and other brush. Follow the trail up-

Sawmill Lake from 6,200'. The dam is at the far northwest end of the lake.

This boater came prepared! There is no campsite with an easy boat access at the northeast end of the lake.

ward and it quickly disappears once you are on the barren rock shelf. The rest of the route is an easy scramble through a small pile of talus before the final pitch to the top (see map).

Once on top, what a grand view! At this 6,240' elevation the entire lake and surrounding forest is open for inspection. The clarity of the water is such, that even from here you can readily spot the old logs that lie on the bottom. The jutting finger of tree-covered rock that separates the main lake from the smaller upper section is clearly defined. It creates a bold statement as it thrusts outward onto the body of the lake. Stretching across the horizon from northwest to southeast, the massive longitudinal body of a ridgeline dominates the scenery. Its tail ended at Canyon Creek Gorge and its head was the broad mass of English Mountain (8,373'). Separating the distance between the ridge and this knoll is the glacially widened floor of Canyon Creek Valley. Snaking its way up the valley, portions of the road to Lake Faucherie (Paddle Location 15) are visible.

Back on the water, paddle to a small inlet bordering the shoreline of the outthrust finger of rock visible from above the knoll. From a pile of eroding granite, you can study the breadth of the main lake and its many coves. The top of this jutting peninsula is level and screened from the wind by stands of pine. Where stacks of boulders lie piled, old fire rings are visible and several maturing Jeffrey Pine stand sentinel. If you tire of the view on one side of the lake, just walk a few steps and you have a new vista to study.

Walk to the point of the outthrust rocky projection, and keep your eyes on the ground. Near a small boulder outcrop you may see a scattering of worked chert and a nice core of yellow jasper. Apparently even before the construction of the reservoir, this local was in use by former Native inhabitants. From the small inlet of the upper lake, it is a short paddle to the mouth of Canyon Creek.

The tip of the peninsula you just explored and the mainland borders the narrow entrance. Paddling into the now, drowned channel of the river, after a few short zigzags the channel opens onto a small but lovely beach. The location of the beach tucked in a small pocket and enclosed by walls of granite, provides its user with ample seclusion. This discovery is not lost on those users who enjoy sunbathing in the nude.

Prior to leaving this end of the lake, I noted that the point on the mainland and opposite the peninsula provided a choice sheltered campsite.

Once on the main lake, paddle west toward the small island visible from shore. The water depth between the island and the peninsula can be deceiving. In some areas the water is deep and free of obstruction. Then, without warning a rocky bar makes its appearance and necessitates some artful paddle strokes to prevent scrapping the hull. Depending on the water level of the lake, the island retains a small sedge-covered swale dry enough to sit and enjoy a break. Otherwise it serves as a nesting spot for Canada Geese, mallards, and the Common Merganser (Mergus merganser). Upon leaving the island, follow the peninsula's shoreline into two picturesque coves that are visible either from the top of the ridge hiked to earlier, or the top of the outthrust peninsula. The first cove contains two islands that are difficult to spot from the main lake. Standing in the lake behind the islands are several fire-ravished snags. Their bleached color and unique position, surrounded by water, make them very photogenic.

Behind the islands are several smaller inlets whose level ground and sheltered location make excellent campsites. These same inlets provide the camper with private swimming areas free from the afternoon wind. Prior to passing the northern point of the third cove is one of the best campsites on the lake. Not only is the view spectacular, but you have the site and sounds of a grand waterfall to appreciate (Spring through early Summer only). The falls in the adjacent cove are far enough away that you don't have to share your campsite with other visitors yet close enough to admire its beauty and still speak without shouting.

If you do paddle into the cove where the falls are located, beach your boat on the cobble bar in front of the pool. If the large snag is still standing on the cobble bar, sit quietly for a moment to observe the comings and goings of the bird using the snag for a nest. One year it was inhabited by a Tree Swallow (Tachycineta bicolor), and the following year a Nuttall's Woodpecker (Picoides nuttallii) claimed the site, *Note: To avoid stressing the parent birds, please keep a proper distance: at least fifty feet from the nest.* Darting overhead

The narrow entrance to the upper end of the lake is also the drowned channel of Canyon Creek.

in search of insects or landing briefly to obtain some mud for their nests swallows *(Family Hirundinidae)* and swifts *(Family Apodidae)* appear to be everywhere.

The paddle between the waterfall and the end of the lake where the dam is located follows a steep and heavily wooded shoreline. There are no easy landing sites or places of easy access into the interior. Only when you reach the cove marking the location of a small stream, do you have a place to take-out. Here you intersect a trail leading to the dam and joining the main Sawmill Lake Trailhead (see map). From here you may access the dam or enjoy the view of the lake, English Mountain rising on your left, and the pointed peak of Haystack Mountain (7,391') on the right. In the spring or during a very wet year, you will have the added attraction of watching the water spill down the multi-hued broad channel of Canyon Creek.

If you are up for a hike, I recommend following the trail that borders

Canyon Creek for a distance of approximately 1 mile (see map). Your reward will be several spectacular falls and pools with a chance to swim or dive into them. (For a detailed description, see Paddle Location 12-B: Upper Bowman Lake.) The last section of shoreline—from the dam to your campsite—follows the section of lakeshore containing numerous campsites located above the steep bank.

Area References

Grater, Russell K. *Discovering Sierra Mammals*. Yosemite Association and Sequoia Natural History Association, 1978. 174 pp.

Petrides, George A. & Olivia, *Trees of the California Sierra Nevada Backpacker Field Guide*. Williamston, MI: Explorer Press, 1996. 79 pp.

Storer, Tracy I. & Robert L. Usinger, *Sierra Nevada Natural History*. Berkeley, CA: University of California Press. 1963, 13th printing. 374 pp.

Canada Geese are common and plentiful near Sawmill Lake.

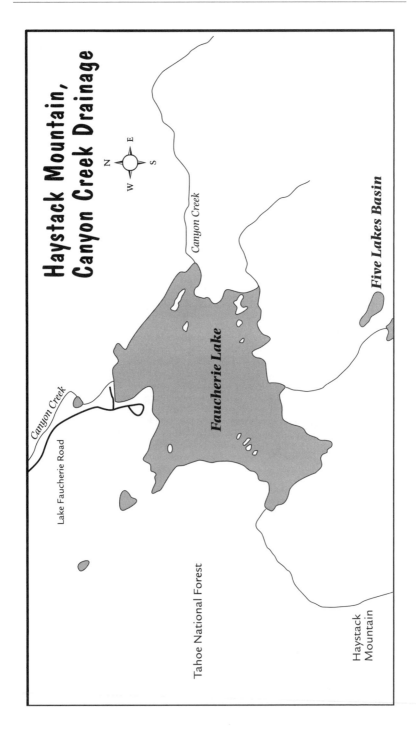

Haystack Mountain, Canyon Creek Drainage

Canyon Creek

Five Lakes Basin

Faucherie Lake

Canyon Creek

Lake Faucherie Road

Tahoe National Forest

Haystack Mountain

Area 8

Haystack Mountain
& Canyon Creek Drainage

PADDLE LOCATION 15
Faucherie Lake

Difficulty: No major problems. Strong late afternoon gusting winds more of a nuisance rather than a safety factor.

Trip Length: Excellent day paddle, but the driving time makes this destination more enjoyable as a weekend trip.

Lake Size: one mile long, one mile wide

Paddle Distances (see map): From the put-in / take-out:
The island: 0.26 mile
Canyon Creek and hike: 0.43 mile
Waterfall: 0.77 mile
2nd waterfall and hike: 1.16 mile
3rd waterfall: 1.67 mile
Take-out for hike: 2.19 mile
Faucherie Group Campground as part of the complete loop: 2.49 miles.

Elevation: 6,132'

Season: In the Spring, when the snow melts off the road, to the first snows of fall.

Historical Background: Named after Benoist Faucherie, a French hydraulic engineer of the 1850's and 1860's. He and others obtained water rights to the Canyon Creek Drainage. Storage dams were constructed on Lake Faucherie and French Lake. The water was then carried by means of pipes, flumes and ditches or canals, down to the hydraulic mining operations along San Juan Ridge. In the early 1960's, Nevada Irrigation District (NID) constructed the present dam to hold and store the waters that drained into the Middle and South Forks of the Yuba River.

County: Nevada

National Forest: Tahoe National Forest, (Nevada City Ranger District: (530) 265-4531)

Maps: USGS 7.5' Topographical Sections: English Mtn, Calif. Quadrangle

National Forest Map: Tahoe National Forest Service Map

Road Map: Compass Maps, Inc.: Nevada and Sierra counties

American Auto Assn. (AAA) Maps: Northern California/Bay and Mountain sections

Access: Take Interstate 80 East, drive past the exit for Yuba Gap, turn off onto Highway 20 west. Continue on Highway 20 for 4 miles and turn right on Bowman Lake Road (Forest Service Road: 18N18) Follow the road for 15 miles until 18N18 ends at the mile marker #15 at Bowman Reservoir.

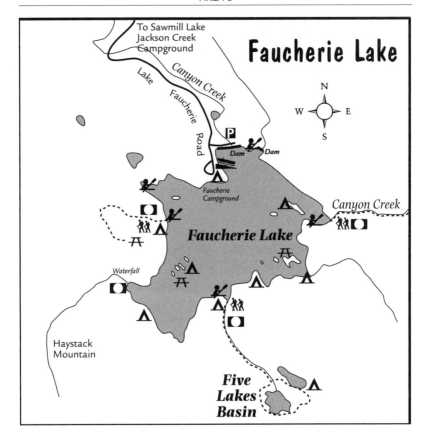

Continue on the same road, paralleling the reservoir, now designated as County Road 843 (Graniteville Road). *Note: At mile marker 10.5 the pavement ends and a rough corrugated cobble strewn road begins. Although the remaining road to Sawmill and Faucherie Lakes are recommended for high clearance vehicles, a 4x4 is not necessary.* Approximately 1/2 mile after passing the turnoff for Bowman Lake Campground, you will have to negotiate your first of several stream crossings. Road 843 continues past Bowman Lake, parallels Jackson Creek, and enters the open flat of Jackson Creek Campground. Make a right turn at the road junction, near the information board and toilets. You are now heading south off of Road 843, and are on Faucherie Lake Road. A short distance after your turnoff you will come to the second stream crossing. Unlike the first one, here you have a cement ramp to drive across. Continue on past the crossing point for 2 miles. You will pass the shoreline of Sawmill Lake. Continue past the lake and you will ascend to the 5,990' elevation point. Here you will pass the turnoff for Canyon Creek Campground (an alternative campground if not boat camping at Faucherie Lake). Continue for an additional 2 miles. When you reach the ridgeline overlooking the basin of Faucherie Lake, take the road across the dam on your left. Park in the turnout; your put-in and take-out is on your left as you face the lake.

Heads Up:

- One of the few high-Sierra lakes accessible by family vehicle
- Campfire permit is required if camping outside the campground during the off-season.
- Faucherie Lake has one established campground: a group campground only.
- Reservations are a must if utilizing campground from late spring through summer.
- Fee sites are operated by: Sierra Recreation Managers, PO Box 273, Pioneer, CA 95666. (209) 295-4512
- ParkNet Reservation Number: 1 (877) 444-6777 or: www.reserveusa.com
- An alternative campground is Canyon Creek Campground located approximately 2 miles before the lake.
- Basic supplies are available off Interstate 80 at the Country Store, Yuba Gap Exit to Crystal Lake Road at the entrance to Kelly Lake.
- Numerous spectacular waterfalls.
- Bear country: pack and camp smart!
- Lots of hiking (see map) and mountain biking possibilities.
- Close proximity to other lakes and campsites.

Put-in at the base of the dam, Faucherie Lake.

Description:

Faucherie Lake is one of the very few high Sierra lakes that is accessible via a Forest Service road that can accommodate almost any type of vehicle. So many campers and their families make this drive that the Forest Service had to place Faucherie Lake Campground on a reservation system. With a little planning and forethought, however, a paddler may make the drive and enjoy the lake without the crowds. If you seek solitude and quiet, plan on paddling Faucherie Lake in the spring when the road opens. The trade-off will involve putting up with some snow-covered ground and cold nights.

Time your arrival with the sunrise. As you drive over the last ridge, you will be treated to a spectacular sight of the entire west end of the lake drenched in a molten hue. The reflection of the snow-covered granite walls bordering

Lake Faucherie contains many small islands suitable for exploration.

the lake will be depicted in sharp detail on the still surface. Drive across the dam and park in the sheltered turnout located on the east end of the dam (see map). From here, it is only a short walk to the water. Later in the season, when the campground is open, you may launch from the sites that border the lake. When you paddle this lake on the colder days of early Spring your reward is the accessible camping on the islands that border the lake. During peak season, these same islands come under heavy use and camping is discouraged.

Launch from the put-in marked on the map and you will spot the small dam and waterfalls that mark the former channel of Canyon Creek. The dam is tucked into a small narrow gorge around the first bend northeast of the put-in. You will hear the cascading water before spotting the dam. From here, you may continue following the shoreline or paddle directly to the islands, visible in the foreground. If you are making this paddle in the early Spring before the area is crowded with campers and plan to spend the night, I recommend the island sitting apart from the chain as your camping destination. You can spot this island by the six conifers growing along its ridge. Your take-out is a submerged small granite shelf on the east end, facing the cove. Because this spot is on the leeward side, your boat is protected from the wind. The gentle slope also allows easy access into and out of the boat. Located just up from the take-out underneath two pines, is a ready-made fire ring and level site for the tent. This campsite is also tucked below the granite ridge that blocks most of the prevailing wind blowing off the lake.

On a full moon night, the moon's bright reflection shimmers on the quiet surface like a bobber at the end of some fishing line. The polished granite of the surrounding basin casts a pale silvery sheen over the entire lake, not unlike a nightlight in a child's room. In the morning, you will rise to the view of the sun's glow on the rocky slopes of Haystack Mountain (7,391') and the distant tips of Sand Ridge (7,428'). As you slowly adjust to your surroundings, you may feel a sense of vertigo when you view the detailed but upside-down reflection of the sky and shoreline on the still surface of the lake.

Your morning paddle may take you to the small cove located directly behind the island where you camped. The sound of the waterfall may have enticed you to explore the area in more detail. Carefully negotiate the submerged granite boulders as you enter the partially hidden inlet. You may be startled by the sudden honk and flight of the small flock of Canada Geese that use this spot for shelter. The cause of the noise becomes apparent when you enter the boulder-strewn inlet. A cascading series of falls, rushing and tumbling down a short but steep gradient delights the eye and sweetens the ear. If you paddle this section of the lake in the spring, when the snow melts, you will weave your way through many such sites of cascading waterfalls.

Eventually you will reach the busy island-filled cove at the extreme southeast end of the lake. Here is a good spot to take out for a hike. If you follow the streambed of Canyon Creek that flows down from the granite ridge you will reach the ridge top and be rewarded with a view of Faucherie Lake with the gorge of Canyon Creek in the background. However, the real treat is the view to the south—the magnificent splendor of French Lake shimmering in its white granite bowl.

Continue along the south shore of Faucherie Lake, paddle past the last island on this end of the lake and enter the now open and exposed area of the lake. Round a finger of weathering granite with its lone dead standing conifer and you first hear, then see the broad, frothy, tumbling whitewater. Almost hidden in a glen of tall pines, this intermittent stream creates a spectacular show, but only during the early months of spring.

In the spring, waterfalls like this are a common sight around the lake.

There is another reason, well . . . actually two reasons why a stop here is advisable. The first reason becomes apparent when you enter the tree-covered bower surrounding the area of the waterfall. Nestled in a small clearing is an exquisite campsite complete with fire ring and crude log benches made by former campers. From here, not only do you have a lake view, but in the spring you will be lulled to sleep by the falls.

The Hike to the Tarns

The second reason for a stopover is not as evident as the first. It involves a hike following the same streambed that provides those picturesque falls. For this activity, arriving here in late spring or in the summer is a better choice. When the streambed flows at a slow trickle or becomes dry, following its course upward becomes easier then attempting to climb the surrounding talus. With that kind of introduction, why would anyone want to go through the trouble to make the climb?

Two words: awesome beauty! The trail leads to and then circles two beautiful tarns that are set in a glacier-carved amphitheater of sparkling granite (see map). Surrounding the dark blue waters of the glacial lakes are carpets of Pinemat Manzanita. Bursts of bright wildflowers grow in various deposits of soil either near the lakes or in the many crags of the amphitheater. Standing in majestic aloofness, Lodgepole Pines, with an occasional fir, stand sentinel around each tarn.

As you climb upward and away from Faucherie Lake, each gain in elevation causes the scenery to broaden and become grander in scale. When you reach the first pitch, a level saddle separating a large protruding knob of granite from the main ridge makes the going easier. Following the wide channel of the streambed ever upward is a "no brainer." This allows you to stop and enjoy the unfolding 360-degree vista.

When you reach the narrow cleft where pines cover the entrance, weave through this small grove and stay to your right. Soon you will have a partial view of the first tarn. Here the trail follows a small talus pile before dropping to a grove of Lodgepole Pines that screen the lake. Follow the trail past the pines onto a sloping slab of granite. Pick a spot, sit and enjoy your accomplishment. If you are here on a warm day, the water although brisk, is by no means intolerable.

When you are ready, follow the trail across the small stream channel located on the south end of the tarn. From here you will have to negotiate the rocky rubble that forms the southeastern base of the tarn. Somewhere in the center of your crossing, look north through the gap in the pines. Those saw-toothed peaks on the far horizon are part of the ridgeline that forms the Sierra Buttes (8,587'). Once you are across, look down to the narrow rock cut that provides a natural access between the two tarns. From there, you will regain the trail that follows the western shoreline of the second tarn. Look for a small clearing that provides a natural campsite. The trail follows a rocky ledge then cuts left across it to drop down through a belt of manzanita. At this point, you should recognize the segment of the original trail where it passes through the narrow granite cleft under the grove of conifers.

The Southwest Shoreline

From the cove containing the waterfalls, continue paddling along the shoreline. You will round the same knob whose mass you observed when climbing the streambed to the two tarn lakes. This section of the lake is shaped as a large rectangular cove with numerous smaller scalloped pocket coves. Located in one of these numerous small coves and hidden behind a screen of vegetation are at least two campsites well protected from wind.

At the opposite end of the larger rectangular cove and facing to the northwest, an intermittent stream empties into the lake. During the spring runoff, the mouth of the stream cascades down as a beautiful waterfall. The falls are tucked into the corner of this large cove so unless you stay close to shore or hear the fall of the water, it is easy to paddle by and miss them. When you turn your boat northward to follow the last section of the lake, two small islands are immediately visible in the foreground. Their location makes them an ideal spot for either a lunch break or, if proper sanitation is practiced, a choice campsite.

If you decide to explore or paddle near the islands, keep a wary eye out for partially submerged rocks in various places surrounding both islands. Their presence becomes more evident in late summer when water levels drop. From the islands, paddle back toward the main shoreline. You may have already noticed that the steep banks that characterized the majority of the southern and southwestern shore are gone and replaced with a gently sloped granite bench. This is due in part to the work of the former glacier that carved its way down through this now-broad canyon. If you are on this part of the lake in the late afternoon of a sunny day, it is worth your while to take out at any point along this western shoreline and hike to the top of the readily visible predominate knoll. On the map provided in this Paddle Location, I chose a route with a starting point from a small cove found just before you pass the last small island at the mouth of a finger cove. From the shore, you will find a trail that winds its way through the brush and rubble to the top of the knoll.

On your way up, take note of the trees growing in small isolated stands, known as islands, throughout the floor of the canyon. The pines are predominately Jeffrey whose characteristic scent of vanilla, pineapple or butter-

At first glance, this Western Juniper looks more dead than alive.

Boaters have turned this little island into a sculpture garden. Before leaving the lake, add your own "message" to the Spirit of the Lake.

scotch may be enjoyed by partaking a deep sniff within a furrow of the living trunk. The second species of conifer, and one whose presence you probably have not seen thus far on your paddle, is the Sierra Juniper or Western Juniper. Under ideal conditions, the Jeffrey Pine may grow to a height of 160 feet. Here however, where there is little or no shelter from severe winds and temperature fluctuations, the trees that survive are all stunted or distorted. Those that are upright are flat-topped or broken at their crown. An excellent example of this characteristic may be seen when you reach the top of the knoll. Growing in regal isolation surrounded by its much younger progeny is an ancient juniper. If the surrounding younger trees survive they will become the legacy of this older mature tree and eventually form one of the tree islands that dot this area. At first glance, the juniper looks more dead than alive. The entire crown has been shattered by repeated lightening strikes. The only evidence that this "patriarch" is still alive comes from the small branchlets whose green scale-like leaves contrast sharply with the desiccated appearance of the trunk. The entire tree appears to glow in a golden light highlighted by the late afternoon sun. This same light casts its magic on the vista of the lake and surrounding basin. You can trace your paddle route and hike to the tarns from this vantage point. Slowly the cobalt blue of the sky begins to darken and the clouds take on a reddish hue. It is time to hike back to the boats and complete your paddle.

If you haven't already passed the last island before your take-out at the dam, it is worth checking out. You will notice something odd about the island's appearance even before you get near it. Upon reaching its location, those odd shapes whose silhouettes have attracted your attention are now revealed. People have created dozens of rock sculptures that now dot the length of the island. Some are simple rock piles while others are more elaborate and unique. If you are so inclined, you may "cap" your day by leaving behind a sculpture of your own. From the island, you will notice the forested headland on your left (northeast). Depending on the season you are paddling here, you may spot tents and other gear set up in the clearing. As you make your way to the tip of the headland you will pass by the only established group campground on the lake. Be careful as you round the headland—a partly submerged shallow rocky reef extends outward from the point. Upon rounding the headland, you will pass by the official boat ramp. Look for the dam with its characteristic shape. Follow its length and you will spot the cove containing your take-out to the right of the dam.

Area References

Arno, Stephen F. & Ramona P. Hammerly, *Timberline Mountain and Arctic Forest Frontiers.* Seattle, WA: The Mountaineers, 4th printing, August 1993. 304 pp.

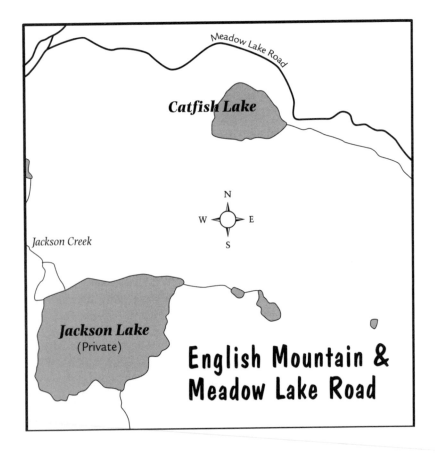

English Mountain & Meadow Lake Road

PADDLE LOCATION 16

Catfish Lake

Difficulty: All skill levels
Trip Length: The lake is too small for anything but a casual day paddle. However, because the drive is so long, this lake should be treated as an overnight trip.
Lake Size: 1000'
Paddle Distance:
From the put-in to the granite outcrop across the lake: 0.15 mile
Elevation: 6460'
Season: Spring through fall
County: Nevada
National Forest: Tahoe National Forest, Sierraville Ranger District (530) 994-3401
Maps: USGS 7.5 Minute Series: English Mountain Quadrangle.
Road Maps: Compass Maps Inc.: Nevada and Sierra Counties
American Auto Assn. (AAA) Maps: Northern California/Bay & Mountain sections

Access: Catfish Lake may be accessed from two directions. The first involves Interstate 80 East, exiting at Yuba Gap onto State Highway 20 West. After 4 miles exit right onto Bowman Lake Road (Forest Road 18N18). At the 10.5 Mile Marker, the pavement ends and the road becomes a hardscrabble dirt and cobble-strewn road. Continue on this road for approximately 10 miles beyond the 10.5 Mile Marker. Look for a road turn to the right approximately 2.75 miles after passing Jackson Creek Campground. Catfish Lake is the first lake on the right, two miles from the turnoff. The first sight of the lake is also the location of the boat launching area. A campsite sits to the right of the boat launch. Additional campsites are located around the southern shore, a short distance past the boat launch.
Alternative Route
Take Interstate 80 East past Truckee, exit onto State Highway 89 North towards Sierraville. Continue on Highway 89 until you exit left (west) onto Henness Pass/Fibreboard Road at Little Truckee Summit. *Note: at this junction of the road and highway there is an OHV staging area complete with toilet/wash facility. A signboard with the latest weather and forest road conditions is posted in front of the toilet facility.* Stay on Henness Pass /Fibreboard Road for approximately

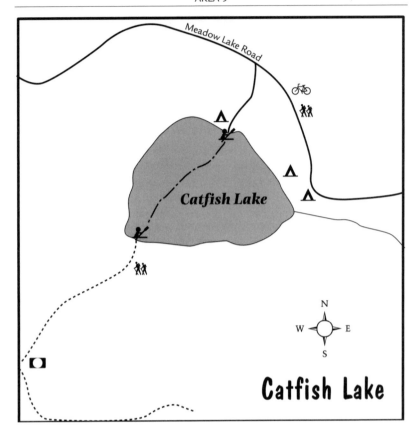

Catfish Lake

10 miles and exit onto Webber/Meadow Lake Road at Webber Lake. Follow this dirt road driving past the private entrance and residence of the ranch/ owners of property surrounding the lake. *Note: If you are interested in paddling or fishing on this lake, check with the owners who run a private campground adjacent to the ranch.* The road joins the main section of Meadow Lake Road a short distance from the private campground. You are now on the last stretch before reaching Meadow Lake. Stay on this road for approximately 10 miles. Upon reaching the northeast shoreline, the road begins to follow the outline of the lake. Look for a turnoff at the southwest end, just past a dilapidated historical sign depicting the history of Meadow Lake. Continue on Meadow Lake Road past the turnoff for H. Hartley's Grave Site. At approximately 4/10ths of a mile, you will come upon a small tarn lake partially hidden by a screen of conifers. (Although this body of water is not described in this book, it is worth the stop to hike past the tarn to the granite ridge beyond for an awesome view of French Lake and the surrounding peaks. In addition, as you hike through the thin pines bordering the northeast edge of the tarn, look for a tree with a yellow metal K-Tag. Located directly below the tag is an older

incised blaze inscribing the Township and Range directly onto the trunk of the pine). From the tarn to Tollhouse Lake, the first Paddle Location is another 1.1 miles. Catfish Lake is an additional 3.76 miles further. If you continue on this section of Meadow Lake Road you will reach Jackson Creek Campground followed by Bowman Lake and eventually, State Highway 20.

Heads Up:
- Easy access from Forest Service roads.
- Dispersed, primitive camping only, a campfire permit is necessary.
- No toilet or running water.
- Bear country: pack and camp smart.
- Small and wind protected, great for beginners and kids.
- Nearby logging roads make for great mountain biking and the granite ridges are perfect for hiking.
- Easy access to nearby lakes.

Description: This picturesque bowl-shaped lake, with a name more conducive to a body of water on the Delta, provides an opportune break from the long, hard drive into the area. The lake is situated at a crossroad that leads into the major access areas within the Yuba River Drainage. You can't but help pass by this lake at least once on any drive into the more remote parts of the forest. Because of this close proximity to the surrounding areas, campers use Catfish Lake as their base camp.

The lake itself is small and oval. You can paddle its entire breadth under thirty minutes . . . maybe an hour, if you dawdle to explore and admire the scenery. With so little to go with, why bother to stop? Located just off the roadway, the lake's quiet setting gives off a serene feeling. Sitting under a massive knoll of granite, surrounded by stately conifers, Catfish Lake offers something special on your way to bigger and more remote lakes. Its extremely easy access, just off the roadway, provides the weary paddler a chance to enjoy a quick paddle with little to no preparation. A couple of hours spent here sweeps the tension and stress out and allows the body and mind to slow down and become adjusted to "river-time."

If you wish to spend the night, I suggest using one of the campsites located on the south end of the lake. They are away from the road and dust that is kicked up by passing vehicles. To access any of these sites, drive a short distance past the clearing that contains the boat launch and look for side roads on your right. If you are feeling ambitious or have energy to burn, traverse the granite ridge bordering the lake for a spectacular view of Jackson Lake and the surrounding saw-toothed ridges. Unfortunately, Jackson Lake is surrounded by private property and therefore, not accessible to public use.

When you feel like exploring surrounding lakes, another conifer-shrouded

Your view of Catfish Lake from Meadow Lake Road.

tarn, Tollhouse Lake (Paddle Location 17) is situated approximately 3.75 miles further down on Meadow Lake Road. An additional 1.83 miles takes you to Meadow Lake (Paddle Location 18). If you backtrack from Catfish Lake on Meadow Lake Road to the crossroads, and turn left (west), you will reach the lakes that border Jackson Creek Campground located approximately three miles down the road. (See Paddle Locations: 12-A through 15.) By turning right (east) at the same crossroad you will access the paddle area of Jackson Creek Reservoir and Milton Reservoir, described in Paddle Location 19.

Finally, I have searched the shallow areas along the shore of the lake, but as yet have not seen any of the small Black Bullhead (I. Melas), that may have given the lake its name and are common to other nearby lakes, specifically Middle Lindsey Lake (Paddle Location 9).

Area References

Durham, David L., *Durham's Place-Names of California's Gold Country Including Yosemite National Park.* Clovis, CA: Quill Driver Books/Word Dancer Press. 2000, 369 pp.

PADDLE LOCATION 17

Tollhouse Lake

Difficulty: All skill levels
Trip Length: The lake itself is too small for anything but a casual day paddle. However, because the drive is so long, this should be treated as an overnight trip.
Elevation: 7,050'
Season: Late Spring through fall before the first snowfall.
Historical Background: Named for a toll house nearby that collected tolls for use on a private road leading to the community of Meadlow Lake.
County: Nevada
National Forest: Tahoe National Forest, Sierraville Ranger District (530) 994-3401
Maps: USGS 7.5 Minute Series: English Mountain Quadrangle.
Road Maps: Compass Maps Inc.: Nevada & Sierra counties
American Auto Assn. (AAA) Maps: Northern California/Bay & Mountain sections

Access: Tollhouse Lake may be accessed from two directions. The first involves Interstate 80 East, exiting at Yuba Gap onto State Highway 20 West. After 4 miles exit right onto Bowman Lake Road (Forest Road 18N18). At the 10.5 Mile Marker, the pavement ends and the road become a hardscrabble dirt and cobble-strewn road. Continue on this road for approximately ten miles beyond the 10.5 Mile Marker. Look for a road turn to the right approximately 2.75 miles after passing Jackson Creek Campground. The first lake you will pass is Catfish Lake. Tollhouse Lake is an additional 3.76 miles.
Alternative Route
Take Interstate 80 East past Truckee, exit onto State Highway 89 North towards Sierraville. Continue on Highway 89 until you exit left (west) onto Henness Pass/Fibreboard Road at Little Truckee Summit.
Note: at this junction of the road & highway there is an OHV staging area complete with toilet/wash facility. A signboard with the latest weather and forest road conditions is posted in front of the toilet facility. Stay on Henness Pass/Fibreboard Rd for approximately 10 miles and exit onto Webber/Meadow Lake Road at Webber Lake. Follow this dirt road driving past the private entrance and residence of the ranch owners of property surrounding the lake. *Note: If you are interested in paddling or fishing on this lake, check with the owners who run a private campground adjacent to the ranch.* The road joins the main section of Meadow Lake Road a short distance from the private campground. You are now on the last stretch before reaching Meadow Lake. Stay on this road for approximately 10 miles. Upon reaching the northeast shoreline, the road begins to follow the outline of the lake. Look for a turnoff at the southwest end, just past a dilapidated historical sign depicting the history of Meadow Lake. Continue on Meadow Lake Road past the turnoff for H. Hartley's Grave Site. Approximately 4/

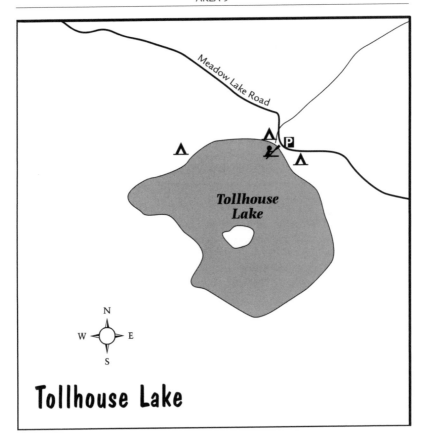

Tollhouse Lake

10ths of a mile, you will come upon a small tarn lake partially hidden by a screen of conifers. From the tarn to Tollhouse Lake is another 1.1 miles. If you continue on this section of Meadow Lake Road you will pass Catfish Lake, then reach Jackson Creek Campground followed by Bowman Lake and eventually, State Highway 20.

Heads Up:
- Easy access off Meadow Lake Road.
- Dispersed camping only, therefore a campfire permit is necessary.
- Bear country: pack & camp smart.
- No toilet or running water.
- Outstanding Sierra scenery of the forest, lake and nearby granite ridge.
- Protection from wind makes this small lake a great place for beginners & children.
- Meadow Lake is less than a mile down the road.

Description: People usually pass Tollhouse Lake on their way to the much larger Meadow Lake (Paddle Location 18) less than a mile down the road. This is unfortunate, but then again, maybe not. If you just paddle Meadow Lake without experiencing the somber beauty of little Tollhouse Lake, well . . . it's like the pie without the whipped cream topping. You get flavor, but not the full-taste sensation. On the one hand, paddling Meadow Lake gives you the chance to exercise and fulfill a complete paddling workout; subsequently, on Tollhouse Lake, you soak in a small feeling of being in the Sierran wilderness.

As soon as you launch your boat, you can't help but feel the lake's setting begin its effect on you. This small, but very alluring tarn fed by snow-melt, sits in a shady slump partially hidden by moss-covered conifers and flanked on the west by a glacially worked granite ridge. Only the north and south ends of the lake are open to full sun, and therefore have carpets of green sedges extending outward from the shore.

Almost mid-center, but across the lake on the west side, is a small rocky island that resembles a Japanese Bonsai. On a clear morning at sunrise, the still surface of the lake acts as a mirror reflecting both the island with its tall spires of fir and the surrounding granite wall. This reflection is so perfect in detail, that for a moment, especially if you have just risen from your sleeping bag, a feeling of vertigo can set in. The paddle on this lake is similar in scope to the paddle on Catfish Lake (Paddle Location 16). A short number of strokes puts you on the opposite shore, regardless the direction of travel. The real joy comes from the ability to take your craft out to the middle of the

On Tollhouse Lake you feel you're in the midst of a true Sierran wilderness.

Your reward at the end of the trail is a panoramic view of French Lake and the smaller Weil Lake.

lake or behind the island and then "let 'er drift" as you soak in the sights and sounds of the forest.

I try to time my paddles on this pocket lake either in the early morning when the mist is still rising, or on a full moon night . . . either time, the setting provides the paddler with a feeling that is nothing short of exhilarating. Of course, having a thermos of one's favorite hot brew just adds to the occasion! As an added bonus, hike the granite ridge that borders the western shoreline. Route yourself to the northwest heading for a level area of high ground. From there you obtain a clear view of upper French Lake and surrounding peaks. Although French Lake is on Forest Service land and open to the public, a closed gate coupled with a deeply abraded access road over a mile long, precludes easy passageway to the lake. A portage, using a boat cart is possible, but extremely difficult. With that said, for those willing to make the effort, it's a lake of unparalleled beauty.

Area References
Durham, David L., *Durham's Place-Names of California's Gold Country Including Yosemite National Park.* Clovis, CA: Quill Driver Books/Word Dancer Press. 2000, 369 pp.

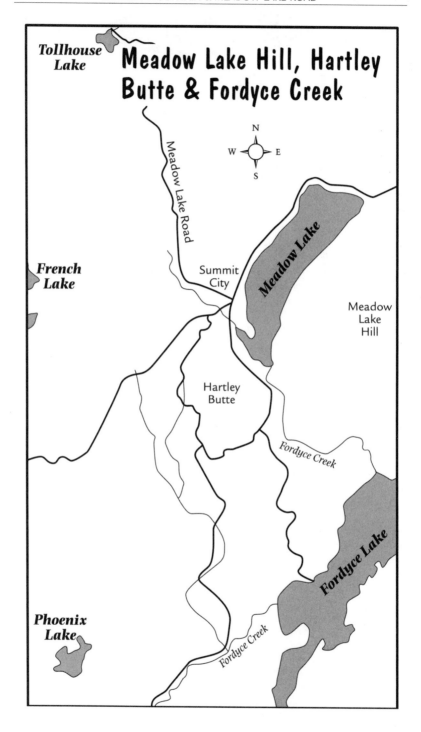

Tollhouse Lake

Meadow Lake Hill, Hartley Butte & Fordyce Creek

N
W — E
S

Meadow Lake Road

French Lake

Summit City

Meadow Lake

Meadow Lake Hill

Hartley Butte

Fordyce Creek

Fordyce Lake

Phoenix Lake

Fordyce Creek

Area 10

Meadow Lake Hill, Hartley Butte & Fordyce Creek

PADDLE LOCATION 18
Meadow Lake

Difficulty: Due to the open setting, the wind may be a significant hazard. If a storm or thunderclouds are eminent, lightening strikes may be a hazard.

Trip Length: Although the lake may be paddled without difficulty in one day, the time it takes to reach it insures this destination to be planned for two or more days.

Lake Size: 1.5 miles long by 5 miles wide

Paddle Distances: (see map)

From the take-out at the boat launch and campground to:

The campsite mid-center and southeast side: 0.75 mile

Take-out for ridge hike: 1.26 mile

The dam site: 0.31 miles

Across the lake mid-center: 0.33 mile

Elevation: 7,254'

Season: Late spring through summer

Historical Background: Your first impression of Meadow Lake, set in a wide meadow surrounded by a ridge of moraine on one side and granite outcrop on the other, is of a typical high-country tarn created by a glacier. This lake, like the town that once stood here, stands testimony to first impressions that lead to false assumptions. To understand this statement one has to go back to 1860, when an ill recluse by the name of Henry Hartley moved up here, built a cabin, and eked out a living as a free trapper. In 1863 Hartley found some reddish gold-bearing rock approximately one half mile southeast of the present site of the lake. The surface deposit appeared of enough value to warrant further exploration. Hartley obtained a couple of partners and they started a mining venture they called the Excelsior Company. Their modest return of gold ore attracted another company—the California Company—and soon nearby claims were staked out and being worked by a host of various groups and individuals.

In 1865 a combination of outside events led to a mass arrival of several thousand people to the cluster of rough cabins called Summit City. They were looking to strike it rich!

"The first public meeting was called at this group of cabins in July. The mining laws of California's Nevada County were adopted and boundaries were defined for a town site to be known as Meadow Lake." —*Sierra-Nevada Lakes*, pg. 239.

By March of 1866, the town of Meadow Lake was officially named and incorporated. By August of 1866, there were 500 buildings, many of them brick. The town boasted over ninety saloons, a theater house, multi-story hotels, and the staple of every gold rush era town: a newspaper (The Meadow Lake Morning Sun). It also had a

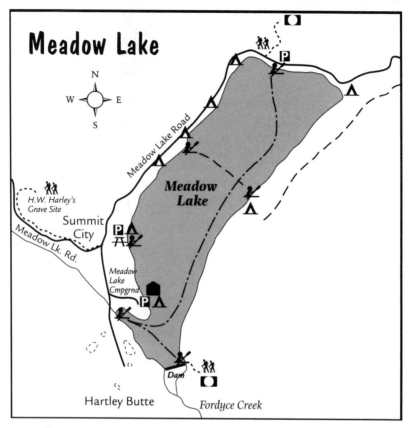

post office, Wells Fargo office, and a bank. By the first week of December 1866, the town's first public school opened accommodating 51 pupils. In the vicinity, four sawmills were in operation. The crowning achievement, however, was the small double-decked steamboat that plied the waters of the new miniature lake. On Saturday nights it carried boisterous miners and townies to the upper end of the lake, where they disembarked onto a wharf leading to several "hurdy-gurdy" houses.

All this high-living on speculation of a shallow surface deposit of ore came to a screeching halt in 1867. After repeated attempts to separate the gold from the sulphides:

" . . . The strangely obdurate ore would not yield to any known process of reduction. It was now clear that a mixture of arsenic, antimony, lead and other metals neutralized the effects of quicksilver and prevented amalgamation. . . By September it was freely acknowledged that Meadow Lake was "played out." — *Sierra-Nevada Lakes*, pgs. 245-246.

By 1872, the town was dead. Only Hartley the Hermit remained. In September of 1873, a transient started a fire in the Excelsior Hotel. By that time only a few houses remained.

Today, the shards of glass and pottery are all that's left of where the town once stood. The lake, however still bears testimony to the artificiality of the entire project. Like the thin layers of ore that created a speculative boom of grandiose proportions, the lake is nothing more than a ". . .mere pothole, seventy-five feet deep and fourteen feet wide, in the grassy center of the high, saucer-like depression, and from it trickled a small stream tributary to the Yuba." —*Sierra-Nevada Lakes*, pg. 233. The "lake" was created in 1858 when the South Yuba Canal Company built the 300 feet long by 42 feet high all-granite dam across the stream to provide water for downhill placer diggings.

County: Nevada

National Forest: Tahoe National Forest, Sierraville Ranger District (530) 994-3401

Maps: USGS 7.5 Minute Topographical Sections: English Mtn. and Webber Peak.

US Forest Service Maps: Tahoe National Forest Map

Road Maps: Compass Maps Inc.: Nevada and Sierra counties

California Auto Assn. Maps: Northern California/Bay and Mountain sections

Access: From Sacramento and the West, the shortest in terms of mileage, is also the more difficult route. It involves approximately 30 miles of off-road driving, two stream crossings and a high-clearance vehicle. The second longer route takes you into Truckee then north and West before exiting onto a washboard dirt and gravel road for the last 10 miles of dirt road.

Meadow Lake has a unique history as this sign depicts.

The Short and Dirty Route

The most direct route from the west on Interstate 80, involves driving I-80 East to State Highway 20 toward Nevada City. Exit onto Highway 20 at Yuba Gap. Continue for 4 miles, exit onto Bowman Lake Road/Forest Service Road 18. The pavement ends at the 10.5 Mile Marker. From here to Meadow Lake, the road becomes a rough secondary road best suitable for high-clearance vehicles. The scenery, however, is spectacular! At Bowman Lake, Forest Service Road 18 becomes FR 843 (on the Compass Map it is listed as Meadow Lake Road). Continue on FR 843 until you reach Jackson Creek Campground. Stay to the left. You will soon begin climbing as you follow Jackson Creek. Stay on 843/Meadow Lake Road for approximately 2.75 Miles. Meadow Lake Road turns sharply to the right. Look for a small directional sign with arrows and mileage to Catfish, Tollhouse and Meadow lakes. Stay on this road for another 7.5 miles until it enters the southwest shoreline of Meadow Lake. Look for a road turn to the right. The newly rebuilt campground and boat launch is located at the end of this road. If you stay on FR843/Meadow Lake Road, you will parallel the lake before following it out and onto Henness Pass Road, about 12.75 miles away.

The Long But Sane Route

Take Interstate 80 East to the State Highway 89 North (Sierraville) exit east of Truckee. Continue on Highway 89 until you exit left (west) onto Henness Pass/Fibreboard Road at Little Truckee Summit. *Note: at this junction of the road and highway there is an OHV staging area complete with toilet/wash facility. A signboard with the latest weather and forest road conditions is posted in front of the toilet facility.* Stay on Henness Pass /Fibreboard Road for approximately 10 miles and exit onto Webber/Meadow Lake Road at Webber Lake. Follow this dirt road driving past the private entrance and residence of the ranch owners of property surrounding the lake. *Note: If you are interested in paddling or fishing on this lake, check with the owners who run a private campground adjacent to the ranch.* The road joins the main section of Meadow Lake Road a short distance from the private campground. You are now on the last stretch before reaching Meadow Lake. Stay on this road for approximately 10 miles. Upon reaching the northeast shoreline the road begins to follow the outline of the lake. Look for a turnoff at the southwest end for the newly rebuilt campground and boat ramp. If you stay on this end of Meadow Lake Road you will reach State Highway 20 some 20 bone-jarring miles.

Description: Paddling on Meadow Lake is like running the Colorado River. You appreciate the whole venture if you know the history behind the scenery. On one level it is a grand view of the surrounding ridge, the tall conifers and the open vista of the grassy swale, but understand too, that a mere century ago, an entire town supported a population of 5,000 souls along with their accouterments on this same site. To add an additional "bit-of-spice" to our location, on the same lake that your paddle craft sits so daintily, a real "huffin-puffen" steamboat used to make daily runs* . . .now that really boggles the mind! Today, paddling Meadow Lake is not in itself a big deal. You paddle it because of its scenic beauty, and in an attempt to capture a historical moment in time. Unless a stay at the Forest Service campground is necessary, load your craft and paddle across Meadow Lake to camp with a night view of the southwest end of the lake (see map).

The former town of Meadow Lake stood bordering the southwest end. At night with little or no distractions you can recreate the town site and picture the incredible image of a steamboat churning its way on the water. By day, explore the west end of the lake first. The rising sun highlights this end first leaving the southeastern side in shadow. Paddle to the flat area

Meadow Lake from the former town site of Summit City/Meadow Lake.

where the town once stood. Take out anywhere along the flat beach and slowly walk its length. With careful observation, you may spot shards of pottery, china or glass, rusted bits of metal, and chunks of algae-covered brick. With luck and a good eye, you may even find an old coin.

If you have the time and inclination, hike the half-mile up Meadow Lake Road to the gravesite of Henry Hartley known as Hartley The Hermit, and the man who found the initial ore deposit. The site is on a small knoll at the base of the main north-south running ridge that borders the northern shoreline. A marker and sign points you in the proper direction (see map). If you decided to stay on the lake, then proceed up the lake following the shoreline. Hidden amongst the Lodgepole Pines are numerous campsites complete with their own beach.

When you bank around the northwest corner of the lake, you will pass a thicket of alder. Immediately past the thicket is a stretch of beach that becomes a clearing leading across the road and upslope through the forest. Secure your boat, grab the daypack and camera and follow the clearing up through the pines. On the map, I included an approximate route to the ridge. There is no trail to follow just the clearing leading into the trees. The forest is not very dense and it is easy to pick your path around the trees. Stay to the right and aim for the ridgeline that is visible on the horizon. Once you break through the cover of pine, you enter a small clearing. Depending on the time of year you visit, the entire clearing is covered with wildflowers. Woolly Sunflowers *(Eriophyllum lanatum)* intermixed with Woolly Mule Ears *(Wyethia mollis)*, Pride of the Mountain, *(Penstemon newberryi)* with gorgeous red blossoms, and one of my personal favorites, the splendid Applegate's Paintbrush, sometimes called the Wavy-Leaved Paintbrush (*Castilleja applegatei*), all provide a showcase of color and form. Growing above the flowers, tall-branched stems of Ranger's Buttons (*Sphenosciadium capitellatum*), with their umbrella-shaped flower clusters, bob in the breeze.

Walk through the flower garden and you'll come to the edge of the ridge with the glaciated valley below. You are now standing on a basalt knob that was once an ancient lava flow. To the left and receding onto the hazy horizon is the wide valley of the Middle Yuba River. The bowl-shaped basin with its tree covered channels, marks the headwaters of the river. To the right is the eroding flank of Lacy Peak (8,216'). Gazing down and across the valley, you can just barely see the location of Moscove Meadows. For this view alone, the short hike from the lake is worth every step!

Back at your boat, you may see the late afternoon sun profiling the Basin of Meadow Lake and Hartley Butte (7,450'). The Butte is named after Henry Hartley whose grave rests off the Meadow Lake Road not far from the butte. Now that the sun's rays have removed the shadows from the lake's southeastern shore, begin your exploration of that side of Meadow Lake. Ever since I read about the steamboat and its noisy journey, filled with rollicking miners, across the lake to the "hurdy-gurdy" houses I have been looking for the remnants of the wharf where the boat docked. Several places based on the terrain, appear promising. So, maybe the south side of the lake will reveal the site. Paddle around the entrance of one of the run-off streams that empty into the lake and follow the northwestern flank of Meadow Lake Hill (7,821'), whose ridgeline frames the shoreline on this side of the lake. Several places on this ridge bear the unmistakable sign of recent logging.

The clear-cut areas, while ugly in appearance, provides an unobstructed path to the top of the hill. The hike is steep but short. On the way up, you'll pass several seeps whose presence was marked by a riot of greenery: Ranger's Buttons, (S. capitellatum); Crimson Columbine (A. Formosa); and the predominant Mountain Mule Ears (W. mollis). In the drier areas Anderson's Thistle (C. andersonii) grows in small clusters. Flitting around the flower heads and taking nectar you may see the orange and black speckled Fritillary Family of butterfly (Genus Speyeria).

Get back on the water and paddle straight for the dam site. Using a protruding outcrop of granite as your reference, aim straight for it and you'll soon find yourself in a small cove located at the south wing of the new dam. I say new, because the original dam, dramatically described in the Hinkle's' classic book on Sierra Lakes, was built entirely of local granite. This newer version is a combination of rock, some granite, and concrete. Studying the granite outcrop at the edge and above this dam you'll see that the area was once quarried. Whether this was part of the area where the early engineers obtained their stone or part of a modern effort, I can't tell.

A butterfly on Anderson's Thistle near Meadow Lake.

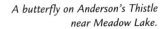

Hike past the wing of the dam and trek over a small earthen berm to enter the conifer forest. After short trek, you'll enter a steep clearing covered with Mule Ears *(W. mollis)*. Below the clearing the view unfolded onto a barren granite valley. You can look across the basin containing Fordyce Reservoir and onto the granitic slopes of Magonigal Summit (7400+'). As the late afternoon sun begins to set, you should think about paddling back to your camp.

*Based on information provided in *Sierra-Nevada Lakes* by Hinkle, pg. 242.

Area References

Gudde, Erwin G., *California Gold Camps.* Berkeley, CA: University of California Press, 1975. 467 pp.

Hinkle, George & Bliss, *Sierra-Nevada Lakes.* (re-printed ed.). Reno: NV: University of Nevada Press, 1987. 383 pp.

Howe, William H., *The Butterflies of North America.* Garden City, NY: Doubleday & Company, Inc., 1975. 633 pp.

Whitney, Stephen, *Western Forests,* National Audubon Society Nature Guide. New York, NY: Alfred A. Knopf, Inc., 1997. 670 pp.

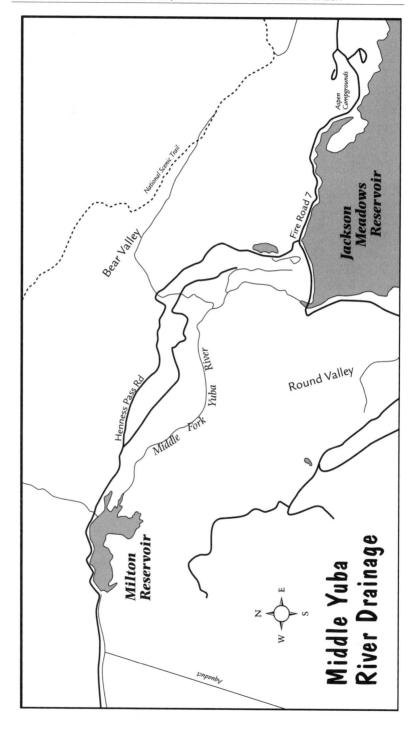

Aspen Campgrounds

Jackson Meadows Reservoir

National Scenic Trail

Bear Valley

Fire Road 7

Henness Pass Rd

Middle Fork Yuba River

Round Valley

Milton Reservoir

Aqueduct

Middle Yuba River Drainage

N E S W

Area 11

Middle Yuba River Drainage & Bald Ridge

PADDLE LOCATION 19

Milton Reservoir

Difficulty: All skill levels

Trip Length: The reservoir is too small for anything but a day paddle. However, the long driving time to the reservoir makes it an overnight destination spot.

Lake Size: 2000' X 1000'

Paddle Distance: All points of interest are located a short paddle from your put-in.

Elevation: 5,690'

Season: From the time the snow melts through fall. Optimum time is late spring for the wildflowers and birds or early fall for the color change.

Historical Background: Milton Reservoir is a dammed portion of the Middle Fork of the Yuba River that flows out of the larger Jackson Meadows Reservoir. It is named after a stopping place called Milton on the nearby Henness Pass Road (1868) (See Intro: Lakes of the Grouse Ridge Region.) The stopping place was also listed as a ranch with the same name.* In Fall, 1981, an experimental fishing program was adopted at the reservoir. The purpose of the program is to maintain a healthy balance of trophy-sized trout and reduce the proliferation of non-game fish. A full description of this program is provided on the Information Board when you arrive at the lake.

County: Bordering on Sierra and Nevada counties.

National Forest: Tahoe National Forest, Sierraville Ranger District, (916) 994-3401.

Maps: USGS 7.5 Minute Topographical Section: Haypress Valley Quadrangle.

National Forest Service Map: Tahoe National Forest.

Road Maps: Compass Maps, Inc.: Nevada and Sierra counties, Nevada-Sierra Counties Street and Road Atlas.

American Auto Assn. (AAA) Maps: Northern California/Bay and Mountain sections

Access: You may reach Milton Reservoir from two diverse directions. The first and primary access is by taking Interstate 80 East to Truckee and exiting onto California State Highway 89 North (a.k.a. The Yuba-Donner Scenic Byway) toward Sierraville. Continue on 89N for approximately 15 miles. Exit left onto Forest Road 07 (Fiberboard/Henness Pass Road). *Note: For current road/weather conditions and campground availability, check the Information Board located in front of the toilet facilities at the OHV Staging Area located to your right immediately after turning onto FR 07.*

The turnoff for Milton Reservoir (there is NO sign for the turnoff heading north on 07) will be on your right just before you cross Jackson Meadow

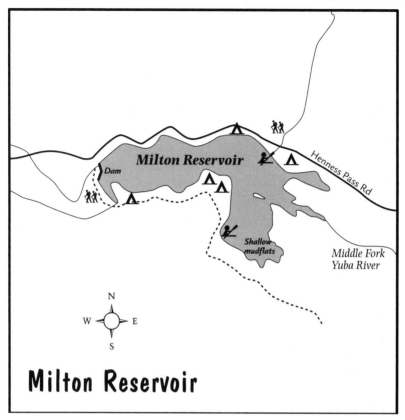

Milton Reservoir

Dam, approximately 19 miles from the 89/07 junction. You are now on Henness Pass Road. Here the pavement ends. The corrugated dirt road is suitable for all vehicles but if you are towing a trailer or are in a large RV, the turn around spaces are very limited. Milton Reservoir is located 2 miles down Henness Pass Road.

The Down and Dirty Route

A secondary access, but the most direct route if arriving from the west on I-80, involves driving I-80 East to State Highway 20 toward Nevada City. Exit onto Highway 20 at Yuba Gap. Continue for 4 miles, exit onto Bowman Lake Road/Forest Service Road 18. The pavement ends at the 10.5 Mile Marker. From here to Jackson Meadows Reservoir the road becomes a rough secondary road best suitable for high-clearance vehicles. The scenery, however, is spectacular! At Bowman Lake, Forest Service Road 18 becomes FR 843, also listed as Meadow Lake Road. Continue on FR 843 until you reach Jackson Creek Campground. Stay to the left. You will soon begin climbing as you follow Jackson Creek. Stay on 843 billowing great plumes of dust until you cross Jackson Meadow Dam and the Spillway. Exit left, immediately after

The road to Milton Reservoir turns off from the dam at Jackson Meadows Reservoir.

crossing the dam. Finally, you are now on Henness Pass Road, the access road to Milton Reservoir. Continue down this gravel road for approximately 2 miles. Look for a left exit to the first camping area adjacent to the river (see map). Milton Reservoir is a short distance from this first camping area.

Heads Up:
- Fire permit required for any fire or stove use.
- No toilet or water facilities—bring your own.
- Dispersed camping, limited number of sites.
- Bear country: pack and camp smart!
- Best sites are along the edge of the reservoir near the Information Board or across the lake.
- Great for kids. Pets are OK.
- Good fishing, especially the fly-fishing.
- Birding is outstanding. Numerous wildflowers in the spring. Fall brings out the color change from nearby aspen.
- Other lakes are located only a short driving distance.
- Great hiking and mountain biking trails nearby.

Description: Some paddle destinations require meticulous preparation, with maps to be studied and mounds of gear acquired. These trips will then be described in the miles paddled over various water and weather conditions. Then there are those destination places that are savored for their intimacy and smallness of place. Where "to drift" is a better description than "to paddle," Milton Reservoir is such a place. Here, paddling becomes secondary to the floating of your canoe or kayak on the wind-driven surface. Maybe a fishing line is cast ... maybe not. A good pair of binoculars or a camera is more important than the paddle in your hands, or the kind of boat you have. Milton Reservoir is a great place to relax and take the family for the weekend or on an extended vacation. Due to the recent deepening of the reservoir, and the implementation of a fish program to re-build the lakes stock of trophy trout, this reservoir has become a favorite destination for fisherpersons. The reservoir is kidney-shaped with the upper end being the widest but also the shallowest. This shallowness is created by the accumulation of silt deposited by the braided in-flow of the South Yuba River. As a result, a wet marsh-like condition prevails close to the tail of the reservoir; subsequently, at the edges where the land is drier, a meadow forms. Unfortunately, because of the shallow depth, you may explore this area only by foot.

For a paddle on the reservoir when it is calm and glassy, be on the water before ten in the morning or wait until after five in the afternoon. Once on the water, unless you are planning to fish, plan your paddle away from the people flyfishing in the deeper sections of the lake. The fly fisher-person uses at least ten to twenty feet of space around his/her boat to cast his/her line. If you position yourself with the lighting just right, you may obtain a great action photo of a fisherperson standing in his or her canoe, line whipping in the air and highlighted by the sun.

When paddling the upper end of the reservoir, almost the entire end is shallow enough to touch the bottom with a paddle. Look out for rock outcrops—layers of silt usually camouflage their presence. If the light on the water is right, you may spot the ellusive goal of all the fisher-persons. Some of the Brown Trout (Salmo trutta) swimming casually past your boat looks easily to be twelve or more inches. As you become engrossed with the fish, it's easy to imagine this scenario. You quickly look up in time to spot a lone Bald Eagle (Haliaetus leusocephalus), as it glides onto a limb of a bleached dead conifer, standing at the edge of the lake. The presence of the eagle quickly stirs a fuss with the nearby waterfowl. A family of Canada Geese hover protectively around their two goslings. One of the adult pair, possibly the male, straightens its neck, opens then flaps its wings, hissing in the direction of the perched eagle. This action, in turn, agitates the small flock of Mallards into leaping into the air and streaking toward the shelter of the meadow. A small band of Mud Hens, American Coot (Fulica Americana), startled by all the commotion, begin their unique "run" across the surface of the lake before disappearing around the bend of the lower reservoir. Only the spunky Red-winged Blackbird begins a one-bird dive-bombing mission on the eagle. Finally, like an irritant mosquito buzzing around, the aggressive blackbird forces the eagle to leave its perch and fly easterly over the nearby ridge.

When this exciting bit of drama is over, you notice that you are not alone. Nearby fisherpersons also caught the action, and with the brazen blackbird's success at vanquishing the much larger bird of prey, we all spontaneously gave a hand clap and a vocal cheer in appreciation of the smaller bird's "chutzpa."

The small size of the reservoir allows for ample time to paddle its length while exploring the nearby shore. From the area where the South Yuba flows into the reservoir, paddle slowly to a nearby cove on the reservoir's west end. This particular cove is important because of is accessibility to the interior of the wet meadow that makes up the greater portion of the upper end of the reservoir. In addition, the rocky knob that juts out from the cove's northern end contains two nice camp spots with a great overview of this end of the reservoir, the wet meadow, and the high ridge that flanks the northeast side of the reservoir. There are several such sites located along the southern shore of the reservoir. All are compact and require packing your gear then paddling across the reservoir to reach them. In addition to the outstanding views, you also have privacy and quiet from the sounds of arriving and departing vehicles, not to mention extraneous noise from adjoining campsites (see map for location of these sites).

As you continue with your exploratory paddle along the shoreline, you round the rocky headland of the cove containing the above campsites and follow a conifer-covered bank before entering the second and last small cove on the reservoir. This last cove also contains the third campsite. Look for a protruding rocky knob. The site is on the level bank to the right of the knob. From the slick rock and staining patterns on the knob, I suspect that a waterfall will grace the rocky surface during spring runoff.

A view to the west of upper and lower Milton Reservoir.

Your put-in near the mouth of the South Yuba River where it empies into the reservoir.

From this portion of the reservoir you have a clear view of the dam, the string of orange buoys that mark off the no-entry zone, as well as the section of Henness Pass Road where it crosses the Yuba River below the dam. If you continue to explore the opposite (northeast) shoreline back to the upper reservoir, be vigilant for partially submerged rocks sitting just offshore from the lake's bank; subsequently, keep an eye out for fishing line belonging to people fishing along the brush-covered shoreline.

Area References

*Gudde, Erwin, G., *California Gold Camps*. Berkeley, CA: University of California Press. 1975. pg. 216.

Durham, David L., *Place-Names of California's Gold Country Including Yosemite National Park*. Clovis, CA: Quill Driver Books/Word Dancer Press, Inc. 2000. 369 pp.

Freeman, Jim, *North Sierra Trout Fishing: A Chronicle Tackle-Box Guide*. San Francisco, CA: Chronicle Books. 1972. 80 pp.

Storer, Tracy I. & Robert L. Usinger, *Sierra Nevada Natural History*. Berkeley, CA: University of California Press. 1963. 374 pp.

Appendix 1

Maps & Map Sources

The most common map for the paddler and backpacker is the topographic (contour) map series published by the United States Geological Survey (USGS). The type that shows the most detail and is the easiest to use, be it on the water or on the trail, has a scale of 1: 24,000. This map series is also known as the **7.50 minute Topographic Quadrangle** often called a *quad*. The scale: 1: 24,000 is to be interpreted as a scale of reference to mean that one inch on the map represents 2,000 feet on the ground. The 7.5' refers to the corresponding number of minutes of longitude and latitude this map quadrangle covers at a scale of 1: 24,000.* The symbol ' refers to a minute of either longitude or latitude; subsequently, the term minute pertains to a placement in space that is divided into 60 minutes, rather than time. For a more precise location, the minutes are subdivided further into 60 seconds with the use of the symbol: ".

For example, the Webber Peak Quadrangle lies between: 120°30' and 120°22'30" Longitude and 39°30' and 39°22' 30" Latitude. Each one of the 7.5-minute quadrangles covers an area of 49 to 70 square miles. Within this area, symbols are used to designate all features natural and manmade. For example: land and water features are shown as a series of lines called contours.The shape, distance between these contours, their width and color *(brown for areas above sea level and blue for features below sea level)* all describe how a specific three-dimensional terrain feature looks on a flat piece of paper—the 7.5-minute quadrangle topographical map sheet.

Unfortunately, many of the topographic maps paddlers, hikers and other users of the backcountry require are out of date. *(USGS is updating its map series based on budgetary availability and area priorities)*. Besides the government agencies, private map companies also publish maps that cover many of the popular lakes and reservoirs of California. Almost all of these maps use the USGS topographical quads as their base map and then overlay their information onto the existing data. As a result, although you may obtain a map with current roads, structures and even some terrain changes, the primary data is only as current as the original topographical quadrangle. In addition, these maps are aimed at the sportsperson. Hence, the majority of overlaid data pertains primarily to choice fishing and hunting areas.

What you _do_ obtain with these private company maps, besides places to fish, current roads and buildings, is a larger scale map of the lake or reservoir itself without any extraneous details. Unfortunately, no known private company maps exist that cover the lakes within the Yuba River Drainage. The closest map that pertains to the Yuba River Drainage is the recently published (2000) South Yuba River Recreation Guide. This excellent map is put out by the US Forest Service and may be purchased at any of their offices. (See **Government/Private Sources For Maps and Map Products**). Unfortunately the map depicts only two of the lakes described in this volume: Fuller and Rucker lakes.

If a current map is required, the best available type is made by remote sensing techniques, either from aerial photography or from satellite imagery. A listing of these sources is available in the appendix under **Maps from Satellite Imagery**. However, for the places described in this book, the cost for satellite imagery maps does not seem warranted.

*Editor's Note: _The higher the map scale ratio, the smaller the detail available. One inch on a map scale of 1:24,000 represents 2,000 feet; one inch on a scale of 1: 250,000 represents about 4 miles. A large-scale map = greater detail. This terminology is often misunderstood._

MAP QUADRANGLES FOR VOLUME III
Note: _A free listing of individual 7. 5-minute map sheets for California and other states may be ordered From USGS by requesting a: California (or other state) Index to Topographic and Other Map Coverage._

USGS 1: 250,000 Map Series:
Chico, California

USGS 7.5-minute Quadrangles Listed by Area
Area One:
USGS 7.5-minute series:
Blue Canyon Quadrangle, photo revised: 1979

Areas Two through Five:
USGS 7.5-minute series:
Graniteville Quadrangle
English Mtn. Quadrangle

Area Six
USGS 7.5-minute series:
Graniteville Quadrangle

Areas Seven, Eight & Nine
USGS 7.5-minute series:
English Mtn. Quadrangle

Area Ten
USGS 7.5-minute series:
English Mtn. Quadrangle
Webber Peak Quadrangle

Area Eleven
USGS 7.5-minute series:
Haypress Valley Quadrangle

GOVERNMENT/PRIVATE SOURCES FOR MAPS and MAP PRODUCTS

Note: *A separate heading is provided for map sources on the Internet*

USGS (local office)
Earth Science Information Center
345 Middlefield Road, Mail Stop 532
Menlo Park, CA 94025-4309
Hours: (M-F) 7:45- 4:15
Phone: (650) 329-4309
Fax: (650)329-5130

USGS (Western Regional Office)
USGS Map Sales
Federal Center
Box 25286
Denver, CO 80225
Phone: (888) ASK-USGS or (303) 202-4700/800-872-6277
Fax: (303) 202-4693
For a list of all the public phones and worldwide web sites, request the US Geological Survey Sources of Information and US Geological Survey World Wide Web Information Fact Sheet. To understand all the symbols used on the topographical

map sheets, request a free copy of Topographic Map Symbols. To obtain the index to all of California's 7.5-minute quadrangles, request a free copy of the California Index to Topographic and other Map Coverage.

California Division of Mines and Geology
Geological Information and Publications
801 K Street, MS 14-33
Sacramento, CA 95814-3532
Phone: (916) 445-5716
Fax: (916) 327-1853

San Francisco:
California Division of Mines and Geology
185 Berry Street, Ste. 210
San Francisco, CA 94107-1728
Phone: (415) 904-7707
Fax: (415) 904-7715
Information only e-mail:
dmglib@consrv.ca.gov
DM&G provides a variety of maps and publications pertaining to the state's geology, mineral resources and seismic hazards.

US Bureau of Land Management (BLM)
(California State Office)
2800 Cottage Way, Room W-1834
Sacramento, CA 95825
Phone: (916) 978-4400
E-mail: gcatledg@ca.blm.gov
Web page: http://www.ca.blm.gov/caso/maps_pubroom.htm
BLM in California Web site: www.ca.blm.gov/caso

USDA Forest Service
All national forests and wilderness areas maps may be obtained at the following address:

USDA Forest Service
Attention: Map Sales
1323 Club Drive
Vallejo, CA 94592
Phone: (707) 562-USFS (8737)

Tahoe National Forest (Supervisor's Office)

631 Coyote Street
PO Box 6003
Nevada City, CA 95959-6003
Phone: (530) 265-4531
www.r5.fs.fed.us/tahoe/

District offices within the Tahoe National Forest

Downieville Ranger District

North Yuba Station
15924 Highway 49
Camptonville, CA 95922
(530) 288-3231

Nevada City Ranger District

PO Box 6003
Nevada City, CA 95959
(530) 265-4538

Sierraville Ranger District

PO Box 95, Hwy. 89
Sierraville, CA 96126
(530) 994-3401

Truckee Ranger District

PO Box 399
Truckee, CA 95734
(530) 587-3558

Truckee Ranger Station

10342 Highway 89 North
Truckee, CA 96161
(530) 587-3558

MAPS FROM SATELLITE IMAGERY

Aerial Images Inc.

Raleigh, NC
http://www.spin-2.com
A US firm selling Russian satellite imagery poster sized and printed by Kodak.

Customer Services
USGS EROS Data Center
47914 252nd Street
Sioux Falls, SD 57198-0001
Phone: (800) 252-4547
Fax: (605) 594-6589
This center houses aerial photos and satellite imagery of the earth.

MAP SOURCES ON THE INTERNET*

*Primary source for these sites came from the Nov./Dec. 1999 issue of California Geology in an article titled: Maps: The Earth On Canvas, *written by Evelyn M. Vandendolder.*

http://math.rice.edu/~lanius/pres/map/mapres.html
Contains links to other websites pertaining to maps and map sales. Includes information on USGS GIS (Geographic Information System) data.

http://infomine.ucr.edu/search/mapssearch.phtml
U. C. Riverside Library *as a reference tool developed INFOMINE. Contains a collection of links to map sources and GIS information. Other California universities and libraries contributed to this website.*

http://www.jpl.nasa.gov
JPL/NASA/CALTECH *contains satellite imagery of earth.*

http://lcweb.loc.gov/rr/geogmap/
LIBRARY of CONGRESS *vast quantities of maps for educational and research purposes without copyright laws.*

http://www.mercatormag.com/links.html
MERCATOR'S WORLD Magazine *with links to map sources. Links are categorized into subjects including: Earth Science, Geography, and Weather.*

http://www.lib.berkeley.edu/EART/MapCollections.html
UNIVERSITY CALIFORNIA BERKELEY Website *claims to be largest depository of maps for Northern California with over 360,000 maps. Site provides links to other map sources.*

http://edcwww.cr.usgs.gov/content_products.html
US GEOLOGICAL SURVEY Website provides information on USGS maps and publications. Handles online map orders.

http://geology.wr.usgs.gov/wgmt/scamp.html
USGS-SCAMP a website devoted to the joint mapping project between Calf. Division of Mines and Geology and USGS to produce a database of digital maps, and an overall database of state maps at either a 1:100,000 or 1:24,000 scales.

PRIVATE MAP COMPANIES

Compass Maps Inc.
1172 Kansas Ave.
Modesto, CA 95351
(209) 529-5017
Excellent road maps of California and counties.

De Lorme Mapping Company
PO Box 298
Freeport, ME 04032
Phone: (800) 452-5931/ (207) 865-4171
Web: www.delorme.com
In 1999 put on the market: 3D topographical quads on compact disk of various states. The De Lorme Company is also known for their excellent shaded relief atlases depicting cultural features and terrain. Their format is similar to the USGS quadrangle maps.

Earth Visions
655 Portsmouth Avenue
Greenland, NH 03840
Phone: (800) 627-7236
Web: www.earthvisions.com
Producers of maps on CD-ROM.

Horizon Maps/REI.com
A product of Recreational Equipment Incorporated (REI); online service that allows you to download USGS quads.

MAPTECH/TOPO!
Digital mapping Technology
655 Portsmouth Avenue
Greenland, NH 03840
Phone: (800) 627-7236
Fax: (603)433-8505
Web: www.maptech.com/topo
Uses the USGS quadrangles as its base and covers the entire state on CD-ROM.
Bought out TOPO! Utilizes their symbology and graphics.

National Geographic TOPO! Sync USA
PO Box 4357
Evergreen, CO 80437-4357
Phone: 1(800) 962-1643
Web: www.nationalgeographic.com/topo
Ability to organize photos, notes and weblinks directly onto the map.

Thomas Bros. Maps
Offices in: Irvine, CA: (714) 863-1984
Los Angeles, CA: (213) 627-4018
San Francisco, CA: (415) 981- 7520
A well-established map company; makers of excellent maps. I particularly like their California Road Atlas and Driver's Guide. Their emphasis is on the road networks, depicting many small secondary roads. Does not show relief.

RETAIL MAP SALES

California Surveying & Drafting Supply
4733 Auburn Blvd.
Sacramento, (Carmichael) CA 95841
Phone: (800) 350-6277/(916) 344-0232/Fax: (916) 344-2998
Sells USGS topographical sheets, BLM maps, road maps, (Compass Maps and others), and maps on CD-ROM.

Recreational Equipment Incorporated (REI)
1790 Exposition Parkway
Sacramento, CA 95815
Phone: (916) 924-8900
Fax: (916)924-9070
In addition to standard map sales, REI maintains its own online service related to

map needs, (see: Horizon Maps at REI.com) A very popular store for outdoor enthusiasts of many different sports.

Sierra Outdoor Center (SOC)
440 Lincoln Way
Auburn, CA 95603
Phone: (530) 885-1844
Fax: (530) 885-0451
E-Mail: -sierraoc@jps.net
In addition to a retail, rental and kayaking/rafting school, SOC also carries a full line of USGS topos, guidebooks and paddle-related literature.

Appendix 2

Paddling Clubs & Organizations

American Canoe Association (ACA)
7432 Alban Station Blvd. Ste, B-232
Springfield, VA 22150
Phone: (703) 451-0141
Fax: (703) 451-2245
E-mail: ACADirect@aol.com
The "Big Dog" of canoeing organizations. A new membership may include a free years subscription to Paddler Magazine, *in addition to the newsletter: American Canoeist. Membership grants you discounts and keeps you abreast on "what's happenin'" in the sport.*

American Red Cross (Sacramento Chapter)
PO Box 160167
Sacramento, CA 95816
Phone: (916) 368-3167
Fax: (916) 368-3224
Still a leader in First Aid, CPR training and canoeing classes.

Becoming an Outdoors Woman
Sponsored by: Calif. Dept. of Fish and Game
and University of Wisconsin-Stevens Point, College of Natural Resources
PO Box 1945
Sacramento, CA 95812
Phone: (916) 657-4333
This program consists of a series of workshops focused on outdoor skills; canoeing is just one of the courses taught. Designed primarily for women, 18 yrs. or older. Sign up early because the canoeing class is extremely popular.

CSUS Aquatic and Boat Safety Center.
1901 Hazel Ave.
Rancho Cordova, CA 95670
Phone: (916) 985-7239
Fax: (916) 985-7312
Rentals and lessons in canoes, kayaks, rowing shells and sailboats.

California Floaters Society
2208 Athens River Ct.
Rancho Cordova, CA: 95670
Phone: (916) 482-8548
Web: www.cfsonline.org

Central California Canoe Club
C/O: Holly Wenger
3655 Bausell Street
Sacramento, CA 95821
Phone: (916)482-5592

Chico Paddle Heads
Attn.: John Alden
12428 Centerville Rd.
Chico, CA 95928-8320
Phone: (530) 345-2453
E-mail: paddlenet@AOL.com
A combination of touring and white water enthusiasts sponsored in part, by North Rim Adventure Sports in Chico, CA. A new club with members excited about all aspects of paddling.

Marin Canoe Club
C/O: Louisa Arndt
810 Idylberry Rd.
San Raphael, CA 94903
Web: marincanoe@aol.com

Western Waters Canoe Club
Web: www.westernwaterscanoeclub.org

Retailers and Outfitters

On Line Sites:
http://paddling.about.com/recreation/paddling
About.com articles and links

http://www.paddling.com
Directory for sites on canoeing, kayaking and rafting events, classifieds, outfitters, manufacturers and other paddling related sites.

http://www.paddling.net
Covers all aspects of canoeing and kayaking, guides, classifieds, product reviews, links, and books.

http://www.sit-on-topkayaking.com
Database with statistics of all sit-on-top boats, forums, articles, book excerpts, links and club listings.

http://www.amateurkayakers.com
A links list of kayaking and paddling resources, books, videos, partners, maps, guides, message boards, and web rings for the novice paddler.

http://wwwhometown.aol.com/cat.adp?cid=15203
Home pages of AOL members interested in canoeing and kayaking.

http://www.canoeamerica.org
Paddlers database with trip reports, slide shows, maps, equipment, clubs and outfitters.

http://www.kayakforum.com
Allows users to discuss various aspects of sea kayaks and kayaking.

http://www.kayakonline.com
Includes kayak buying tips, information on manufacturers and links to clubs and events.

http://www.kayakeronline,com
Articles for the beginner on all aspects of kayaking including paddle strokes.

http://www.onwatersports.com
One of the first websites devoted to watersports. Still the place to obtain information on boats, gear and technique.

Adventure Sports
1609 Watt Avenue
Sacramento, CA 95864 - 2963
web: www.sierrgear.com
Phone: (916) 971-1850
Fax: (916) 971-1942
Sales, rentals on canoes, kayaks and inflatables and outdoor gear. Demos, classes and trips offered in kayaking and canoeing.

North Rim Adventure Sports
346 Broadway
Chico, CA 95928
Phone: (530) 345-2453
Fax: (530) 345-0369
Retail sales of paddle craft, bike and climbing gear. Classes in kayaking are also offered.

California Canoe & Kayak, Sacramento
Nimbus Winery
12401 Folsom Blvd. Ste. 205
Rancho Cordova, CA. 95742
Phone: (916) 353-1880
Fax: (916)353-5171
E-mail: CalKayak@aol.com
Web: www.calkayak.com
Classes and trips: 1(800) 366-9804
Retail sales, rentals and guided trips. The Sacramento store carries the largest selection of name brand canoes in Northern California.

California Canoe & Kayak, Oakland
Jack London Square
409 Water Street
Oakland, CA 94607
Phone: (510) 893-7833
Fax: (510) 893-2617
E-mail: Calkayak@aol.com
Web: www.calkayak.com
Classes and trips: 1(800) 366-9804
Retail sales, rentals and trips. The Oakland store specializes in sales, repair and outfitting of sea kayaks as well as recreational, touring kayaks and canoes.

Current Adventures/Kayak School & Trips
PO Box 828
Lotus, CA 95651
(530) 642-9755
Fax: (530) 642-9725
Web: www.kayaking.com
To book a reservation or obtain information:
Toll Free: 1-888-4-kayaking
ACA Instruction/Certification programs available.
Kayak classes from beginner through advanced available in sea kayaking and white water. Classes in Safety/Rescue available. Summer kids program in kayaking. Trips: local and exotic.

Klepper West/Western Folding Kayak Center
6155 Mt. Aukum Rd.
Somerset, CA 95684-0130
Phone: (530) 626-8647 (local)
Toll Free: (888) 692-8092
Web: www.klepperwest.com
Sales and repair on new as well as used folding kayaks. Exclusive dealer in folding kayaks in the Sacramento and Bay areas.

Mountain Hardware
11320 Donner Pass Road
PO Box 2913
Truckee, CA 96160
Phone: (530) 587-4844
Carries Wenonah and Current Designs canoes and kayaks.

Mr. Canoe's Paddlesports
POB 1555
Forestville, CA 95346
Phone: (707) 887-7416
E-Mail: mrcanoe@jps.net
Web: www.MrCanoesPaddlesports.com
Sell, buy, rent, trade and consign: canoes, kayaks and accessories. ACA Certified Instructors.

REI, Sacramento
1790 Exposition Parkway
Sacramento, CA 95815
Phone: (916) 924-8900
Fax: (916) 924-9070
A major chain in the West specializing in quality outdoor gear and accessories. In addition to retail sales, has a rental program, provides classes and trips.

Tahoe City Kayak Shop
265 North Lake Blvd.
Tahoe City, CA 96145
Phone: 530-581-4336
Sells paddling gear and boats, rents boats and gear, outfits trips.

Tahoe Paddle & Oar
Tahoe City, CA 96145
Phone: 530-581-3029
Sells and rents paddle craft and gear, outfits trips.

The River Store
Box 472/1032 Lotus Rd.
Lotus, CA 95651
Phone: (530) 626-3435
Fax: (530) 626-7036
Web: http://www.coloma.com/riverstore
Retail sales, demos, and guided trips. Specializes in white water and touring kayaks.

Sierra Outdoor Center (SOC)
440 Lincoln Way
Auburn, CA 95603
Phone: (530) 885-1844
Fax: (530) 626-7036
E-mail: -sierraoc@jps.net
In addition to retail, rental, a school, and trips; SOC carries a full line of local USGS topographical quads. SOC is well recognized for their knowledgeable staff on raft sales and repair. SOC offers both white water kayak and raft guided trips.

Sports Fever/Ski ' N ' Sport
682-C Freeman Lane
Grass Valley, CA 95949
Phone: (530) 477-8006
Fax: (530)477-8318
Retail sales of canoes, kayaks and other sports.

Wolf Creek Wilderness
595 E. Main Street
Grass Valley, CA 95945
Phone: (530) 477-2722
Fax: (530) 477-6038
Web: www.wolfcreekwilderness.com
Retail sales rentals and guided trips. The owners specialize in trips within Northern California, as well as on other lakes and rivers in the state. A winter sports program, sales and rentals available.

Appendix 3

Wildflowers

I list the wildflowers by color that I had noted and photographed when researching the area in the months of May through August. This list represents only a fraction of the numbers visible during my forays around the lakes. The color, shape and size of the many varieties of wildflowers provide an additional bonus to all outdoors enthusiasts as they pass through meadows, forests or stream banks. Their presence enhances and complements a landscape already stunning in its beauty.

This statement becomes evident when passing through the same region in late summer or early fall, long after the blossoms have withered and dried. The scenery, while still captivating, seems to have lost some subtle presence that made it come alive in sight and scent.

On your next outing in one of the Paddle Locations described in this guidebook, take the time to stop and study one of the wildflowers in bloom. Who knows, that one action may set the rhythm for the day and turn a promising outing into a memorable event.

Blue and Purple to Violet Flowers:
Stickseed; Sticktight; beggarticks *(Hackelia velutina)*
Blue Penstemon *(Penstemon laetus)*
Harlequin Lupine *(Lupinus stiversii)*
Brewer Daisy *(Erigeron peregrinus)*/Leafy Daisy *(E. foliosus)*
Brewer's Lupine *(Lupinus breweri)*
Torry's Lupine *(Lupinus lepidus var. sellulus)*
Baby Blue-Eyes *(Nemophila menziesii)*
Aster Fleabane *(Erigeron peregrinus)*
Alpine Aster; Dwarf Purple Aster *(Aster alpigenus)*
Anderson' Thistle *(Cirsium andersonii)*
Jacob's Ladder *(Polemonium californicum)*
Sky Pilot *(Polemonium eximium)*
Swamp Onion *(Allium validum)*
Western Mountain Aster *(Aster occidentalis)*

Pink/Red to Orange Flowers:
Anderson's Thistle *(Cirsium andersonii)*
Bush Monkeyflower; Sticky Monkeyflower *(Mimulus aurantiacus)*
California Fuchsia *(epilobium canum)*
California Poppy *(Eschscholzia californica)*
Crimson Columbine *(Aquilegia formosa)*

Scarlet Monkeyflower *(Mimulus cardinalis)*
Scarlet Gilia; Skyrocket; Foxfire *(Ipomopsis aggregata)*
Scarlet Penstemon; Beaked Penstemon *(Penstemon rostriflorus)*
Pride of the Mountain; Mountain Pride *(Penstemon newberryi)*
Leopard Lily; Panther Lily *(lilium pardalinum)*
Live-Forever *(Dudleya cymosa)*
Mountain Spiraea *(Spiraea densiflora)*
Lemmons Paintbrush *(Castilleja lemmonii)*
Alpine Lily *(Lilium parvum)*
Alpine Shooting Star *(Dodecatheon alpinum)*
Fireweed *(Epilabium angustilfolium)*
Snow Plant *(Sarcodes sanguinea)*
Spreading Phlox *(Phlox diffusa)*
White-veined Mallow *(Sidalcea glaucescens)*
Whitney's Locoweed *(Astragalus whitneyi)*
Giant Red Paintbrush *(Castilleja miniata)*
Green Manzanita *(Arctostaphylos patula)*

Yellow Flowers:
Musk Monkeyflower *(Mimulus moschatus)*
Rabbitbrush; Rubber Rabbitbrush *(Chrysothamnus nauseosus)*
Stonecrop *(Sedum obtusatum)*
St. John's Wort *(Hypericum formosum)*
Tinker's Penny *(Hypericum anagalloides)*
Oval-Leaved Eriogonum *(Eriogonum ovalifolium)*
Pyrrocoma *(Pyrrocoma apargiodes)*
Woolly Mule Ears; Mountain Mule Ears; Western Mule Ears; *(Wyethia mollis)*
Wooly Sunflower *(Eriophylleum lamatorum)*
Arrow-Leaved Balsamroot *(Balsamorhiza sagittata)*
Common Sunflower; Mirasol *(Helianthus annuus)*
Golden Aster *(Chrysopsis villosa)*
Creek Goldenrod *(Solidago canadensis)*
Evening Primrose *(Oenothera elata)*
Water Plantain Buttercup *(Ranunculus alismaefolius)*
Yellow Pond Lily *(Nuphar lutea ssp. polysepala)*
Sulfur Flower; Sulfur Buckwheat *(Eriogonum umbellatum)*
Mountain Violet *(Viola purpurea)*
Yellow Wood Violet; Pine Violet *(Viola lobata)*
Harlequin Lupine *(Lupinus stiversii)*
Northern Goldenrod *(Solidago multiradiata)*
Nodding Microseris *(Microseris nutans)*
Wandering Daisy *(Erigeron peregrinus)*
Western Wallflower *(Erysimum capitatum)*
Lomatium *(lomatium utriculatum)*

White Flowers:
American Dogwood *(Cornus serica)*
White-Flowered Bog Orchid; Sierra Rein Orchid *(Plantanthera leucostachys)*
Oval-Leaved Eriogonum *(Eriogonum ovalifolium)*
Corn Lily *(Veratrum californicum var. californicum)*
Mountain Dogwood *(Cornus nuttallii)*
Mountain Misery; kit-kit-dizze *(Chamaebatia foliolosa)*
Deer Brush *(Ceanothus integerrimus)*
Western Pasque Flower *(Anemone accidentalis)*
Western Labrador Tea *(Ledum glandulosum)*
Leichtlin's Mariposa Lily *(Calochortus leichtlinii)*
Plainleaf Fawn Lily *(Erythronium purpurascens)*
Ranger's Buttons; Button Parsley; Swamp White Heads *(Sphenosciadium capitellum)*
Granite Gilia; Prickly Phlox *(Leptodactylon pungens)*
White-Veined Pyrola; White-Veined Wintergreen *(Pyrola picta)*
Pinedrops *(Pterospora andromeda)*
Yarrow; Woolly Yarrow; Wild Tansy *(Achillea millefolium)*

Brown and Green Flowers:
Single-Stemmed Groundsel *(Senecio integerrimus)*
Western Pasque Flower *(Anemone accidentalis)*

References
Blackwell, Laird R., *Wildflowers of the Sierra Nevada and the Central Valley.*
Edmonton, AB: Lone Pine Publishing, 1999. 288 pp.

Horn, Elizabeth, *Sierra Nevada Wildflowers.* Missoula, MT: Mountain Press Publishing Company, 1998. 215 pp.

Spellenberg, Richard, *Audubon Society Field Guide to North American Wildflowers Western Region.* New York, NY: Alfred A. Knopf, Inc., 1979. 862 pp.

Wiese, Karen, *Sierra Nevada Wildflowers A Falcon Guide.* Helena, MT: Falcon Publishing, Inc., 2000. 187 pp.

Glossary

This glossary provides a quick and handy reference to the reader for scientific, nautical or other bit of jargon. To provide the Reader with the source from which I used a word or phrase in question, the field of study is written in parenthesis following the word. Some of these words may have similar definitions but are used in a different context depending on the discipline they derive from. Whenever possible, I include a website that covers the subject in more detail.

Abutment (engineering): A masonry mass receiving the arch, beam or truss at each end of a bridge. The same mass may also be used as a support against the continual pressure of water against a bridge or pier.

Afterdeck (nautical): The part of a ship's deck past the midsection towards the stern (back).

Alluvium (geology/mining): From the word *alluvial* meaning: formed or deposited by the action of running water. Various materials that are eroded, transported and deposited by streams. Also known as an alluvial deposit.

Area (geography): Any particular extent of surface; geographical region or tract: Grouse Ridge Area, the area near the Yuba River Drainage Region.

Bar (geology/hydrology/geography/mining): A mixture of unconsolidated materials such as mud, sand, gravel, cobbles and other sediments that form mounds, ridges or banks and are partially or fully submerged in stream channels, river mouths, estuaries and along the coast.

Basalt (geology): Extrusive igneous rock formed on the surface from volcanic activity such as lava flows, dikes, shield volcanoes and cinder cones. www.geo.mtu.edu/volcanoes/

Batholith (geology): A large mass of plutonic rock at least 40 square miles in extent, composed of coarse-grained rock that originally crystallized below the surface. The Sierra Nevada Batholith is made up of many smaller *plutons*, intrusive masses composed largely of granitic rock. See: http://www.colorado.edu/GeolSci/Resources/WUSTectonics/Tectintro.html

Bedrock (geology): The solid rock underlying the top layer of soil or other unconsolidated material. Sometimes incorrectly called "country rock."

Bench (geology): A flat or gentle slope of land usually narrow in width bounded by steeper slopes below it and above it.

Berm berme (geology/geography): A narrow ledge or shelf along a slope.

Blaze (forestry/backpacking): A symbol cut or notched into the trunk of a tree to indicate direction of travel (see also: duck).

Broach (nautical): A turning of your boat broadside (sideways) to the wind and waves. The effect to this movement may cause the boat to capsize.

Canal (mining/engineering): In the Northern mines, the terms canal, ditch and flume were used to describe a specific type of man-made water conveyance system that carried water for the purpose of hydraulic mining operations. See: www.cwo.com/~ditches/index.htm

Cap Rock (geology): A hard layer of rock overlying softer more erosion-prone layers.

Chasm (geology/geography): A deep crack or narrow gorge in the earth's surface.

Chert (geology/archaeology): A hard, dense crystalline rock of sedimentary origin composed of chalcedony and quartz. The rocks ability to hold a sharp edge similar to obsidian made it a sought-after tool source by Stone-Age Cultures.

Chinking (construction/engineering): Filling the empty spaces of a structure such as a log cabin, or a rock wall with a substance like mud, mortar, small rocks or even paper.

Claim (mining): That portion of the land that a miner claims for the purpose of removing mineral ore in accordance with mining laws.

Cobble (geology): A stone with a diameter between 2.5 and 10 inches (64 and 256 mm).

Contour (cartography): An imaginary series of lines used on a topographic map that run along the ground points having the same elevation. The color of these lines indicates above or below sea level, with brown for ground points and blue for features below sea level.
See: http://www-sci.lib.uci.edu/SEP/CTS98/topographic.html

Country Rock (geology): Rock that surrounds or is penetrated by various mineral veins; rock surrounded by an igneous intrusion such as magma.

Core (archaeology): A stone from which workable flakes are removed. These stone flakes are, in turn, worked into a variety of tools. As more flakes are removed, the core becomes progressively smaller. When flakes of workable size can no longer be removed, the core is discarded.

Cove (geography): A small sheltered bay in the shoreline of a sea, river or lake.

Cribbing (mining/engineering): Wooden or metal framework used to strengthen or provide support. Many of the flumes built onto the sides of ravines had cribbing that supported the actual flume.

Deciduous (botany/biology): Trees or other plants that lose their leaves annually at a particular season.

Dike (geology): Cracks or fissures in the earth that are filled with molten matter. As the molten material cools and hardens it forms into various minerals. In Sierran granite, dikes composed of pegmatite or aplite are common.

Diorite (geology): A medium to coarse-grained intrusive rock.

Dry Stacking (construction): The placement of materials such as stone one on top of the other without the use of mortar, cement or other binding agents. Sometimes the stone is *dressed* or shaped to fit better before it is stacked.

Duck (backpacking): A stack of rocks, one on top the other, to be used as a trail marker. Sometimes called a *cairn*.

Flank (geography): A side or lateral part: *the flank of a mountain*.

Flume (mining/engineering): A wooden or metal structure with a center channel for carrying water. In the area covered by this volume, flumes were constructed where ditches could not be dug, along the side of steep ravines at a prescribed gradient.

See: www.cwo.com/~ditches/index.htm

Fungus, pl. fungi (biology): Any group of organisms that include moulds, yeasts, rusts, smuts, mildews, mushrooms and toadstools. They are not considered true plants because they have no leaves or roots. They contain no chlorophyll, therefore are not able to make their own food (photosynthesis); they also reproduce by spores rather than pollination. Fungi are either parasites, or saprotrophs (living on dead matter).

See: www.herb.lsa.umich.edu.kidpage/factindx.htm

Specific to California and the Sierra Nevada fungi: www.mykoweb.com

Gneiss (geology): Coarse-grained metamorphic rock, formed under conditions of high temperature and pressure, often associated with schists and granites.

Gradient (geology/hydrology): The rate of descent or ascent of any topographic feature; the steepness of slope. In hydrology, the term applies to the grade or fall of a stream. Gradient is expressed in feet per mile.

Granite (geology): A plutonic igneous rock consisting primarily of the minerals quartz, feldspar and biotite.

Granitic: Of or like granite but containing less or additional minerals that is associated with true granite. *The Sierra Nevada Mountains are a former batholith; when it cooled the rock became a granitic intrusion.*

Greenstone (geology): An old-field term describing an altered igneous rock green in color due to presence of chlorite, hornblende, or epidote.

Gruss; grus (geology): Loose fragments of coarse rock associated with the weathering of granite.

Gunnel; gunwale (nautical): Structural supports that run end to end along the top of the hull. Can be made out of wood, vinyl, or aluminum. Inside strips of the gunnels are called "inwales" and the outside strips are "outwales." Derived from an old English word pertaining to the area on a warship that braced the guns.

Hanging Valley (geology/glaciology/geography): A tributary valley that joins the main valley at an elevation above the main valley. Formed when a small tributary glacier cannot deepen its valley as fast as the main glacier can. Waterfalls are often characteristic of hanging valleys (see Paddle Location 13). For more about glaciers:

www.nsidc.colorado.edu/NSIDC/EDUCATION/GLACIERS / www.ship.edu/~cjwolt/geology/slides/gl20c.htm

Hornblende (geology): Green or black rock-forming mineral. It is a silicate composed mainly of calcium, iron, magnesium, and aluminum. Hornblende is found in both igneous and metamorphic rocks.

Hurdy-gurdy houses (slang): Western dance halls with bars, dancing and prostitutes.

Hydraulic Mining (mining): An extraction process whereby high-pressure hoses wash enormous amounts of earth and other overburden. This form of mining required huge amounts of water to wash the soil into sluice boxes for extraction of the ore. To meet the demand for a continous flow of water, rivers gorges and existing small sierra lakes were dammed; deep reservoirs were constructed and vast tracts of land were criss-crossed with ditches, canals and flumes. See: www.calgoldrush.com/graphics/evolution.html

Igneous rock (geology): Rock formed by the cooling and solidification of magma or lava. *Intrusive* or plutonic igneous rock forms and crystallizes beneath the earth's surface such as the intrusive *igneous rock* that makes up the Sierra Nevada Batholith. *Extrusive igneous rock* occurs as a result of volcanic action on the earth's surface. Examples of this type of rock are varieties of lava, volcanic ash, cinders and the glass-like obsidian. See: www.geo.mtu.edu/volcanoes/

Intermittent stream (geography/hydrology): A body of water that flows on a seasonal or irregular basis.

Jasper (geology): An opaque to slightly translucent cryptocrystalline *(having crystals too small to see with an ordinary microscope)* quartz, containing iron impurities giving the minerals a red, yellow or brown coloration.

Joint (geology): Fractures (cracks) in a mass of rocks that do not show displacement on one side or the other.

Knob (geology): A prominent usually isolated rounded hill.

Knoll (geology): A small rounded hill; hillock.

K-Tag (forestry): A yellow metal surveyor's tag depicting the section, township and range of an area.

Leeward (nautical): A sheltered or protected place out of the wind; opposite of windward.

Lichen (biology): Organisms that consist of both a specific fungus and a specific alga living together in a mutually beneficial relationship *(symbiotic relationship)*. The alga providing the food and the fungus provides water and protection. Lichens are a sponge-like mass, somewhat resembling moss. They grow in patches on trees, rocks, and other surfaces. See: http://mgd.orst.edu/hyperSQL/lichenland/index.html

Matrix (geology): The rock in which minerals, gems or fossils are embedded.

Mélange (geology): A mixture of assorted rock fragments having a variety of shape, size and composition.

Metamorphic rock (geology): Rock formed by the transformation of preexisting rock in response to increased heat, pressure or chemical change. The Scottish geologist Charles Lyell coined the term in 1833. The process that creates this form of rock is termed *metamorphism*.

Mill, Stamp (mining): A plant or structure designed to reduce ore into smaller bulk for treating by other methods to capture valuable minerals within the ore body. Of the various mill designs, the stamp mill crushed ore with individual heavy iron stamps that were lifted by cams and then dropped onto the ore. See: www.calgoldrush.com/graphics/evolution.html

Moraine, glacial (glaciology/geology): A ridge of unsorted primarily rocky debris, called *till*, in or on a glacier, or deposited by an older glacier. Moraine piles are given a variety of names dependent on where the moraine was deposited. As an example: a lateral moraine lies on the side of a glacier; an end moraine forms around the frontal edge of the glacier's snout and sometimes connects to the lateral moraine.
See: www.ship.edu/~cjwolt/geology/slides/gl23.htm and gl25.htm

Node (geography/geology): A protuberance or *knob*.

Ore (mining): The naturally occurring material from which economically valuable minerals can be extracted at a profit.

Pegmatite (geology): An exceptionally coarse-grained igneous rock or vein that consists largely of quartz, alkali, feldspar and mica. Pegmatite and pegmatite dikes are relatively small and light (white to pink) in color and most are of granitic composition.

Pitch (mountaineering): A stretch of rock or snow, usually of some technical difficulty. In mountaineering a pitch has a measurement not longer than a rope's length. The term has been broadened to include any section of difficult ground to be covered.

Placer (mining): A sedimentary deposit containing economic minerals such as gold that have weathered out from bedrock and been concentrated usually by the action of streams.

Plate Tectonics; Continental Drift (geology): Theory developed in the 1960s in part from an earlier hypothesis published by Alfred Wegener in the early 1900s, to explain the phenomena of continental drift, seafloor spreading and the formation of many of the physical features of the earth's surface.
The earth's outermost layer, called the lithosphere, is similar to a jigsaw puzzle of major and minor "plates" that move relative to each other probably due to influence of convection currents in the mantle beneath the lithosphere. At the margins of these plates, where they collide or move apart, major landforms such as mountains, volcanoes, ocean basins, trenches and ridges are created.
See: http://www.seismo.unr.edu/pub/louie/100/plate-tectonics.html
http://www.ucmp.berkeley.edu/geology/tectonic

Pluton (geology): A single massive body of plutonic rock (rock formed at considerable depth and usually medium to coarse-grained such as granite) consisting of intrusive igneous rock of a size that may be mapped. An assemblage of plutons is a *batholith*. The Sierra Nevada Mountain Range is an example of a granitic batholith.
See: http://www.colorado.edu/GeolSci/Resources/WUSTectonics/Tectintro.html

Pocket cove; lake (introduced): A term coined by a local Sacramento scientist to describe relatively small bodies of water removed from any major drainage source and located in a protected shallow basin.

Portage (Old French): Synonymous with carry. To carry a canoe and gear overland to a distant river, lake or around an obstacle in the water.

Put-In (paddling): The location on a body of water where a canoe or kayak is placed prior to a paddle. See: **Take-Out.**

Quadrangle (cartography): The rectangular area represented by U. S. Geological Survey topographical and geological maps. The two common sizes depict tracts about 13 miles wide by 17 miles north to south and 6.5 miles wide by 8.5 miles north to south.
See: http://mac.usgs.gov/mac/isb/pubs/booklets/topo/topo.html

Quartzite (geology): A granular rock composed mainly of quartz and formed by the metamorphism of sandstone.

Race (mining): An English term used to define the varied features of water conveyance systems. These systems include flumes, canals and ditches.
See: http://www.cwo.com/~ditches/index.htm

Ridge (geology/geography): An elongated, narrow and steep sided elevated feature on the earth's surface.

Saddle (geography/geology): **1.** A gap that is broad and gently sloping on both sides. **2.** A relatively flat ridge that connects the peaks of two higher elevations.

Scrape zone (geography/construction): The area around the boundary of a dam-filled reservoir that has been cleared of trees and vegetation. The area to be scrapped begins as close to the bottom of the reservoir as possible and extends outward to the reservoir's high water line.

Scree (geology): A mound of loose angular material less than 4 inches in size.

Section Map (cartography): A description or scale drawing of the successive rock layers or geological structures as they would appear on the surface or if their appearance was cut through and their bedding exposed.

Seep (geology): A small area where water or another liquid percolates slowly to the surface.

Slash (forestry): Remnants of a logging operation. This vegetative debris consists mainly of treetops, limbs and brush piles.

Springboard (lumbering): A board inserted into a notched trunk of a large tree to be cut for lumber. Lumberjacks used the springboard as a platform to provide footing as they cut the tree.

Striations (glaciology/geology): Are scratches cut into the surface area of the bedrock a glacier moves over.
See: www.ship.edu/~cjwolt/geology/slides/gl10.jpg

Swale (geology/geography): A slight depression, sometimes swampy, in the midst of generally level ground.

Take-Out (paddling): Opposite of a *Put-In.* The place where a canoe or kayak is removed from the water.

Talus (geology): A.k.a. rubble; scree. Coarse and angular rock fragments derived from and accumulated at the base of a cliff or steep slope.

Tailings (mining): The pulverized remains of rock and other waste material extracted from mining operations.

Tarn (geology/glaciology): A small lake occupying a depression eroded by a glacier or dammed by the mound of debris scooped aside by a glacier's movement. Tarns are common in cirques.

See: www.shipedu/~cjwolt/geology/slides/gl11b.jpg

Tectonics (geology): The study of movements of rocks on the earth's surface.

Terrace (geology/geography): A flat raised level of land bordered by vertical or sloping sides, especially one of a series of such features placed one on top of the other.

Terrain (geology/tectonics): Any tract of land in respect to its breadth and natural features.

Terrane (geology): A region of crust with well-defined margins, which differs significantly in composition from neighboring regions. The terrane may be thought of as having once been all or part of a tectonic plate that may have traveled some distance before melding to the continent at its present location.

Tertiary Gravels (mining/geology): Stream and riverine deposits from former rivers and streams that flowed during Tertiary Time (between 65 to 30 million years ago). Early miners discovered that many of these former channels contained a great deal of placer gold.

Thwart (nautical): A wooden or metal support piece attached horizontally across the inside hull of a canoe.

Topography (geography/cartography): the surface features of a place or region, including hills, mountains, valleys, streams, lakes, bridges, tunnels, roads etc. In cartography the term applies to the detailed description or drawing of the surface features of a place or region.

Topographic Map (cartography/geography/geology): A map showing the elevations as well as the positions of the physical and cultural features of a given area, often in color and with contour lines.

See: http://mac.usgs.gov/lsb/pubs/booklets/symbols

Vertigo (medical): Dizziness; a whirling sensation accompanied by a loss of balance or any contact with the ground.

Windward (nautical): The weather side; the side from which the wind blows. Opposite of leeward.

ANNOTATED BIBLIOGRAPHY OF TECHNICAL REFERENCES

Aiken, Zora and David, *Simple Tent Camping: Basics of Camping from Car or Canoe,* Camden, ME: Ragged Mountain Press, (n.d.).
A simple introductory guide to camping. Contains excellent tips for beginners insuring that the first trip won't be the last.

Alt, David D. and Donald W. Hyndman, *Roadside Geology of Northern California.* Missoula, MT: Mountain Press Publishing Co. 1994, 17th printing, 251 pp.
The entire Roadside series of books are an excellent introduction to the geology of California and the United States. All the books provide maps with geologic features superimposed over the roads and highways of the state. The text is clearly written and easy to comprehend.

"A River Runner's First-Aid Kit," Dan Schaffer, MD, *River Magazine,* May 1999 Vol. II, Issue 4. pg. 48.
An up-to-date well thought out article on how to plan and pack a useful first-aid kit.

Bakker, Elna, *An Island Called California,* Berkeley, CA: University of California Press, 1972, 357 pp.
A classic introduction to the natural history of the state. I refer to this book constantly when researching a paddle area.

"Canoeing Tandem Talk," staff, *Canoe & Kayak Magazine,* December 1996. Pg. 14
Good communication skills make for a more enjoyable time on the water, not to mention improving your learning curve in the boat.

"Car-topping With Comfort; Roof Racks Guaranteed to get Your Paddle Craft to the Put-In," Aaron Bible, *Paddler Magazine,* July/August 1998 Vol. 18, No. 4. pg. 70.
Comparison and description of major rack systems currently on the market.

Clark, William B., ed. *Gold Districts of California, Bulletin 193*, San Francisco, CA: California Division of Mines And Geology, 1970. 186 pp.
A newly revised ed. of this excellent bulletin came out in 1998. It contains historical and geological inf. on the gold districts of the entire state.

Coale, John, *Canoeing the California Highlands A Quiet Water Guide to Paddler's Paradise,* Cedar Ridge, CA: Changing Sky Publications, 1998. 126 pp.
A coffee table book that doubles as a basic guide to the many lakes in California.

Daniel, Linda, *Kayak Cookery: A Handbook of Provisions and Recipes,* originally published in: Chester, CT: The Globe Pequot Press, 1988.
Current edition printed by Menasha Ridge Press, Birmingham, AL, 2nd ed. 1st printing. 208 pp.
Not only do the recipes work, and the outcome deliciously satisfying, the book has some excellent tips on packaging and stowing the foodstuff prior to touring.

Dennis, Jerry, *From a Wooden Canoe: Reflections on Canoeing, Camping, and Classic Equipment.* New York, NY: Thomas Dunne Books, 1999. 204 pp.
Personal commentary on all aspects of canoeing and camping. A book to take with you and read on your own trip.

Diaz, Ralph, *Complete Folding Kayaker,* Camden, ME: International Marine/ Ragged Mountain Press, 3rd edition, 1994.
The only book available devoted exclusively to the folding boat kayaker. Although the author covers different folding kayak designs, his emphasis is toward the Klepper style of kayak.

"Do It Yourself: Cockpit Customizing with Foam," Ken Rasmussen, *Sea Kayaker Magazine,* February 1998, Vol. 14, No. 6. pg. 42.
Describes how to make your kayak comfortable and safe for long distance touring.

"Downside of Gold Fever: The Environmental Aftermath." David Carle, *Sierra Heritage Magazine,* January / February 1999, Vol. 18, No. 4. pg. 42.
Desire to get to the gold meant destroying watersheds and natural flow of rivers and streams. Describes how this was done, explains some of the technology that was used.

Dowd, John, *Sea Kayaking A Manual for Long-Distance Touring,* Vancouver, BC: Greystone Books, revised ed., 2nd printing, 1997. 264 pp.
A very readable primer by an individual who has kayaked for 35 years all over the world. He has the ability to communicate his knowledge clearly without the use of jargon. The chapter on: Sea Kayaking for People with Disabilities, is worth the price of the book.

"Focus On Photography; Photographic tips and techniques for Paddlers," Lowell Jones, *Sea Kayaker Magazine,* June 1998, Vol. 15, No. 2. pg. 32.
How to use a camera from a moving canoe or kayak, proper storage of cameras and film, and the right lens for the right moment.

Getchell, Annie, *The Essential Outdoor Gear Manual,* Blacklick, OH: McGraw Hill Companies, International Marine, 1987. 134 pp.
The best reference book on the repair, maintenance and care of outdoor gear being sold today. I rely heavily on this book before I attempt any boat repair or description of how to repair any damaged gear. Every serious outdoors person should have a copy of this book.

Hansen, David & Judy, *Canoe Tripping with Children: Unique Advice for Keeping Children Comfortable,* Merrillville, IN: ICS Books, 1990.
Great common sense ideas on how to entertain the kids without losing your own enjoyment of the trip.

Hill, Mary, *Geology of the Sierra Nevada.* Berkeley, CA: University of California Press, 1975, 232 pp.
An excellent source book for the reader interested in how California's landscape came to be.

The author skips the jargon and makes the complex easy to understand.

Hoover, Mildred Brooke, Hero Eugene Rensch & Ethel Grace Rensch, *Historic Spots in California*, Berkeley, CA: University of California Press, 4th printing, 1962. 411 pp.
The emphasis is on the historical background. to the many communities that sprung up at the time of the Gold Rush and after. Many of these places no longer remain except as "names on the side of the road." I find this book to be extremely valuable when researching the names of the sites destroyed by the reservoirs.

Jacobson, Cliff, *Canoeing and Camping Beyond the Basics*, Merrillville, IN: ICS Books Inc., 1992.
You will never be wrong purchasing a book written by this author. He is opinionated, but those opinions carry the weight of: "been there, done that." This handy little booklet contains the same practical inf. as his primer.

_____*The Basic Essentials of Map and Compass*, Merrillville, IN.: ICS Books Inc., 49 pp.
(This short but easy to comprehend guide will give you the confidence to plan and read a route using a map and compass)
_____*"Custom Touches for Your Canoe,"* Paddler Magazine, October 1997. Pg. 80.
It's always those little things that make the difference between an OK trip and a GREAT trip. Outfitting a canoe properly, is one of those small things that will enhance a canoe trip.
_____ *"Canoes for Rent,"* Canoe & Kayak Magazine, August 2001. pg. 38
Tips on being prepared prior to renting a canoe.

Johnston, Verna, R., *Sierra Nevada The Naturalist's Companion (revised edition)*. Berkeley, CA: University of California Press, 1998. 206 pp.
A thoroughly enjoyable natural history of the Sierra Nevada, written with an eye for detail that covers the work of early naturalists and explains updated material.

Mason, Bill, *Song of the Paddle: An Illustrated Guide to Wilderness Camping*, Minocqua, WI: Northwood Press, Inc., 1988. 186 pp.
A follow-up to the author's first volume. Stunning photography followed by clear advice and information on wilderness canoe camping.

Mckowan, Doug, *Canoeing Safety & Rescue: A Handbook of Safety and Rescue Procedures for Lake and River Canoeists*, Calgary, CAN: Rocky Mountain Books, 1999
Written for the canoeist: both flat water and river runner. Solid information with good illustrations and photos.

McPhee, John, *The Survival of the Bark Canoe*, Warner Books Edition, published by Farrar, Straus And Giroux, 1975 ed. 114 pp.

The author builds a history of the birch bark canoe around the biography of Henri Vaillancourt a modern day canoe builder who follows the traditional methods and uses the same tools that the Indians used in the construction of his birch bark canoes.

Mills, Sheila, *The Outdoors Dutch Oven Cookbook*, Camden, MA: Ragged Mountain Press, 1997. 170 pp.
If you have ever tasted a meal properly prepared in a Dutch oven, then you know this book will be a favorite resource guide. I received this book as a gift and am preparing and eating my way through it.

Montgomery, M. R., *Many Rivers to Cross of Good Running Water, Native Trout, and the Remains of Wilderness*, Simon & Schuster, 1995. 254 pp.
More than just a book on trout fishing . . . there is a contemplative wisdom on the meaning of wilderness and what we stand to lose, eloquently written.

"No Yelling Allowed; Good Agreements Make Good Paddling Partners," Steve Salins, *Canoe & Kayak Magazine,* October 1998, Vol. 26, Issue 5. pg. 15.
There is a good reason why doubles, both canoes and kayaks, are derisively called: "divorce boats." This article provides some common sense tips on how to avoid making the mistakes that lead to an ugly time on the water.

"Osprey: The Fish Eagle," Dennis Flath, *River Magazine.* April 1999, Vol. II, Issue 3. pg. 40.
Concise description of the behaviors and characteristics of the premier fish catcher in the hawk family. . . . the eyewitness description of a power play between ospreys and Canada Geese is worth the read.

"Outfitting Family Trips," Alan S. Kesselheim, *Canoe & Kayak Magazine,* May 1997, Vol. 25, Issue 2. pg. 52.
Ensuring the comfort and safety of children when preparing a family canoe trip.

"Paddling with Deaf and Hard of Hearing Kayakers," Elizabeth Van Dyke, *Sea Kayaker Magazine,* December 1997 Vol. 14, No. 5. pg. 52.
Upon reading this informative and personal article, you come to realize that the term: "handicapped" is, in part, only a state-of-mind.

Pickett, Edwin R., *Birds of Central California, Sacramento,* CA: Sacramento Bee Newspaper Reprints, 1972, 2nd printing. 160 pp.
If you come across this out-of-print gem, snag it immediately. The book is a compilation of articles written for Sacramento Bee *under the heading: "The Bird Watcher." I have yet to find a source book that covers the subject in such depth. 160 birds are described.*

"Planning Your River Canoe Trip," Joanie, McGuffin, *River Magazine,* March, 1999 Vol. II, Issue 2. pg. 48.

Some sound advice on how to prepare for your first overnight or longer canoe trip. Information is good for lakes and rivers.

Powell, Jerry A. & Charles L. Hogue, *California Insects,* Berkeley, CA University of California Press, 1979, 388 pp.
A technical but thorough source book on "bugs of California."

Roberts, Harry, *The Basic Essentials of Canoe Paddling,* Merrillville, IN: ICS Books, Inc., *Part of the Basic Essentials Series of books. This volume is a fast paced introduction to canoe paddling. No philosophy on paddle grips or scientific treatise on wood vs. synthetics—just how to paddle a canoe properly.*

Rowlands, John J., *Cache Lake Country Country life in the North Woods, (Wilderness Edition),* John J. Rowlands, W. W. Norton & Company, Inc., 1959. 270 pp.
Amongst the thoughtful homespun observations on living in the woods, are some practical woodcraft that any aspiring woods person should know.

Ruark, Robert, *The Old Man and the Boy and The Old Man's Boy Grows Older,* Robert Ruark, Stackpole Books, Classics of American Sport Series, 1989 ed. 630 pp.
These two classics on growing up are a must read for any outdoors person. A real "hoot" to carry and read on a paddle trip.

Schoenherr, Allan A., *A Natural History of California,* Berkeley, CA: University of California Press, 1st pub. Printing, 1995. 772 pp.
The "unofficial" study of the natural history of the state. This book is absolutely crammed with data on the state. Definitely one to have as a source book.

Seidman, David, *The Essential Sea Kayaker: A Complete Course for the Open Water Paddler.* Camden, ME: Ragged Mountain Press (Division of McGraw-Hill Companies), 1992 12th printing. 144 pp.
For a while this book was the only descent introductory instruction book on the American market. The updated version is still an excellent source of information on "getting started" on all aspects of the sport.

Spielman, Andrew, Sc. D. & Michael D'Antonio, *Mosquito A Natural History of Our Most Persistent and Deadly Foe,* New York, NY: Hyperion Books, 2001. 247 pp.
*Everything . . .and some things you wish you didn't know . . . about that #% * little denizen of Nature.*

Stratton, George, *Camping California's National Forests* (formerly: *The Recreation Guide to California's National Forests*) Helena, MT: Falcon Press, 1991. 258 pp.
A basic guide to what's available at our National Forests. Includes information on camping, sports and some historical background.

"*The American Dipper,*" Graham Neale, *River Magazine.* September 1998 Vol. 1, Issue 5. pg. 34.
Background on John Muir's favorite bird, formerly known by its British name of Water Ouzel.

"*The Trials and Tribulations of Paddling Double,*" ed. staff, *Sea Kayaker Magazine,* February 1997. pg. 56.
All the do's and don'ts of paddling in a double kayak.

"*The Uniqueness of Sierra Saprophytes,*" Lee Gardner & Will Hart, *Sierra Heritage Magazine.* May/June 1999, Vol. 18, No. 5. pg. 24.
Beautiful plants that live on organic matter and do not require chlorophyll to sustain life.

"*Trout: An Expression of River Patterns,*" Rich Mcleary, *River Magazine.* August 1998, Vol. 1, Issue 3. pg. 32.
The natural history and biology of trout.

"*Using the UTM System,*" *Canoe & Kayak Magazine,* December 1994, pg. 23.
How to read maps that contain the Universal Transverse Mercator grid system. All-revised 7.5 minute topographical map sheets contain this easy to use system, while on land or in the water.

Walbridge, Charlie, *Knots for Paddlers,* Birmingham, AL.: Menasha Ridge Press, 1995.
Knot tying specifically for boaters. Written by a well-known ACA instructor and paddler.

Whitney, Stephen, *The Sierra Nevada,* San Francisco, CA: Sierra Club Books, 6th ed., 1979. 526 pp.
Still the best classic on the natural history of the Sierra region. I rely on it constantly . . . and it packs well too.

Wyatt, Mike, *The Basic Essentials of Sea Kayaking,* Merrillville, IN: ICS books, Inc., 1996, 2nd Ed.
An excellent introduction to the sport. The material is well researched without the techno jargon. Lots of helpful sketches and photos.

Periodicals

Canoe & Kayak Magazine
PO box 420825
Palm Coast, FL 32142-0825
Phone: (800) 829-3340
Web: http://www.canoekayak.com
A buyer's guide is published with every December issue.

Canoe Journal
Published annually by *Canoe & Kayak Magazine.*
(Same address as *Canoe & Kayak Magazine.*)
Covers in-depth history of all aspects on canoes and canoeing.

Paddler Magazine
C/O Paddlesport Publishing Inc.
7432 Alban Station Blvd., Ste. B-232
Springfield, VA 22150
Phone: (703) 455-3419
Fax: (703) 451-2245
Paddler on-line: www.aca-paddler.org/paddler
A buyer's guide is published with every Jan/Feb issue. By joining the American Canoe Association, you receive a free one-year subscription.

Sea Kayaker Magazine
PO Box 17170
Seattle, WA 98107-9948
Phone: (206) 789-9536
Fax: (206) 781-1141
Web: http://www.seakayakermag.com
E-mail: mail@seakayakermag.com
The magazine is known for its in-depth review of kayaks with every issue.

Sierra Heritage Magazine
PO Box 263
Auburn, CA 95604-9900
Phone: (800) 35-SIERRA or (530) 823-3986
Fax: (530) 823-0209
Web: http://www.sierraheritage.com
E-mail: sierra@ns.net
A magazine that covers the past and present history of the Sierra Foothills and the Sierra Range.

Outdoor Guidebooks & Maps

from FineEdge.com

PADDLING GUIDEBOOKS

Up the Lake with a Paddle, Vol. 1: **Sierra Foothills,
Sacramento Region** by Van der Ven, ISBN 0-938665-54-5, $18.95
Up the Lake with a Paddle, Vol. 2: **Tahoe Region, Crystal Basin
& Foothill Reservoirs** by Van der Ven, ISBN 0-938665-70-7, $21.95
Up the Lake with a Paddle, Vol. 3: **Tahoe National Forest—West**
by Van der Ven, ISBN 0-938665-82-0, $19.95

RECREATION TOPO MAPS

The Great Flume Ride, ISBN 0-938665-75-8, $3.95
Eastern High Sierra, 2nd Ed., ISBN 0-938665-77-4, $8.95
Santa Monica Mountains, ISBN 0-938665-69-3, $8.95
San Bernardino Mountains, ISBN 0-938665-78-2, $8.95
San Gabriel Mountains, ISBN 0-938665-13-8, $8.95
North Lake Tahoe Basin, ISBN 0-938665-34-0, $8.95
South Lake Tahoe Basin, ISBN 0-938665-68-5, $8.95

MOUNTAIN BIKING GUIDEBOOKS

Mountain Biking Northern California's Best 100 Trails
by Fragnoli & Stuart, ISBN 0-938665-73-1, $18.95

Mountain Biking Reno & Carson City Best Trails
by R. W. Miskimins, ISBN 0-938665-66-9, $15.95

Mountain Biking Southern California Best 100 Trails, 2nd Ed.
Fragnoli & Douglass, Eds., ISBN 0-938665-53-7, $16.95

Mountain Biking the Eastern Sierra's Best 100 Trails
by Hemingway-Douglass, Davis, & Douglass, ISBN 0-938665-42-1, $18.95

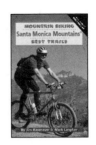

Mountain Biking South Lake Tahoe's Best Trails
by Bonser & Miskimins, ISBN 0-938665-52-9, $14.95

Mountain Biking North Lake Tahoe's Best Trails
by Bonser & Miskimins, ISBN 0-938665-40-5, $14.95

Mountain Biking California's Central Coast Best 100 Trails
by Fragnoli, ISBN 0-938665-59-6, $18.95

Mountain Biking Santa Monica Mountains' Best Trails
by Hasenauer & Langton, ISBN 0-938665-55-3, $14.95

Mountain Biking North America's Best 100 Ski Resorts
by Fragnoli, ISBN 0-938665-46-4, $16.95

Lake Tahoe's Top 20 Bike Rides on Pavement and Dirt
by Miskimins, ISBN 0-938665-36-7, $5.95

Favorite Pedal Tours of Northern California
by Bloom, ISBN 0-938665-12-X, $12.95

**Mountain Biking the San Gabriel Mountains' Best Trails,
with Angeles National Forest and Mt. Pinos**
by Troy & Woten, ISBN 0-938665-43-X, $14.95

Prices are subject to change © 2002 Fine Edge Productions

FineEdge.com
13589 Clayton Lane, Anacortes, WA 98221
Phone: 360.299.8500, Fax: 360.299.0535
Website: www.fineedge.com

For trail information, check www.MountainBikingPress.com

About The Author

Born in Pau, France and raised in San Francisco and Santa Cruz, California, Bill has enjoyed surfing, snorkeling, backpacking & museum viewing since he was a teenager. Having completed his Air Force commitment with a tour in Vietnam as an Aerial Reconnaissance photographer, he graduated from San Francisco State University with a Bachelor of Arts Degree in Anthropology (Archaeology) followed by a teaching credential.

Bill worked as a caretaker at the Calico Early Man Site under the tutelage of Ruth DeEtte Simpson. He also participated in several projects and field surveys conducted by the Paleontology and Geology Department of the Museum of Northern Arizona with William J. Breed as curator. In the early 1980's Bill volunteered as a docent, then became a paid staff member at the Ano Nuevo State Reserve, in San Mateo County, California.

Bill's love of nature, archaeology and geology, plus his skill as a photographer, brought excitement to the classroom where he taught social studies, science and history classes for over ten years. In 1984, he moved to Sacramento where he worked for California Canoe & Kayak. He is a Naturalist/Guide for Current Adventures, a kayak school & trip outfitter. Married to Louise Anne Cherry, Bill is the father of 15-year-old Peter Karl who is attending high school, and stepfather of Eric, who is a sergeant in the Army.